AF730230

Hindu Music

FROM VARIOUS AUTHORS

Compiled by
Rajah Comm. Sourindro Mohun Tagore

Two Parts Bound in One

Low Price Publications

2010

First Published 1882

Reprinted in **LPP** 1990, 1994, 2010

Tagore, Sourindro Mohun (1840-1914)

ISBN 10: 81-7536-513-7
ISBN 13: 978-81-7536-513-1

Published by
Low Price Publications
A-6, Second Floor, Nimri Commercial Centre,
Ashok Vihar Phase-IV, Delhi-110052
Ph.: 011 27302453 Fax.: 011 4706 1936
e-mail: info@Lppindia.com
website: www.Lppindia.com

Printed At
D.K. Fine Art Press (P) Ltd.
Delhi

PRINTED IN INDIA

PREFACE TO THE FIRST EDITION

The very deep interest which the European Public have of late evinced with regard to my humble labors towards the revival of Hindu Music, has created in me a desire to present to them a collection of all that have ever been written on the subject by the Oriental Scholars of Europe, together with my own comments on their views and on those of our ancient Sanscrit musical writers.

The whole will consist of two parts: The first part contains extracts from almost all the eminent works on Hindu Music extant in the English language.

It is therefore hoped that the present collection, notwithstanding its short-comings, will be received with indulgence by those interested in the subject. Should his hope be realised, I purpose soon to publish the second part which will contain a dissertation on our ancient Sanscrit musical works and a criticism on the different views taken by the European writers on Hindu Music, together with further collections if available.

All the extracts bear the name of the works from which they have been taken. With regard to one taken from the "Ain-i-Akbari," a valuable translation of which has lately been published by H. Blochmann, Esq., M. A., I have only to add that my best acknowledgments are due to that learned gentleman for his kind permission to make use of his work.

SOURINDRO MOHUN TAGORE

Calcutta,
Pathuriaghata,
The 28th January, 1875.

PREFACE TO THE SECOND EDITION

The increasing interest which has of late been evinced by the Public in the Music of India, has led me to bring out a second edition of this work. I have incorporated with this a further collection of the views of foreign writers on Hindu Music, which has been placed in the second part. As I have already published a Dissertation on Indian Music under the designation of "Six Principal Rágas of the Hindus," I have thought it unnecessary to give in this work my own views on the subject, such as I had promised to do, while bringing out the first edition.

My acknowledgements are due to the learned writers, extracts from whose works from the subject of Part II.

SOURINDRO MOHUN TAGORE

Calcutta,
Pathuriaghata Rajbati,
20th October 1882.

CONTENTS.

CONTENTS.

CONTENTS.

CONTENTS.

GLOSSARY

OF

THE MOST USEFUL MUSICAL TERMS.

B.

Bishnoopud. A species of Hindu divine songs, p. 106.

Bugeed, Bur. A species of song, vide curca, p. 107.

Bum. The bass end of a drum.

Bunsee or Banslee. A flute.

Byree, *m.* Byrum, *f.* An onomy. Crishnu's flute, the Pupeeha, and some other birds are thus designated by the females of Hindustan, as being the enemies to their repose

C.

Charbyt. Songs in the Oordu, comprising four couplets, p. 107.

Chhund. A sort of ancient songs, chiefly in the Sungscrit, p. 101.

Chutoorung. Songs consisting of four strains in different styles. 1, Kheal ; 2, Turana ; 3, Surgum ; 4, Tirwut, p. 106.

Cool. A sort of songs, p. 107.

Curtar, castanets made of wood, ivory, &c.

Cymbals and Castanets. Jhanjh, Munjeera, Curtar, &c.

D.

Dadra. Original songs of Boondelkhund and Bhughelkhund, p. 107.

Gholkee. A sort of drum.

Dhoon, from ध्वनि a sound. It is used in contradistinction to Rag and Raginee : any piece of melody not strictly in conformity with the established melody is thus characterised.

Dhoorpud. A species of song on the ancient fashion. It is not generally understood or relished, and its use seems to be about to be superseded by lighter compositions, as Tuppa, p. 101.

Drums are of various sorts, the chief of them are Nukara, Mridung, Tubla, and Dholkee. For their construction, &c., see the Chapter on Musical Instruments, p. 90.

F.

Flageolet. Ulghozub.

Flute. Bansulee or Bunsee. The famous instrument played upon by the god Krishnu. It is seldom used, and there are few tolerable performers on it now.

G.

Gamut. The native term for this is Surgum.

Geet. A species of ancient songs, chiefly in Sungscrit, p. 101.

Ghuzel. Persian lyric poetry, and in imitation of it, those in Oordu, p. 106.

Gramsthan. The first or lowest note of an octave is called *gram*, and is in some measure equivalent to our key note. The extent of Hindu music being limited to three octaves, the notes of the lowest octave are said to belong to *Khuruj*, or *mundar gram*, and the sounds supposed to proceed from the umbilical region, which is its *gramsthan*; those of the middle octave, to *muddhum gram*, and are supposed to proceed from the throat immediately: and the notes of the highest octave are believed to have their origin in some of the cavities of the scull or brain, and thence denominated *tarook gram*.

Griha. The key note.

Grunth. Native treatises on music.

Guitar. See Rubab. Sitar, &c.

H.

Holee, or Horee. A species of song, p. 103.

I.

Instruments (Musical). These are divided into four classes : 1, "Tut ;" 2, "Bitut ;" 3, "Ghun ;" and 4, "Sooghur." For a description of these, vide the Chapter on musical instruments, p. 90.

J.

Jhanjh. Large cymbals.

Jut. A species of song, p. 105.

K.

Khadoo. A Rag or Raginee, which comprises in its course only six soors or notes.

Kheal. A species of songs, p. 102.

L.

Letters and Syllables, unpropitious.

The following eight letters are reckoned unpropitious, and should not begin any piece of Hindu poetry or song, *viz.*, इच घनधरखभ. Words consisting of three letters or syllables, (which is the same in Nagree,) of the following sorts, are believed to be equally unlucky ; 1. Those which have the middle syllable long, and the first and third short, and are called "*Jugun*," as मलिन ; 2. Those which have the two first syllables short, and the last long, denominated "Sukun," as ललिता ; 3. A short syllable between two long ones, "*Rukun*," as मोहनी ; 4. "*Tukun*" the two first long and the last short, as पाताल.

M.

Moorchhuna. A term expressive of the full extent of the Hindu scale of music, and as this extends to three octaves, there are consequently twenty-one Moorchhunas, having distinct names. A Moorchhuna differs from a *soor* in this respect, that, there are twenty-one of the former and only seven of the latter, so that every *soor* has the same name whether it belong to the lowest, middle, or highest octave; whereas every individual sound through the whole range of three octaves has a distinct name when it is considered as Moorchhuna, by which way of naming them the octave of any particular sound has a distinct appellative. A *Khadoo Rag* for instance, q. v., extends to six *soors* or notes; but it may comprehend within its compass seven, or eight, or more Moorchhunas, according to the number of notes which are repeated in another octave.

Mridung. A sort of drum, appropriately used to accompany Dhoorpuds, and other solemn species of music.

Munjeera. Little cymbals used to mark the time.

Muqamat Farsee. Persian music. These are said to have their origin from the prophets, whilst others ascribe them, as well as the invention of musical instruments, to philosophers. Although the Muqamat Farsee are originally of Persia, yet as they are now known in this country, it seems necessary to say a few words respecting them. The natives of Persia, like those of Hindustan, reckon their ancient music as comprising of twelve classes or Muqams, each of which has belonging to it two Shobuhs and four Goshuhs. The Muqams being generally considered equivalent to the Rags of Hindustan, the Shobuhs being esteemed their Raginees, and the Goshuhs their Putras and Bharjyas.

The annexed table exhibits all the Muqams and Shobuhs, and thirty of the Goshuhs, the rest being unknown.

Names of Moqamat.	*Shobuh.*	*Goshuh.*
Kehavee, ...	Nourozi Urub, ...	Buhare nishat.
	consists of 6 notes, ...	Ghureeb.
	Nourozi Ujum, ...	Suwara.
	6 notes, ...	Ghumzooda.
Hoosynee, ...	Doogah, ...	Nubate Toork.
	2 notes, ...	Surfuraz.
	Moohyyer, ...	Busta nigar.
	8 notes, ...	Nubate Coordaneea.
Rast, ...	Mooturuffe, ...	Nihavunduk.
	8 notes, some say 9.. ..	Sufa.
	Punjgah, ...	Dilbur.
	5 notes, ...	Ouje Cumal.
Hijaz, ...	Sigah, ...	Nigar.
	3 notes, ...	Visal.
	Hisar, ...	Shuhuree.
	8 notes, some say 10, ..	Usheeran.
Boozoorg, ...	Hoomayoon, ...	Ghizul.
	4 notes, ...	Turub ungez.
	Noohzut, ...	Buhre Cumal.
	8 notes, ...	Buhre uslee.
Cochuk, ...	Rukb, ...	Etedal.
	3 notes, ...	Golistan.
	Tyatee, ...	Sureer.
	5 notes, ...	Hyran.
Iraq, ...	Mookkalif, ... or	Jumalee.
	Rooe Iraq, ...	Rooh ufza.
	5 notes, ...	
	Mughloob, ...	Hyrut.
	8 notes, ...	Moatedilah.
Isfuhan or Isfuhang	Tubreez, ...	Muanuvee.
	5 notes, ...	Puhluvee.
	Nushapooruk, ...	
	6 notes, ...	
Nuva, ...	Nourozi Khara, ...	
	5 notes, ...	
	Mahvur, ...	
	6 notes, ...	
Ooshshaq	Zabœl, ...	
	3 notes, ...	
	Ouj, ...	
	8 notes, ...	
Zungooluh, ..	Chargah, ...	
	4 notes, ...	
	Ghizal, ...	
	5 notes, ...	
Boosuleek,.. ..	Usheeran, ...	
	10 notes, ...	
	Suba, ...	
	5 notes, ...	

Music. The science of. This in Sungscrit is termed Sungeet. The invention of it is attributed to demi-gods, and amongst others to Narud, Sumeshwur, Hunooman, and Coolnath. Several treatises were written and are in existence, but they are so obscure, that little benefit is to be expected from them to the science.

Musicians. These are divided into classes by the Hindu authors, agreeably to merit and extent of knowledge.

I. *Nayuk.* He only has a right to claim this denomination who has a thorough knowledge of ancient music, both theoretically and practically. He should be intimately acquainted with all the rules for vocal and instrumental compositions, and for dancing. Should be qualified to sing Geet, Chhund, Prubund, &c., to perfection, and able to give instruction.

II. To this class belong those who understand merely the practice of music, and is subdivided into—

1. *Gundhurb.* One who is acquainted with the ancient (*Marg*) *Rags*, as well as the modern (*Desee*), and
2. Goonee, or Gooncar. He who has a knowledge of only the modern ones.

III. *Culavunt, Gundharbs,* and *Gooncars,* who sing *Dhoorpuds, Tirvuts, &c.,* to perfection, go by this appellation.

IV. Quvval, excels in singing Qoul, Turana, Kheal, &c.

V. Dharee, sings Curca, &c.

VI. Pundit. This term literally signifies a Doc. Mus., and is applied to those who profess to teach the theory of music, and do not engage in its practice.

(Culavunt and Quvval are modern terms.)

N.

Nucta. A species of song, sung in Boondelkhund, &c., p. 107

Nuqaruh. A sort of large drum played upon with sticks.

It is one of the instruments of the Noubut Khanuh.

Nuy: Literally a reed, Persian. A Mahomedan musical instrument.

O.

Oodoo. A Rag or Raginee which consists of only five notes.

Oopuj. An ad libitum passage.

Oorohee. Descending scale.

Ootpunnu. Origin (of sounds).

P.

Palna. Cradle hymns, p. 107.

Prubund. A species of ancient songs, p. 101.

Q.

Qoul ... } Species of song, p. 107.
Qulbana ... }

R.

Rag. A Hindu tune, p. 61 et seq.

Ragsagur. A species of composition, p. 103.

Rekhtah. Poetry in the tongue called Rekhtah, set to music, p. 106.

Ritoo. Seasons. The poets and musicians of Hindustan divide their year into six seasons, and one of these is allotted to each Rag, with his Raginees, Pootras, and Bharjyas. The seasons are:

Busunt,	Comprising the months.	Chyt and Bysakh.
Greeshmu,		Jeth and Usarh.
Burkha,		Sravun and Bhadru.
Surut,		Ashwin and Cartic.
Hem,		Ughun and Poos.
Shishir,		Magh and Phalgoon.

The Rags allotted to the seasons are

Bhyron	Surut.
Malcous	Shishir.
Hindol	Busunt.
Deepuc	Greeshmu.
Sree	Hem.
Megh	Burkha.

Rohee. Ascending scale.

Rubab. A guitar strung with gut strings.

It is a Mahomedan instrument, and particularly liked by the Puthans.

S.

Sarungee. The Hindustanee fiddle, a modern invention.

Seasons, vide Ritoo.

Sitar. An instrument of the Guitar species, invented by Umeer Khosrow of Delhi.

Sohla. A species of song, p. 107.

Soor. A sound, the key-note, and the octave alt of the Khuraj.

Soor-bhurna. To produce a sound from the throat, generally meant to sound the key-note.

Srooti. The chromatic scale of the Hindus, consisting of the sub-divisions of the seven notes of the gamut into twenty-two parts.

T.

Tal. Time or measure of melody.

Thoomree. One of the more modern species of song, p. 103.

Time. Tal.

Tirwut and Turana. Modern compositions; the style said to be invented by Umeer Khosrow, p. 106.

Treatise on music is called a grunth.

Tubla. Small drums. These are used two at a time, one played upon with each hand; the right is used for the treble (Zeer) and the left for the bass (Bumb). It is of modern invention.

Tumboora. A stringed instrument used to prolong the key-note, and fill up pauses in song.

Tuppa. One of the very modern species of song brought to perfection by the late Shoree of Lukhnow, p. 103.

V.

Veen. The most ancient, extensive, and complicated musical instrument of Hindustan. Its invention is attributed to the Mooni Narud.

Z.

Zeĕr. The treble end of a drum.

Zicree. A species of song originally of Goojrat, introduced into Hindustan by Qazee Muhmood, p. 107.

PART I.

PREFACE.

By music minds an equal temper know,
Nor swell too high nor sink too low;
Warriors she fires with animated sounds,
Pours balms into the bleeding lover's wounds.—POPE.

Poets themselves must fall, like those they sung,
Deaf the praised ear, and mute the tuneful tongue.—POPE.

A general view of the plan and contents of the work.

A TREATISE on the Music of Hindoostan is a desideratum which has not yet been supplied. Although several eminent Orientalists have endeavoured to penetrate this elegant branch of Indian science, scarcely any part of it has been elucidated or rendered familiar to Europeans. It is this chasm which I have endeavoured to fill; how far I have succeeded in an undertaking so difficult (for reasons which shall presently appear), it is for the public to determine.

It is impossible to convey an accurate idea of music by words or written language; that is, the various degrees of acuteness or gravity of sounds, together with the precise quantity of the duration of each, cannot be expressed by common language, so as to be of any use

A

to performers, and as the musical characters now in use, which alone can express music in the manner that could be desired, is a modern invention, of course all attempts to define music anterior to the invention of this elegant and concise method must have necessarily proved abortive.

How far the ancient philosophers of this country advanced towards the perfection of this science will appear in the course of this work; but as they were something similar to the awkward attempts made in Europe previous to the invention of the system now in use, they were insufficient for practice. The musical scale, invented by Magister Franco, and the time table, were both known here, and it only required a trifling degree of ingenuity to connect the one with the other, so that one individual character might instantly express both. This step was wanting, and it is this which has rendered all their treatises on music an unintelligible and almost useless jargon.

During the earlier ages of Hindoostan, music was cultivated by philosophers and men eminent for polite literature, for whom such general directions and rules for composition sufficed, after a course of musical education acquired from living tutors; indeed, the abhorrence of innovation, and veneration for the established national music, which was firmly believed to be of divine origin, precluded the necessity of any other; but when, from the theory of music, a defection took place of its practice, and men of learning confined themselves exclusively to the former, while the latter branch was abandoned entirely to the illiterate, all attempts to elucidate music from rules laid down in books, a science incapable of explanation by mere words, became idle. This is the reason why even so able and eminent an Orientalist as Sir William Jones has failed. Books alone are insufficient for this purpose—we must endeavour to procure solutions from living professors, of whom there are several, although grossly illiterate. This method, although very laborious, and even precarious, seems to be the only one by which any advance can be made in so abstruse an undertaking. Should the public consider this work as at all conducive to the end to which it achieves to aspire, it is the intention of the author to lay before them specimens of original Rags and Raginees, set to music, accompanied with short notices, which will serve to elucidate the facts advanced in this volume.

The causes which induced a defection of the theory from the practice of music in Hindoostan will be developed in the course of the work, and it is sufficient here to notice that such a defection has actually taken place, and that a search for one versed both in the theory and practice of Indian music would perhaps prove as fruitless as that after the philosopher's stone. The similitude will hold still further if we take the trouble to second our search with due caution, for there are many reputed Kemiagurs in this country, all of whom prove themselves to possess no more knowledge of the auriferous art, than the reader can himself possibly be possessed of.

A taste for the classics is imbibed by us from our school education. No philologer will, I believe, deny that impressions contracted in early infancy, or tender age, will, if possible, be effaced with the greatest difficulty.

It is therefore hard for us to divest ourselves of the idea that whatever is of Greek or Egyptian origin must be deserving of respect and imitation. The near connection between poetry and music should not be forgotten. To the antiquarian such researches afford a two-fold interest. From this source should be derived that veneration for ancient music which all classical scholars entertain, and for which several have laboured.

The similitude between the music of the classical nations and that of Hindoostan has never, I believe, been traced, and the following labour will, I presume to hope, be productive of some fruit.

There is no doubt that harmony is a refinement on melody; but much modern music, divested of the harmony which accompanies it, presents to us its blank nudity, and want of that beauty which warranted the expression "and most adorned when adorned the least." Although I am myself very fond of harmony, and it cannot but be acknowledged that it is a very sublime stretch of the human mind, the reasoning on harmony will perhaps convince the reader that harmony is more conducive to cover the nakedness, than shew the fertility, of genius. Indeed, perhaps all the most beautiful successions of tones which constitute agreeable melody are exhausted, and this is the reason of the poorness of our modern melody, and the abundant use of harmony, which however in a good measure compensates by its novelty. At the same time, we are constrained to allow that harmony is nothing but art, which can never charm equally with nature. "Enthusiastic melody can be produced by an illiterate mind, but tolerable harmony always supposes previous study,"—a plain indication that the former is natural, the latter artificial.

To be convinced that foreign music, such as we have not been accustomed to, is always repugnant to our taste, till habit reconcile us to it, we need only refer to the sentiments of the several travellers who have recorded their particular feelings on hearing the music of nations with whom they have had but little intercourse. Europe, the boast of civilization, will likewise throw an additional weight into the balance of impartiality when the music or science of those nations is concerned who are designated semi-barbarous by her proud sons. It should be a question likewise whether they have witnessed the performance of those who were reputed to excel in so difficult a practice.

If a native of India were to visit Europe, and who having never had opportunities of hearing music in its utmost perfection—who had never witnessed an opera, or a concert, directed by an able musician, but had merely heard blind beggars, and itinerant* scrapers, such as frequent inns and taverns—were to assert that the music of Europe was execrable, it would perhaps never have occurred to his hearer that he had heard only such music as he would himself designate by the same title, and; the poor traveller's want of taste would perhaps be the first and uppermost idea that would present itself. But when we possess the contrary testimonies of two enlightened travellers with respect to the same subject, surely we may have reason to appear somewhat sceptical. On the opinions given by Europeans on the music of Hindoostan, I shall produce an example.

Dr. Griffiths, in his Travels in Europe, Asia Minor, and Arabia, 1805, page 115, says,—"There are amongst the Turks some who affect a taste for music; but they understand not 'the concord of sweet sounds,' nor comprehend, according to our system, a single principle of musical composition. An ill-shaped guitar, with several wires, always out of tune,—a narrow wooden case, upon which are fastened two catgut strings,—a tambourine of leather, instead of parchment, ornamented with many small plates of brass, which jingle most discordantly,—and a sort of flute, made without any regard to the just proportion of distance between the apertures, constitute the principal instruments of these virtuosi: yet it is extremely common to see, amongst the lowest orders, performers on the guitar, which they continue for hours to torment with a monotony the most detestable."

In a note on this paragraph, the Doctor says,—"These ideas were committed to paper many years ago: I have since seen Mr. Dallaway's interesting remarks upon the music of the Turks, which I shall transcribe; and only observe, that however correct may be their theory, their execution has always appeared to me (and I had many occasions of attending to it) so far beneath mediocrity, as to merit no kind of comparison with any other music or musical performers. From the division of the semitones into minor tones, Mr. D. says, results that *sweetness of melody* by which they are so much delighted, and which leads them to disparage the *greater harmony* of European music;—but Turkish judgment only can give way to a preference so preposterous; nor can it be supposed that performers, who *play merely from memory*, and *reject notes*, can acquire any eminence in the difficult science of music." Mr. Dallaway says,—"They are guided by strict rules of composition according to their own musical theory."

I have quoted this passage not as the only or most appropriate example, but because it first occurred to me, and the similarity between the Turkish, as described by Dr. G. and Mr. D., and the Indian music, appeared to me to be sufficiently close to warrant its insertion in this place.

From the censure passed by Dr. G. on musicians playing from memory, it should appear, that it did not occur to him that all ancient musicians of Egypt, Greece, and Rome, lived in an age much prior to that of the monk of Arezzo, who is supposed to be the inventor of the modern musical characters, and must consequently have played from memory, notwithstanding which they are celebrated to have acquired eminence. In more modern times we have had several bright examples in men who were either born blind, or were deprived of sight in early infancy, and constantly played from memory, who became great musicians and composers. In fact, several eminent men have been of opinion that the study of music was to be chiefly recommended to blind persons. Saunderson, the algebraist, became blind in his infancy, and Milton was so when he composed his divine poem, which shews what men are capable of doing from memory.

On the acquisition of India to the Europeans, it was generally believed to have been in a semi-barbarous state. The generous attempts made by Sir William Jones and Dr. Gilchrist, together with the elegant acquirements of Mr. H. H. Wilson, have proved it to be an inexhaustible mine, pregnant with the most luxuriant ores of literature. Several French authors have likewise contributed to the more intimate acquaintance of the Europeans with Eastern learning.

The poetry of a nation is almost universally sought after by the traveller and the curious, and it is seldom considered by him that its music deserves a thought; while it should be remembered, that poetry and music have always illustrated and assisted each other, particularly in Hindoostan, where both are subservient to religion, and where the ablest performers of music were Munies and Jogees, a set of men reputed for sanctity, and whose devout aspirations were continually poured forth in measured numbers and varied tone.

Every scrap of Egyptian and Grecian music is treasured up as a relic of antiquity, how despicable soever its merits might be. I at least have not discernment sufficient to comprehend the beauties of the Greek air inserted in the Flutist's Journal, No. 6, page 123, and many other pieces of equal merit, which I could point out, were I inclined to criticise.

That Indian music, although in general possessing intrinsic claim to beauty in melody, is seldom sought after, will be, I presume, allowed; but why? I shall venture to say, because possession cloys. We think it in our power to obtain it whenever we please, and therefore we never strive for it; but may we never, never become a nation so lost and forgotten as the ancient Egyptains and Greeks, whose music can only be gleaned from some imperfect accounts in their writings, although it would enhance the value of the music of this country. I am however convinced, for reasons given above, that an endeavour to comprehend the ancient music of Hindoostan would not prove so easy an undertaking as one would be inclined to promise himself it would.

I have endeavoured to notice the similarity which appears to me to exist between the music of Hindoostan and that of the other two ancient nations—how far my conjectures have been correct, it remains with the learned to decide. Should my labours prove successful in any one instance, I shall feel happy to have contributed even in so small a degree to the development of a science so intimately connected with the *belle lettres*, and which respects a country acting so conspicuous a part on the theatre of the modern world.

Egypt, Greece and Rome are the only ancient countries which the European scholar is taught to reverence as having been civilized and enlightened—all the rest he is to consider as barbarous. India is not generally thought of, as deserving of any approximity in rank; but the acuteness of some has even led them to doubt, whether this country was not in a state of civilization even before the most ancient of those three; nay, whether this was not the parent country—the root of civilization. If a graft from the parent tree, having found better soil, has flourished more luxuriantly, are we to despise the root which gave it birth? In India, to this day, superstition and idolatry prevail: so did they in Egypt, Greece, and Rome; and if the truths of the gospel were not to have been announced to the world for two thousand years longer, we should have found the same things prevailing in Europe. India has besides suffered the persecutions of illiberal Mahomedan princes, who were equally superstitious; and although desirous of eradicating idolatry (the falsity of which they never thought of demonstrating but with the sword), and were thus far certainly iconoclasts, surely were no encouragers to the improvement of sciences. So that all the philosophy and learning of the Hindoos consist in the knowledge of their most ancient writings. If it should appear that in those times they had advanced more towards the perfection of music than did the classical nations, it seems to me sufficient to authorise their bearing the palm, at least in this branch of science.

The theory and practice of music, as far as it is now known and practised in Hindoostan, I hope I have succeeded in describing. A knowledge of what might be wanting here, I presume will be found on inquiry very difficult to obtain;* but I hope some one more able

* "Had the *Indian* empire continued in full energy for the last two thousand years, religion would, no doubt, have given permanence to systems of music invented, as the Hindoos believe, by their gods, and adapted to mystical poetry: but such have been the revolutions of their government since the time of *Alexander*, that, although the *Sanscrit* books have preserved the theory of their musical compositions, the practice of it seems wholly lost (as all the *Pandits and Rajahs* confess) in *Gour* and *Magadha*, or the provinces of Bengal and Behar. When I first read the songs of *Jayadêva*, who has prefixed to each of them the name of the mode in which it was anciently sung, I had hopes of procuring the original music; but the *Pandits* of the south referred me to those of the west, and the *Brahmans* of the west would have sent me to those of the north; while they, I mean those of Nepal and Cashmir, declared that they had no ancient music, but imagined that the notes of the *Gitagovinda* must exist, if anywhere, in one of the southern provinces, where the poet was born: from all this, I collect, that the art which flourished in India many centuries ago, has faded for want of due culture, though some scanty remnants of it may, perhaps, be preserved in the pastoral roundelays of Mathura on the loves and sports of the Indian Apollo."—*Sir William Jones, vol. I, p.* 440.

Sir William Jones, it seems, confined his search to that phœnix, a learned Pandit, who might likewise be a musician; but, I believe, such a person does not exist in Hindoostan for reasons which shall be hereafter noticed.

and persevering will supply the deficiencies, and restore the original music of this country to its primitive state. Many branches of Indian science and literature have been revived by zealous Orientalists, and it seems not quite clear why its music has been so much neglected.

I have not confined myself to the details in books, but have also consulted the most famous performers, both Hindoos and Mussulmans, the first Veenkars in India, the more expert musicians of Lucknow, and Hukeem Sulamut Ulee Khan of Benares, who has written a treatise on music.

The reader will not find this work a translation of any of the existing treatises on music, but an original work, comprehending the system of Hindoostanee music according to the ancient theory, noticing as much of it as is confirmed by the practice of the present day. I have endeavoured, likewise, throughout the work, to assign the motives for several peculiarities in Hindoo music and manners, for which none has been hitherto assigned, such as the confining their Raginees to particular seasons of the year and time of day and night: the difference between the lyric poetry of several nations of Asia, sung in this country: some ancient customs now become wholly or partly obsolete, and practices now out of fashion, or rendered useless in consequence of the security afforded by the British Government.

In the definition of the term "*Rag*," I have taken the liberty to differ from Dr. Gilchrist and Sir William Jones; the motives for which will, I hope, appear sufficiently cogent to have warranted the presumption. Some reasoning on harmony and melody will likewise be found, which I hope will not be unacceptable; but on impartial consideration found to possess some weight. The immense variety in time noticed in the original treatises, a great many of which are still practised, has led me to discuss this subject more largely than I should have done, had its number not been so limited in European practice, and the subject not appeared so important. *All* the species of composition have been noticed, with a short sketch of the distinguishing characters of each; and a brief account of the principal musicians, from the most ancient to the present time, is superadded.

INTRODUCTION.

The verse of Chaucer is not harmonious to us : they who live with him, thought it musical.—DRYDEN.

Music. Its power on the human mind. That of Hindoostan. The opinion of the Natives with respect to their ancient musicians. How a knowledge of it may be acquired. Not generally liked by Europeans. Reasons assigned for this. Native opinion with regard to its lawfulness. Musical instruments. Relation of music to poetry considered. Progress of music in Hindoostan. The manner of life which should be led to insure eminence in this science. Cause of its depravity. Date of its decline. The similarity which the music of this country seems to bear to that of Egypt and Greece. How a knowledge of the music of Hindoostan might conduce to a revival of that of those countries. Comparisons offered. Whether the natives of Greece or Hindoostan had made greater progress in music. Comparisons decide in favor of the latter.

ALL arts and sciences have undoubtedly had very trivial and obscure beginnings, and the accounts given by historians of their inventors are generally to be considered as fabulous; for they certainly are the gradual productions of several, wrought up into a system after the lapse of considerable time, and the confirmation of a variety of experiments. Nature is always gradual in her productions, and the length of time required to bring any thing to perfection is in proportion to the quality of that thing. The stately *bur* tree takes ages to develope its majesty, while the insignificant mushroom springs up in a few hours. With the human mind, it is observed to be the same as with other productions of nature ; time and culture improve it, and the more the adventitious circumstances surrounding it are favorable, the more it flourishes.

"The invention of great arts and sciences have amongst all nations of antiquity been attributed to deities or men actuated by divine inspiration, except by the Hebrews, the only nation upon earth who had the knowledge of the true God. Indeed, there is an awe with which men of great minds, particularly such as exercise them for the benefit of mankind, inspire us, that it is no wonder they were regarded by the ancients as beings of a superior order." Men of limited command have it not in their power to diffuse their benevolence to an extensive circle ; but when princes, or great statesmen and able generals, condescend to employ their leisure in works which are conducive to the benefit, or alleviation of the cares, of society, they evince the natural goodness of their hearts, they gain the particular esteem of the people over whom they exercise control, and are regarded as men of a superior order.

All philologers are agreed, that music is anterior to language. Dr. Burney* says, "Vocal music is of such high antiquity, that its origin seems to have been coeval with mankind ; at least the lengthened tones of pleasure and pain, of joy and affection, must long have preceded every other language, and music. The voice of passion wants but few articulations, and must have been nearly the same in all human creatures, differing only in gravity or acuteness according to age, sex, and organization, till the invention of words

* General History of Music from the earliest ages to the present period, vol. i, p. 464.

by particular convention, in different societies, weakened, and by degrees rendered it unintelligible. The primitive and instinctive language, or cry of nature, is still retained by animals, and universally understood; while our artificial tongues are known only to the small part of the globe, where, after being learned with great pains, they are spoken. 'We talk of love, and of hatred,' says M. de Voltaire, 'in general terms, without being able to express the different degrees of those passions. It is the same with respect to pain and pleasure, of which there are such innumerable species. The shades and gradations of volition, repugnance or compulsion, are equally indistinct want of colors.' This censure should, however, be confined to written language; for though a word can be accurately expressed in writing, and pronounced but one way, yet the different tones of voice that can be given to it in the utterance are infinite. A mere negative or affirmative may even be uttered in such a manner as to convey ideas diametrically opposite to the original import of the word." From this it appears, that music, or at least variety in tone, is the soul of language, and without which no precise meaning can be attached to any particular word.

"* If the art of music be so natural to man that vocal melody is practised wherever articulate sounds are used, there can be little reason for deducing the idea of music from the whistling of winds through the reeds that grew on the river Nile. And indeed, when we reflect with how easy a transition we may pass from the accents of speaking to diatonic sounds; when we observe how early children adapt the language of their amusements to measure and melody, however rude; when we consider how early and universally these

* Encyclopædia Britannica, Art. Music.

practices take place—there is no avoiding the conclusion, that the idea of music is connatural to man, and implied in the original principles of his constitution." The Hindoos attribute the invention of music to Muhadev; but after making due allowances for superstition and ignorance, as well as for the innate pride of man, it seems unnecessary to argue this point any farther.

Every nation, how rude soever, has, we see, its music, and the degree of its refinement is in proportion to the civilization of its professors. She is yet in her cradle with the rude Indians of America, or the "hideous virgins of Congo." With the natives of Hindoostan, she may be said long to have left the puerile state, though perhaps still far from that of puberty, her progress towards maturity having been checked, and her constitution ruined and thrown into decay by the overwhelming and supercilious power of the Mahomedan government; while in Europe, and especially in the luxuriant soil of Italy, she sports in all the gaiety of youthful bloom and heavenly beauty. It is with music, as with painting, sculpture, statuary, architecture, and every other art or science, chiefly ornamental or amusing, that it flourishes best nnder steady and peaceful governments, which encourage them by their patronage. "Literature, arts, and refinements, were encouraged more early at the courts of the Roman pontiffs, than in any other country; and owing to that circumstance, it is, that the scale, the counterpoint, the best melodies, the dramas, religious and secular, the chief graces and elegances of modern music, have derived their origin from Italy."

It is a very ancient observation, that the "greatest masters in every profession and science always appear in the same period of time;" and P. Bossu and Juvenal do not give much credit for doubting "whether any influence of stars, any power of planets, or kindly aspect of the heavenly bodies, might not at times reach our globe, and impregnate some favorite race with a celestial spirit." He also sneers at the assertion of the supernatural conceptions and miraculous nursings of Hercules and Alexander, Orpheus, Homer, and Plato, Pindar, and the founders of the Roman and Persian empires, and attributes the cause to emulation. This latter principle, however, cannot exist without encouragement, which is the source of all emulation. Did Ukbur Shah not encourage and patronize genius, his court would not have been filled with the gems "Nouratun." Why is Italy considered as the school of music? Or why was she with regard to the rest of Europe what ancient Greece was to Rome?

The power of music on the human mind has always been acknowledged to be very great, as well as its general tendency towards the soft and amiable passions. Polibius, speaking of the inhabitants of Cynete, Plato, with his opponent Aristotle, Theophrastus, and other ancient writers, were of this mind. In Arcadia, every man was required by law to learn music, to soften the ferocity of his manners; and her admirers of Hindoostan have not been backward in their praises of it. Most natives faithfully believe that ancient songsters of the period, when their government flourished, had power not only over human beings, and passions, but also over irrational animals and inanimate and insensible creatures. There are professors on record to whom the wild beasts listened with admiration, nay at the sound of whose voice rocks melted and whole rivers forgot to flow.

"I have been assured by a credible eye-witness," says Sir William Jones, "*that two wild antelopes used often to come from the woods, to the place where a more savage beast, *Siraj-ud-Doulah*, entertained himself with concerts, and that they listened to the strain with an appearance of pleasure, till the monster, in whose soul there was no music, shot one of them, to display his archery; secondly, a learned native of this country told me that he had frequently seen the more venomous and malignant snakes leave their holes, upon hearing tunes on a flute, which, as he supposed, gave them peculiar delight; and thirdly, an intelligent *Persian*, who repeated his story again and again, and permitted me to write it down from his lips, told me, he had more than once been present when a celebrated lutanist, *Mirza Mohummud*, surnamed *Bulbul*, was playing to a large company in a grove near *Shiraz*, where he distinctly saw the nightingales trying to vie with the musician, sometimes warbling on the trees, sometimes fluttering from branch to branch, as if they wished to approach the instrument whence the melody proceeded, and at length dropping on the ground in a kind of ecstacy, from which they were soon raised, he assured me, by a change of the mode."

Whatever poets or fabulists might have alleged in favor of music, and whatever extravagant praises the wildness of their heated imaginations, assisted by the dictates of a fertile genius, led them to pronounce, it is nevertheless certain that very few persons have been found in every age whose apathetic bosom did not feel the glow music is wont to inspire. The power of music anciently, it has been supposed,

* On the Musical Modes of the Hindoos, written in 1784, and since much larged by the President, p. 415.

would, from the agreeable surprise, which must have been occasioned by its novelty, add much to the effect that could be looked for in later times; indeed, some have supposed, it could not but be irresistible. With regard to Oriental music, although it has been generally celebrated by almost all scholars of the East, yet it seems to me very doubtful, whether any of those who have thus eulogised the subject fully comprehended its beauties.

The only way by which perfection in this can be attained is by studying the original works, and consulting the best living performers, both vocal and instrumental; and few persons have inclination, leisure, and opportunities sufficient for an undertaking in itself so complicated, and rendered more so from the want of perspicuous definitions. Indeed, without the assistance of learned natives, the search would be entirely fruitless. The theory of music is so little discussed at present, that few even of the best performers have the least knowledge of any thing but the practical part, in which to their credit it must be acknowledged they excel. The reason of which seems to be, that most treatises on Hindoostanee music are written in the manner of "Tartini on Harmony," which men of erudition have lamented was not committed "in a style of greater perspicuity."

Notwithstanding what men of great learning and taste have alleged in favor of Oriental music, persons whose authority should be venerable, there are many who treat it with derision: some that pretend to be connoisseurs, but upon whose judgment I shall leave others to offer their opinion, and will observe in a transient manner, that the only reasoning they have to allege is to remark with a smile that it is *Hindoostanee* music, and not consistent with their natural taste, without satisfying us that their taste is of the most refined nature.

There is a note in Mr. Wilson's translation of the Megha Duta on this passage :

"Not e'en the vilest, when a falling friend
"Solicits help it once was his to lend,"

which I cannot help transcribing.

"The *Hindus* have been the object of much idle panegyric, and equally idle detraction ; some writers have invested them with every amiable attribute, and they have been deprived by others of the common virtues of humanity. Amongst the excellencies denied to them, gratitude has been always particularized, and there are many of the European residents of India, who scarcely imagine that the natives of the country ever heard of such a sentiment. To them, and to all detractors on this head, the above verse is a satisfactory reply ; and that no doubt of its tenor may remain, I add the literal translation of the original passage, "Not even a low man, when laid hold of for support by a friend, will turn away his face with forgetfulness of former kindness ; how therefore should the exalted act thus ?"

If by Hindoostanee music is meant that medley of confusion and noise which consists of drums of different sorts, and perhaps a fife—if the assertoin be made by such as have heard these only, I admit the assertoin in its full extent ; but if it be so asserted of all Hindoostanee music, or of all the beauties which it possesses or is susceptible of, I deny the charge. The prepossession might arise from one or more of the following causes : first, ignorance, in which I include the not having had opportunities of hearing the best performers ; secondly, natural prepossession against Hindoostanee music; thirdly, inattention to its beauties from the second motive or otherwise; fourthly, incapacity of comprehension. It is probably not unfrequent that all these causes concur to produce the effect.

It is certainly not rational in a man to praise or decry any thing before he is perfectly acquainted with its various excellencies or imperfections. There are many things in nature which might appear impossible to a superficial observer of her works—there are likewise several mechanical and philosophical contrivances which present a similar view to the uninitiated. Who would have thought that instinct could lead an irrational animal so far as almost to approach to sense, before proper attention was paid to the various devices and arts employed by different animals? Who should have credited the wonderful effects of gunpowder, which obtained for the Spaniards the appellation of the "mighty thunders" in the wars with the Incas so late as the middle of the fourteenth century? That fire might be literally brought down from heaven was considered a miracle before Dr. Franklin's time, and such a thing as the fulminating silver was not dreamed of before the invention of it by Brugnatelli. What surprising and stupendous effects have of late years been produced by the action of so simple an agent as steam; and to what variety of purposes has it been directed by the ingenuity of man! How it would have rejoiced Captain Savery to have beheld steam, acting as it were from its own impulse and consciousness, resembling that of a reasonable being!

We can easily see how ignorance or incapacity might lead a person to wrong conclusions, yet we do not consider whether those persons who decry Hindoostanee music have had opportunities of hearing it to the best advantage; whether, supposing they had, they were at the time divested of all prejudices against it, and were disposed to judge impartially; whether they possessed the requisite capacity to comprehend its beauties.

Dr. Burney, in his preface to his general History of Music, from the earliest ages to the present period, (MDCCLXXVI.) very justly observes, that "to love such music as our ears are accustomed to is an instinct so generally subsisting in our nature, that it appears less wonderful it should have been in the highest estimation at all times, and in every place, than that it should hitherto never have had its progressive improvements and revolutions." It is perhaps owing to this general want of acquaintance with it, that Oriental music is not so much esteemed as perhaps its merit deserves. Although I have met with some European ladies who eagerly desired to possess a copy of a Hindoostanee song or air, yet it seemed to me that they esteemed it more as a relic of curiosity, perhaps to be sent home, than for its intrinsic worth in their eyes.

The author of "An Inquiry into the Life and Writings of Homer" very justly observes, that "we are born but with narrow capacities: our minds are not able to master two sets of manners, or comprehend with facility different ways of life. Our company, education and circumstances make deep impressions, and form us into a character, of which we can hardly divest ourselves afterwards. The manners, not only of the age and nation in which we live, but of our city and family, stick closely to us, and betray us at every turn when we try to dissemble, and would pass for foreigners. In a similar manner, unless we are perfectly well acquainted with the manners, and customs, and mode of life prevalent amongst a nation, and at the very juncture of time which the poet describes, it is not possible to feel the effect intended to be conveyed."

Various are the opinions which the natives entertain of music with regard to its lawfulness or otherwise. The Hindoos are unanimous in their praises of it, and extol it as one of the sweetest enjoyments of life, in which the gods are praised with due sublimity, kings and princes have their benevolent and heroic actions recited in the most suitable manner, the affluent enjoy its beauties without reproach, the needy by its aid forget their misery, the unfortunate finds relief by giving vent to his sorrow in song, the lover pays the most gratifying compliment to his mistress, and the coy maiden without a blush describes the ardour of her passion.

The Moosulman doctors, however, disagree from them and with each other. The more severe of them prohibit the use of it altogether as irreligious and profane; while others are somewhat more indulgent, and permit it with certain restrictions. A few, convinced of its excellence, but dreading the censure of casuists, have prudently preferred silence. Some have considered it as exhilirating the spirits, and others, perhaps with more reason, declare it to be an incentive to the bent of the inclination, and consequently possessing the property of producing both good and evil. That moral writer Shekh Sadee says,

بگويم سماع اي برادر كه چيست اگر مستمعرا برانم كه كيست

Music is either vocal or instrumental. The former is everywhere acknowledged to be superior to the latter. It is not in the power of man to form an artificial instrument so very delicate and beautiful in tone, and possessing all the pliability of a truly good voice.

When I speak of the beauties of Hindoostanee music, I would have it understood, that I mean its intrinsic and real beauties, uncircumscribed in its acceptation to any individual branch of it. Although nature might not perhaps have bestowed sufficient ingenuity on the natives of India, which might enable them to rival other nations in the nicety of their instrument, (or what appears to me a more attributable cause—a want of patronage from the distracted state of the country and depravity of the times,) she has, however, been sufficiently indulgent to them in their natural organs. The names of Byjoo, Nayuk Gopal, and Tansen will never be forgot in the annals of Hindoostanee music; and time will show whether any of the disciples of the late Shoree will ever rival him. The above observation on the musical instruments of Hindoostan should only be applied to the present times, for we can offer no opinion as to the care bestowed on their manufacture during the flourishing state of the empire. With respect to the voice, there are some in existence whose singing does them great credit, and I have myself had the pleasure of hearing a few both males and females who richly deserve this praise.

It is allowed that 'some compositions contain sentences so pithy, delivered in such beautiful poetry, that they do not at all stand in need of music to set them off to advantage; while there are sometimes such happy effusions of the musician's imagination that they speak for themselves; nor could all the fire of the poet or the persuasion of the rhetoretician add a single grace to those they already possess.'

The natives of India are sensible of this power of music, and have sometimes demonstrated it in their melodies, which if considered in a musical view are really elegant, and engage all our attention ; but when we come to examine the sentiment which has been delivered in so delicate a strain, and which we fancy will be in accordance with the beauty of the melody, we find ourselves sadly disappointed, for they contain odd sentences awkwardly put together. I shall explain how this comes to pass.

The ancient musicians of Hindoostan were also generally poets and men of erudition, and sung their own compositions ; in fact, music and poetry have always gone hand in hand, and as the Egyptain priests, by means of their hieroglyphics, reserved the knowledge of their sciences exclusively to themselves, so the ancient Brahmins of this country threatened with excommunication any of their tribe who should presume to apostatise and betray the sacred writings or Shasters to any but members of the elect, whose mouths only were esteemed sufficiently holy to utter words so sacred ; indeed, the innate pride of man would induce them to keep that to themselves which was the sole cause of all the abject deference and almost adoration paid to Brahmins by all the other tribes. On the other hand, none of the inferior tribes could presume to wish to acquire a knowledge of the sacred writings, as it would be reckoned impious to do so. It was thus that the ancients sung their own composition ; but in progress of time, and especially under the Mahomedan princes, when music became a distinct trade, (and all whose imaginations were fruitful for musical composition were not likewise blessed with talent for poetry,) the musician, relying on the strength of his own abilities in music, and fancying himself a poet of course, scorned to set melody to the poetry of others. The consequence has been what I have noticed in the preceding paragraph; but notwithstanding this disadvantage, they have gained the palm from competitors, who as poets might claim superiority, whilst the melody of the others has preserved its rank for ages.

The history of the world, and of the rise and decline of empires, the biography of eminent men, and the account of the invention and progress of arts and sciences, furnish us with one melancholy and common moral, that nothing sublunary is stable. How trivial and insignificant were the beginnings of nations, who in time grew powerful, and became the terror of their neighbours, or of the world! How different the picture of their flourishing state from that of their decline and fall; even to the time when men inquire of each other, where was Thebes, or Palibothra situated!

The history of music, in common with that of other arts and sciences, furnishes us with similar instruction. Its first origin seems to have been to convey the idea of our passions to others. In progress of time, when language arrived to a certain degree of intelligibility, its use began to be restricted to the worship of the Supreme Being. It was afterwards extended to the commemoration of great events, the celebration of the praises of chieftains and heroes, and lastly to the alleviation of the cares of society, in which the enumeration of the joys of love holds a distinguished place. In Hindoostan, music arrived at its greatest height during the flourishing period of the native princes, just a little before the Mahomedan conquest, and its subsequent depravity and decline since then, closed the scene with the usual catastrophe.

Music has always been highly appreciated, especially when ts charms have not been prostituted to add to the allurement of licentious poetry. Hence it is that after it had been methodised, the greatest men in this country in ancient days admired it, and patronised its professors; till in course of time, these becoming licentious, cast such a stigma on the science, that men of honor disdained to be numbered amongst its professors. At present most native performers of this noble science are the most immoral set of men on earth, and the term is another word for all that is abominable, synonimous with that of the most abandoned and profligate exercises under the sun. The later musicians of Greece and Rome were no better; indeed the parallel will admit of being drawn through the whole latitude.

The author of An Inquiry into the Life and Writings of Homer, treating of bards of the age of that poet, says, "It was indeed no life of wealth or power, but of great ease and much honor. The ΑΟΙΔΟΙ were welcome to kings and courts; were necessary at feasts and sacrifices; and were highly reverenced by the people." The ancient troubadours of Provence were likewise all musicians.* Their subsequent depravity is well known.

The common opinion in Hindoostan is, that to be a great musician, a man must live retired from the world like a Jogee. This opinion is influenced by a consideration of the practices of the greatest professors of antiquity, and is not perhaps without some foundation. We know that some of the greatest poets used to retire to their favorite romantic and wildly beautiful spots, the most attracting parts of which they

* Todos o los mas cavalleros andantes de la edad passada eran grandes Trobadores y grandes musicos. Part I. lib. iii. Don Quixote.

copied from nature, and adopted as the foundation of their enchanting scenes. The aid the painter derives from them is evident. It is not only the poet and the painter, however, that such delightful places befriend, the genius of music likewise inhabits them, and in a special manner patronises her votaries there. This opinion was also common with the Greeks, as will appear from a passage quoted from Plato by Dr. Burney: "The grasshopper sings all summer without food, like those men who, dedicating themselves to the muses, forget the common concerns of life."

The paucity of men of genius has been one reason for the estimation in which they were held. This scarcity has been universally acknowledged. Sir William Temple says, "Of all the numbers of mankind that live within the compass of a thousand years, for one man that is born capable of making a great poet, there may be a thousand born capable of making great generals, or ministers of State, as the most renowned in story."

The musicians of this country of old, who adopted this austere method of living, concerning themselves little about the luxuries and vanities of the world, would not be bribed to display their talents in public as hired professors. No gifts or grants were considered by them as worth accepting, as they cared for nothing. Princes and great men of taste therefore found themselves under the necessity of courting their friendship, and of accepting the fruit of their genius as a favor, for which they possessed no other means of repaying them but with honor and kind treatment. Their tribe likewise screened them from all sacrilegious violence, and insured respect. The religious sentiments of the natives, who considered these persons as voluntary exiles, who had renounced the world, and dedicated themselves to the worship of the gods, added some weight to the admiration they commanded ; and the ease and independence enjoyed by such men would spur the desire of its acquisition in others.

The consideration obtained by these men, in time, induced several of an avaricious disposition to engage as pupils, and after acquiring some knowledge of the art, to set up for themselves ; but the sordidness of their views was soon discovered. They, however, still continued to maintain their ground, till the country became overstocked with professors, who prostituted their abilities for a mere trifle ; and lastly, considering themselves as ministers of pleasure, and seeing that it answered their avaricious views, even engaged in other traffic not at all honorable to a man of any profession, and they might have said, with the Provençal minstrel of the 12th and 13th century—

> I from lovers tokens bear,
> I can flow'ry chaplets weave,
> Amorous belts can well prepare,
> And with courteous speech deceive.

They were become like the minstrels of England in the regin of Edward II. when it was found necessary in 1315 to restrain them by express laws.

Musicians of real merit, however, continued to meet with due honor and patronage till the reign of Mohummud Shah, who is considered the most luxurious of the sovereigns of Delhi, and the splendur of whose court could not be maintained without expert musicians. After the reign of this monarch, his successors had neither tranquillity nor leisure sufficient for such amusements, and became engaged in sports of a quite different nature, replete with dismal reflections.

Dr. Carey, in the preface to his Sanscrit Grammar, Calcutta, 1820, supposes the Egyptians to have been a colony from India. The reasons stated by that gentleman appear very plausible, which may be consulted by the curious reader. Bigland, in his Letters on the Study and Use of Ancient and Modern History, page 67, treating on the difference of castes, says, "This regulation has no where been found in any country of note, ancient or modern, except Egypt and India, which has caused many to suppose that the inhabitants of India were originally a colony from Egypt, or that the Egyptians were a colony from India." And again, p. 69, "These distinctions were sanctioned by religion, and interwoven into its very essence in Egypt as well as in India. In this the Egyptian priests and the Brahmans of India have exactly hit the same mark, and met with equal success."

Although a similarity in the music of the two countries would not have much weight in hazarding such an opinion, yet, added to other resemblances, and to the conjectures of such respectable authorities, it will perhaps not be considered out of place that I have pointed out all the conformity which appeared to me to subsist between the two.

Every person who reads the history of ancient music must be struck with the vast laborious researches made in that branch of science, and cannot but admire the abilities and patience of the authors. But it is a matter of regret that their labours have more generally ended in obscurity, doubt, and conjecture than in ascertaining the desired point. This, however, has been the case with almost all disputed points, of great antiquity, and must perhaps for ever remain so for want of authentic documents, which can never be produced by either party; for none could have existed previous to the invention of letters, and most of what was since committed to writing has been destroyed by revolutions and time. There is, however, another difficulty particularly attending upon the history of music. This is a science which addresses itself exclusively to the ear, and before the invention of the modern method of committing an air to paper, all description of it in books must have been vague, and liable to great uncertainty. The hatred of the natives of India to innovation has prompted them to preserve their ancient practice almost inviolable, and hence perhaps if a thorough knowledge of Indian music is acquired, and some similarity be found between it and that of the nations above noticed, there would perhaps be some hopes of unravelling the practice of those celebrated countries. That great part of ancient music is unintelligible is most generally allowed, and such as have endeavoured to elucidate them, have for the most part made but little progress for want of perspicuous definitions and living performers, who might assist in deciphering the theory.

If a comparison between the ancient music of Greece, which was principally borrowed from the Egyptians, and that of Hindoostan, might be hazarded, it would appear that great similarity exists between the two. The same rythmical measure, the same subdivision of semitones into minor divisions, the same noisy* method of beating time not only

* Many ancient instruments were monotonous, and of little use but to mark the measure: such were the Cymbalum and the Systrum; and it was for this reason, perhaps, that the cymbals were called Æera by Petronius. But it would afford us no very favourable idea of the abilities of modern musicians, who would acquire so much parade and noise in keeping together. "The more time is beat," says M. Rousseau, "the less

with the hand, but also with instruments of percussion; melody without harmony, in its present acceptation; and the similarity of the effects said to have been produced by the music of the two nations. The Diatessaron or 4th of the Greeks was always fixed, while the intermediate sounds were mutable, which equally corresponds with the practice of Hindoostan.

The Greeks divided their diatonic scale into two tetrachords, which were exactly similar to each other, *si ut re mi* and *mi fa sol la*, and the note *mi*, being that by which both were joined, was denominated the conjunctive tetrachord. The Sarungee or fiddle of Hindoostan is always tuned in this manner, and not by 5ths, as is the practice in Europe, and the Greek method is allowed to be more correct in intonation, and in some respects more simple.

If it were inquired whether the nation of Greece or Hindoostan proceeded farther in the cultivation of music, the accounts we have of its state amongst the former, and the living examples at present found in the latter, aided by a review of its flourishing state under the native princes, would decide in favor of Hindoostan. The use of a flute, with holes to produce melodies, was only discovered during the latter ages of Greece, as well as the performance on that

it is kept; and in general, bad music and bad musicians stand most in need of such noisy assistance." Burney's History of Music, vol. i, p. 75. With due deference to such authors, I beg to observe that no allowance seems to have been made for the different styles of music. The music now in use in Europe would certainly be despoiled of all its beauty by such an accompaniment; but the ancient music was on the rythmical principle, in which the greatest beauty consisted in marking the time distinctly. The same train of reasoning will account for the practice of Hindoostan.

instrument as a solo; both of which existed in Hindoostan from time immemorial. It was the instrument on which Krishna played. The Greeks did not play solo, except on the trumpet, till the Pythic games were celebrated, when Sacadas of Argos is said to have been the first who distinguished himself by playing on the flute *alone.**

Agalaus† of Tegea won the crown which was proposed for a player upon stringed instruments without singing. This was so late as the 8th Pythiad, 558 B. C., and seems to be the first instance of such a performance.

'The Greek scale at the time of Aristoxemus extended to two octaves, and was called Systema perfectum, maximum, immutatum.' The Veen, one of the most ancient instruments of India, and on which the Mooni Narud is said to have performed, extends to three octaves and a half.

'There was no instrument amongst the Greeks with necks or finger-board, so that they were not acquainted with the method of shortening strings in playing, so as to produce different sounds; (so their melody must therefore have been confined to from four to ten sounds, as their Cithara had only that number of strings);' while here various musical instruments have existed which possessed these improvements, as will be shewn when I come to treat of them respectively. They did not express the octave of any sound by the same character; these have one common name for the same note in every octave.

'The dancers in Rome were called Saltatores from their frequent leaping and springing.' This is all that is known of their dance; but we have no account of their particular graces. 'The dance of the Greeks was similar, and served

* Burney, vol. i, p. 82.

† *Ibid.*

as the model which their conquerors, the Romans, adopted. Amongst them this class of people were denominated Curetes.' This description is evidently very defective, and gives us no very distinct or graceful idea of this amusement amongst them.

The dance, as it is now practised in Hindoostan, is comparatively of a modern date. Music having been in more ancient times dedicated almost solely to religious purposes, the dance was likewise practised by persons actuated with religious zeal and warlike enthusiasm, till they were subsequently prostituted by interested performers for the entertainment of the luxurious. Dances being accompanied with song, and the theme of the latter being charged from pious hymns to love ditties, the actions of the one were necessarily conformed to the words of the other; and this in a short time could not fail, amongst so voluptuous a people as conquered the degenerate sons of India, to change into that effeminate and meretricious style in which it is at present. Indeed, the want of morals amongst its professors of both sexes is the primary cause of the present derogation of this elegant science amongst the natives from its original dignity. If we consider, however, this branch of music abstractedly, without reverting to any tendency which it might have on the morals of the spectators, it cannot but be allowed that they are accompanied with much grace, and the Bhav, which regards gesticulations expressive of the poetry, is, by expert performers, such as would not disgrace a stage-player.

HINDOOSTANEE MUSIC.

What it is termed in the original. The treatises held in the greatest estimation. Native divisions what, and how many. The arrangement adopted in this work.

MUSIC in Hindoostan is termed "Sungeet" from the Sanscrit, whence this as well as all terms connected with it are derived. There are various original treatises on this science, with translations of several in the Hindee and Persian. The most esteemed of these are the Nadpooran, Ragarnuvu, Subhavinod, Ragdurpun, and the Sungeet Durpun, and other works in the original Sanscrit, and short accounts in the works of Hukeem Salamut Ulee Khan, and the Tohfuht-ool Hind, by Mirza Khan. The native authors divide Sungeet into seven parts :—1, Soor-udhyay, which treats of the seven musical tones, with their subdivisions ; 2, Rag-udhyay, defines the melody ; 3, Tal-udhyay, describes the measures, with the manner of beating time ; 4, Nrit-udhyay, regards dancing ; 5, Aurth-udhyay, expatiates on the signification of the poetry sung ; 6, Bhav-udhyay, confines itself to expression and gesture ; and 7, Hust-udhyay, instructs the method of performing on the several musical instruments.

The first three of these heads are more immediately connected with my design. Something will likewise be cursorily mentioned in the course of the work regarding the 5th and last heads. Those referring to dancing and its appropriate actions, I shall leave aside.

I shall not, however, confine myself to the method adopted in the original works on this subject, but shall treat of its various branches in the order in which they will naturally present themselves.

OF THE GAMUT.

Madam, before you touch the instrument,
To learn the order of my fingering,
I must begin with rudiments of art,
To teach you Gamut in a briefer sort.

Shakespear.

What it is called. The derivation of the word. The subdivisions of tones. Resemblance of these of the Greek diesis. Opinions of Dr. Burney and Mr. Moore on the enharmonic genus. Names of the seven notes. Origin of these. The Gamut invented by Guido and Le Maire. Dr. Pepusch. Srooti.

THE Gamut in Hindoostanee is termed Surgum, which appellation is said to be derived from the four first notes of the scale, as our A B C is from the three first letters of the alphabet, or the word itself from the two with which the Greek letters begin. The number of tones is the same as in the modern music of Europe, but the subdivisions are more in the manner of the ancient enharmonic genus of the Greeks. The difference in the subdivision of the tones which characterised the enharmonic, consisted in the notes of the chromatic genus being divided by the diesis or quarter tone.

To a person versed in the modern music of Europe, the subdivisions of semi-tones into minuter parts will appear incomprehensible, at least inasmuch as to be productive of any melody that would be pleasing to the ear. I shall forbear to say anything on my own authority, but shall quote a passage which I think appropriate.

Dr. Burney, in his general dissertation on the music of the ancients, p. 43, treating of the Grecian enharmonic genus, has this: "How this *quarter tone* could be managed, so as to be rendered pleasing, still remains a mystery; yet the difficulty of splitting a semi-tone into two halves, or even dividing it into more minute intervals, is less, perhaps, than has been imagined. When it is practised by a capital singer or a good performer on the violin or hautbois, at a pause, how wide it seems!"

T. Moore, in his translation of the XLIII. Ode of Anacreon, has the following note on these lines:

> And while the harp impassioned flings
> Tuneful rapture from the strings.

"Barbiton, Anc. Mus. If one of their modes was a progression by quarter tones, which, we are told, was the nature of the enharmonic scale, simplicity was by no means the characteristic of their melody; for this is a nicety of progression, of which modern music is not susceptible."

That such subdivisions exist in Hindoostanee music is certain, but it must be left to time, and more intimate acquaintance with the science, to determine whether it has any claim to the eulogium bestowed by this gentleman on the enharmonic of the Greeks.

The names of the notes are: 1, Khuruj; 2, Rikhub; 3, Gundhur; 4, Muddhum; 5, Punchum; 6, Dhyvut, and 7, Nikhad. In solfa-ing, however, the first syllable only of each is mentioned—*su*, *ru*, or *ri*, *gu*, *mu*, *pu*, *dhu*, *ni*. The Khuruj is called *su*, on account of its being likewise denominated *soor*, or the fundamental note, by way of pre-eminence.

I do not recollect that any of those who have written on Hindoostanee music has informed the public what system has been adhered to by him ; that is, which note of the Surgum has been made to correspond with which of our gamut. It seems to me to be a matter of some consequence to determine this point, for the benefit of those who might wish to make the comparison.

As the number of notes is the same in both cases, the only thing to be determined is, which is to correspond to the first of their scale, or *Khuruj*. Sir William Jones makes the *Khuruj* to correspond to A ;* but in this it appears to me he is guided more by alphabetical arrangement of letters than by any connection it may have with musical arrangement.

If the *Khuruj* is tuned UT or C, it seems to me to be more systematic, it being the key-note of the natural scale.

The musicians of Hindoostan never appear to have had any determined pitch by which their instruments were regulated, each person tuning his own to a certain height, adapted by guess, to the power of the instrument and quality of the strings, the capacity of the voice intended to be accompanied, and other adventitious circumstances. From this it may be observed that it is immaterial which note is designoted by which letter, but it seems to me more systematic that some such definition be made.

The authors of the East, being desirous of tracing every thing to its source, in the want of authentic history, supply its place by fable. In the instance of the origin (oot-punnu)

* See his delineation of the finger-board of the Vina.

of the gamut, they say, that the various sounds of which it is composed are derived from the natural sounds or calls of various animals. The Khuruj, they assert, is in imitation of the call of the peacock; the Rikhub, of the bird called pupeeha; the Gundhur, of the lowing of a sheep; Muddhum, from the call of the bird named Coolung; Punchum, Koel; Dhyvut, horse; and Nikhad, elephant. How far this opinion can be maintained, I leave the reader to determine. I was not aware, before I got a sight of native treatises on music, that the lowing of sheep, the neighing of horses, or the call of the elephant, could be construed into musical sounds.

It will be allowed that the Hindoos have made no despicable advances in music, when it is known that they have seven distinct names for notes which compose their gamut. Guido of Arezzo in Tuscany, a monk of the order of St. Benedict, is allowed to be the inventor of the gamut as it is adopted in Europe, although some dispute this point. The date of this invention is about the year 1022. The syllables ascribed to him are only six in number, taken from the first syllables of the hymn of St. John "Ut queont laxis," the major seventh being then considered merely as a note of grace, and not essential to the scale; and it was not till about the latter end of the sixteenth century that the last *si* was invented by Le Maire, a singing-master of Paris.*

* *Sa, ri,* &c. Three of which syllables are, by a singular concurrence, exactly, though not in the same places, with three of those invented by *David Mostare,* as a substitute for the troublesome gamut used in his time, and which he arranges thus :

Bo, ce, di, ga, lo, ma, ni.—Sir William Jones, vol. i, p. 426.

Solmization, however, in various parts of Europe, still continues to be performed by the tetrachord, as was the practice in Greece, adapting only the Guidonian terms in lieu of the Grecian. In England, the syllables *mi*, *fa*, *sol*, *la*, only were used, so that the octave of *mi*, was *la*, till the eighteenth century, when the whole of the hexachord was introduced by Dr. Pepusch.

The notes of an octave are divided into twenty-two minor subdivisions, instead of the twelve semi-tones, as is done with us. These are called Srootis, and each of them has a distinct name assigned to it, as is specified in the following table.

Soors.	*Comprising Srootis.*
Khuruj	Butra.
	Cumodutee.
	Mundrica.
	Chhunduvutee.
Rikhub	Duyavutee.
	Runjunee.
	Ructica.
Gundhar	Sivee.
	Crodhee.
Muddhum........................	Bujjra.
	Prusarunee.
	Preetee.
	Marjunee.
Punchum	Kshutee.
	Ricta.
	Sidpunee.
	Ulapunee.
Dhyvut	Mundutee.
	Rohinee.
	Rummya.
Nikhad........................	Ooggra.
	Joobhunca.

Here it must be observed that the intervals between the first and second, fourth and fifth, and fifth and sixth notes of the octave are divided each into four parts ; those between the second and third and sixth and seventh, each into three parts, and those between the third and fourth, and seventh and eighth, which with us are reckoned semi-tones, each into two parts.

OF TIME.

Musick do I hear !
Ha, ha ! keep time. How sour sweet musick is,
When time is broke, and no proportion kept.

Shakespear.

Heroes who o'ertime, or die,
Have their hearts hung extremely high :
The strings of which in battles' heat
Against their very corslets beat ;
Keep time with their own trumpet's measure,
And yield them most excessive pleasure.

Prior.

The various measures used in Europe. Difference between them and those of Hindoostan. Their resemblance to the rythm of the Greeks. Similarity between the Greek and Sanscrit languages. The Hebrew unmusical, likewise the Arabic. Melody and metre considered. Tartini's objections against metre endeavoured to be controverted the dignified prose in Sanscrit, and tongues derived from it. Its superiority to the Oordoo. Probable origin of the modern musical measure. Tartini's deduction of measure from the proportions of the octave and its fifth, opposed to the practice of Hindoostan. Whether the rythmical or the musical measure possesses greater advantages. Opinion hazarded thereon. Time table. Characters for expressing time. Their varieties.

TIME in music signifies the measure by which the melody is regulated, and without which there is no music. The importance of this branch of the science is so generally acknowledged, that it is superfluous to expatiate on its merits. I shall not here insist on the different measures in European practice, as it must be understood by all who have any knowledge of music, and to those who are not initiated in that science, it is not my object to enter into any explanation.

A great difference prevails between the music of Europe and that of the Oriental nations in respect to time, in which branch it resembles more the rhythm of the Greeks, and other ancient nations, than the measures peculiar to the modern music of Europe. To all those who are acquainted with the principles of ancient music it will be unnecessary to observe, that this rhythm was no other than the poetical feet which formed the basis of their musical measure.

From the certain knowledge of the rhythm of the ancients, and the similarity observed in the practices of the natives of India, Persia, and other Oriental countries, it inclines one to the opinion that the rhythmical measure is the lawful offspring of nature, found in all parts of the world, which existed much prior to the birth of her younger sister, the modern musical measure.

Much has been said by writers against the use of rhythm, as it confines the melody to certain measures ; but I question, whether there can be any melody without restrictions of that nature, be that the ancient rhythmical, or the present musical, measure. When the great variety of poetical feet in the Greek and Sanscrit languages, as well as in those derived from the latter, is taken into consideration, it seems doubtful, whether the one would not even allow more variety than the other. The Hebrew is acknowledged to be a harsh language, and unfavourable to music, from the paucity of vowels and abundance of consonants ; the same is likewise applicable to the Arabic : the Sanscrit has sixteen vowels, and the language is sonorous beyond a doubt. This should perhaps be one reason for its being particularly adapted for music.

On the contrary, authors have not been wanting who have defended it, perhaps with more zeal than the subject would freely admit. Amongst others, Isaac Vossius is of opinion, that "since the discontinuance of the use of rhythm, and the adoption of the modern musical measure, musicians have lost that power over the passions which the ancients are said to have possessed." I mention this fact only in a transient manner, and leave it on his authority for the decision of others; but I must confess, that I can by no means agree with him, when he ascribes this power to rhythm unassisted by melody.

Sir William Jones* seems to have more reasonably assigned the cause of the power of the ancient musicians. His words are, "It is in this view only that we must consider the music of the ancient *Greeks,* or attempt to account for its amazing effects which we find related by the greatest historians and philosophers; it was wholly passionate or descriptive, and so closely united to poetry, that it never obstructed, but always increased, its influence; whereas our boasted harmony, with all its fine accords and numerous parts, paints nothing, expresses nothing, says nothing to the heart, and consequently can only give more or less pleasure to one of our senses; and no reasonable man will seriously prefer a transitory pleasure, which must soon end in satiety, or even in disgust, to a delight of the soul, being always interesting, always transporting." However, to give all the merit to melody, and deny that rythm has any share in aiding the effects produced by melody in

* Essay on the Arts commonly called imitative, inserted in his works, vol. iv, p. 556.

exciting the passions, cannot be consonant to sound reasoning, as the very idea of the necessity of some sort of measure by which the melody might be regulated is repugnant to it. How different would epic poetry sound if written in the measure peculiar to anacreontic odes, or *vice versâ!* Metre is allowed to have this effect in poetry, and why not in music? It is very well known that a mere transposition of key, without a change in the time, has very little power on the spirits of the hearer.

It has been also alleged in defence of rythm, that "a melody of even very ordinary merit, in which the time is distinctly and accurately marked, is more capable of pleasing and giving satisfaction generally than a more scientific and laboured composition that is deficient in this respect." Many of our songs will prove this assertion.

From the strict regard paid by the ancients to their long and short syllables, Tartini supposes, "they could not have prolonged any note beyond the time allowed to the syllable, and from this cause a fine voice would be unabled to display its powers by passing rapidly from syllable to syllable to prevent the loss of time." How far this may hold good with respect to the music of the Greeks, we possess no existing means of judging; but with regard to Oriental music, this is not the case. For in this respect, there is more liberty allowed than our modern system of time will permit, as I shall endeavour to demonstrate.

The peculiar nature of the melody of Hindoostan not only permits but enjoins the singer, if he has the least pretention to excel in it, not to sing a song throughout more than once in its naked form; but on its repetition, which is a natural consequence, occasioned by the brevity of the pieces in general, to break off sometimes at the conclusion, at other times at the commencement, middle, or any certain part of a measure, and fall into a rhapsodical embellishment called *Alap*, and after going through a variety of *ad libitum* passages, rejoin the melody with as much grace as if it had never been disunited, the musical accompaniment all the while keeping time. These passages are not reckoned essential to the melody, but are considered only as grace notes, introduced according to the fancy of the singer, where the only limitations by which the performer is bound are the notes peculiar to that particular melody, and a strict regard to time. No other rules exist for them, and if measured with the opinion of Dr. Burney,* they appear to be in the right for not confining them to certain forms.

It will perhaps be inquired, how in such cases strict adherence to time can be maintained. The reply is, that when these flights are more lengthened than a single apogiatura, the *ad libitum* movement runs through the full time of a whole measure, or a certain number of measures, reckoning from the instant of its adoption to that when it is dropped, taking up the measure of the rythm at the same foot where it was dropped, or if these passages require more or less time than the complement of the measure requires, allowance is made for it in rejoining the melody.

A great number of pieces are in dignified prose, of an elevated strain, peculiar to the Sanscrit and the languages derived from it. These are not strictly confined to poetical feet,

* Writing down grace is like recording the nonsense and impertinence of conversation, which, bad at first, is rendered more and more insipid and absurd as the times, manners, and occasions which produced it become more distant.—*General History, vol. ii, p.* 151, *note u.*

and admit of much variety. In compositions of this nature, two or more notes are frequently allotted to one syllable, and they resemble more the style of the modern musical measure than the generality of poetical compositions. These pieces, and indeed all those songs called Dhoorpuds and Kheals, as well as those of some other species, are commonly in the language spoken at Vruj and in the district of Khyrabad.

The Vruj Bhasha is peculiar to the Hindoos, and although an extremely elegant and sonorous language, bearing the greatest resemblance of any to the Sanscrit, is nevertheless not so generally understood as the Oordoo. It appears, however, to be far superior for poetical compositions, and there certainly are more numerous works in it possessing genuine poetical beauties than in the other.

I have not seen any account of the origin of the present musical measure of Europe, and am led to believe that it must have had its rise from the following cause. The primitive fathers of the Christian churches being desirous of admitting music in their divine service, in imitation of the Apostles, the Hebrews, and all other nations, were however unwilling to admit the melodies then in use amongst the pagans as profane. The rythmical measure also was objected to, as being too light and lively, and the distinction of poetical feet being laid aside, all notes were rendered of the same length. When music began afterwards to be cultivated for the stage and the cabinet, the insipidity of music composed of notes of equal length was soon felt, and the ancient metrical measure being out of favor, while the adoption of some sort of measure was found necessary, appears to be the most plausible reason for the invention of the measure now in use throughout Europe.

Dr. Burney, in his General History of Music, has the following paragraph, page 82: "Tartini has deduced all measure from the proportions of the octave and its fifth: 'common time, or measure,' says he, 'arises from the octave, which is as 1 : 2; triple time arises from the fifth, which is as 2 : 3.' 'These,' adds he, 'are the utmost limits within which we can hope to find any practicable proportions for melody.' Indeed, many have attempted to introduce other kinds of measure, which, instead of good effects, have produced nothing but the greatest confusion, *and this must always be the case.* Music has been composed of five equal notes in a bar, *but no musician has yet been found that is able to execute it.*" The authorities of Tartini and Dr. Burney are very respectable, yet we may sastisfy ourselves every day that there is *beautiful melody* in Hindoostan, comprising *seven and other unequal* number of notes in a measure, and that they *have* musicians in abundance that are able to execute it. The table prefixed to the end of this article will prove the existence of many very unequal measures successfully employed by them. The above deduction itself of Tartini remains yet to be proved, before we give it our unqualified assent.

From all that has been discussed above, a question naturally arises, namely, which has the advantage—the ancient rythmical or the modern musical measure? This appears to be a point difficult to decide, and will perhaps not be finally settled until the musicians of Europe shall have learned to play the music of Hindoostan in unequal number of notes. In the meantime, perhaps, if we steer a middle course, and allow each its merit, we shall not be far from the truth. The rythmical measure seems to have been quite adapted to the language of the Greeks, which admitted of such variety in the metrical feet, and as the Sanscrit is known to bear a striking resemblance to it in this respect, the use of it may be allowed to be equally advantageous in melodies of that language, and those derived from it, many of the poetical feet of which could not be adapted to the modern melody of Europe.

The time table in Europe was first formed in the eleventh century. Magister Franco, believed to be a native of Cologn, is by some allowed the honor of this invention, although others suppose him only to have improved on the principles of his predecessors. He is, however, acknowledged to have invented the term minim; as only the long, breve, and semibreve were known about that time. Although six different characters for time are generally described in modern time tables, yet no more than four were known till several centuries after the time of Franco.

There are four sorts of characters for time used by the musicians of Hindoostan—the Undroot, the Droot, the Lughoo, and the Gooroo, with marks, which serve as our point to lengthen the preceding note half its value. They reckon a fifth, Ploot, but that I conceive is not a distinct character.

It is certainly very creditable to the knowledge of music in Hindoostan that characters of such different values have subsisted amongst them. The ancient Greeks seem to have had only two, the long and the short, which served to mark the measure both of poetry and music, and in the canto farmo notes of equal value only are found.

Time, in the acceptation it has in music, is called Tal.*

* The origin of this word is said to be from Tand, the dance of Muhadew, and Las, that of his wife, Parvuttee, the first letters of which form the word Tal ताल.

They reckon an immense variety of these, but such as are now practised are limited to ninety-two. These I shall describe in the annexed table. The aggregate quantity or value* fixed in the third column forms one complete measure, but in beating, the commencement of every note given there is struck. The syllables corresponding with a certain number of the strokes of the *Tal*, from its commencement, *Oochchar*, are called *Purun*, the last of which in the measure is termed *Sum*, which is always on an accented syllable, and is the principal note in the measure. In this respect, *Sum* is equivalent to the most emphatic parts of our music denominated accented parts.

* I use the word "Value," not in the double sense ascribed to it by D'Alembert, but simply mean its quantity of duration.

OF HARMONY AND MELODY.

"Thoughts that voluntary move
Harmonious numbers."
Milton.

"The prophet David, having singular knowledge, not in poetry alone, but in music also, judging them both to be things most necessary for the house of God, left behind him a number of divinely indited poems, and was farther the author of adding unto poetry melody in public prayer, melody both vocal and instrumental, for the raising up of men's hearts, and the sweetening of their affections towards God."—*Hooker.*

The origin of harmony in Europe. Opinions of several learned men on the subject of harmony, with that of the author. Claims of melody.

HARMONY, in the present acceptation of the word, is a plant whose native soil is Europe, whence it has been transplanted to some other countries; but all the native culture of music has not been able to make it grow spontaneously in any other part of the world as in its indigenous soil and climate. Wherever else it is found, it is exotic. The only harmony which Hindoostanee music generally admits of, and indeed requires, if it can be called harmony, is a continuation of its key note, in which respect it resembles very much the Scotch pastorals, or the instrument accompanies the voice in unison, as was the practice in Europe, until towards the end of St. Lewis's reign in the thirteenth century.

Many discussions have taken place amongst the learned on the merits of harmony. M. Rousseau and some other authors seem to be of opinion that music is not really improved by the use of harmony. The former produces various arguments to prove that it is a barbarous and Gothic invention. All our reasoning, however, cannot lead us to subscribe to the truth of this great author's assertion when we hear the harmony of a piece judiciously selected, and in which the melody is not overpowered; in short, harmony by which melody is adorned, not overloaded.

Dr. Burney, in a note, p. 459, says: "There is a fashion, we find, not only in melody, but harmony; modern ears are best pleased with Ptolomy's arrangement, though Doni tells us that in the last century, the diapason of Didymus was most in vogue.

"Tartini has asserted, that melody is the offspring of harmony as being deduced from it. I cannot presume to dispute so great an authority, but I would only beg to question, whether melody or harmony was first practised in the world. Every unprejudiced person will, I believe, coincide with me, that although melody can certainly be deduced from harmony, yet the former is the elder sister by many a thousand year. Harmony and melody are not like music and language; there is not the same relation between them.

"Notwithstanding the dependence of melody upon harmony, and the sensible influence which the latter *may* exert upon the former, we must not however from thence conclude, with some celebrated musicians, that the effects of harmony are preferable to those of melody. Experience proves the contrary."*

* Encyclopædia Britannica, Art. Music, p. 531.

It is not in my power to decide a point on which the learned are divided in their opinion. I shall only offer a few obvious remarks, which must naturally strike every person who bestows any degree of attention on the subject.

Many pieces of music, in parts, even by the greatest masters, which are universally admired, would sound quite insipid if divested of that harmony which animates them. This at once decides the merit of harmony, although it may likewise add some weight to the opinion which some entertain, that the modern melody has not the merit of the ancient, and that harmony is used with the view of compensating for its poorness, and diverting the attention of the audience from perceiving the barrenness of genius.

It will be easily allowed that the beauties of a piece of melody are not so perceptible when sung with accompaniment in parts, as when it is performed as a solo. Dr. Burney has some very appropriate sentences, which I beg leave to transcribe.

"Upon the whole, therefore, it seems demonstrable that harmony like ours was never practised by the ancients; however I have endeavoured to shew, that the stripping their music of counterpoint does not take from it the power of pleasing, or of producing great effects; and in modern times, if a Farinelli, a Gizziello, or a Cafarelli, had sung their airs wholly without accompaniment, they would, perhaps, have been listened to but with still more pleasure. Indeed, the closes of great singers, made wholly without accompaniment, are more attended to than all the contrivance of complicated parts, in the course of the airs which they terminate.

"An elegant and graceful melody, exquisitely sung by a fine* voice, is sure to engage attention, and to create delight without instrumental, assistance, and in a solo, composed and performed by a great master, the less the accompaniment is heard the better. Hence it should seem as if the harmony of accumulated vocal parts, or the tumult of instrumental, was no more than a succedaneum to a mellifluous voice, or single instrument of the first class, which is but seldom found. However, to diversify and vary our musical amusements, and to assist in dramatic painting, a full piece and a well-written chorus have their peculiar merit, even among songs and solos, however elegant the composition or perfect the performance."†

* "All these instruments (pianoforte, organ, &c.) were far inferior to the voice, the spontaneous gift of nature, in promptitude, and in the power of obeying every call of sentiment, every degree, as well as every kind of emotion, with which the heart was agitated. The pleasures of harmony, though great, were monotonous, and could not express the momentary variations of sentiment, which are as fleeting as the light and shade of a prospect, while the dappled clouds fall across the sky. The violin and a small number of the simple wind instruments were found to be the only ones which could fully express those momentary gradations of sentiment that give music its pathos, and enable it to thrill the very soul." Supplement to Encyclopœdia, Britannica, vol. ii, Art. Pianoforte.

We may here likewise observe, that as all musical instruments without exception are inferior to that unrivalled gift of nature, a good voice, and a single voice is not able to sing in parts, it may be deduced that music in parts was never intended by nature.

† "It may indeed happen, from the number of performers, and the complication of the harmony, that meaning and sentiment may be lost in the multiplicity of sounds; but this, though it may be harmony, loses the name of music.

"The second department of this division by lively and accentuate nflections, and by sounds which may be said to speak, expresses all the

Melody seems to be as much the child of nature as the rythmical measure already noticed. Indeed, music is found all over the world, and that music, except in Europe, where harmony has been introduced for the space of little more than two centuries, is purely melody, be that of a refined or gross nature, and generally in rythmical measure.*

passions, paints every possible picture, reflects every object, subjects the whole of nature to its skilful imitations, and impresses even on the heart and soul of man sentiments proper to affect them in the most sensible manner. This, continues he, (M. Rousseau,) which is the genuine lyric and theatrical music, was what gave double charms and energy to ancient poetry; this is what, in our days, we exert ourselves in applying to the drama, and what our singers execute on the stage. It is in this music alone, and not in harmonics, or the resonance of nature, that we must expect to find accounts of those prodigious effects which it formerly produced.

"But, with M. Rousseau's permission, all music, which is not in some degree characterised by these pathetic and imitative powers, deserves no better name than that of a musical jargon, and can only be effectuated by such a complication and intricacy of harmony as may confound, but cannot entertain, the audience. This character, therefore, ought to be added as essential to the definition of music; and it must be attributed to our neglect of this alone, whilst our whole attention is bestowed on harmony and execution, that the best performances of our artists and composers are heard with listless indifference and oscitation, nor ever can conciliate any admirers, but such as are, indeed, by pedantry and affectation, to pretend what they do not feel. Still may the curse of indifference and inattention pursue and harrow up the souls of every composer or performer who pretends to regale our ears with this musical legerdemain; still the grin of scorn, or the hiss of infamy, teach them to correct this depravity of taste, and entertain us with the voice of nature."—Encyclopædia Britannica, Art. Music.

* "Music is at present divided more simply into *melody* and *harmony*; for since the introduction of *harmony*, the proportion between the length and shortness of sounds, or even that between the distance of returning cadences, are of less consequence amongst us. For it often happens in

That melody is the production of genius, and harmony of art, will not, I believe, be disputed; nor that the former is more generally comprehended and relished by mankind than complicated harmony.

Music had already been too much circumscribed by rules of art, mathematics was made to supply the place of the ear, or rather in a great measure to supplant its authority altogether, even before the invention of harmony.*

Having advanced all that I thought was necessary on the subject of harmony and melody in general, I shall now introduce the reader to the melodies of Hindoostan.

modern languages, that the verses assume their measure from the musical air, and almost entirely lose the small share of proportion and quantity which in themselves they possess."—*Ibid.*

* "Had the philosophers never meddled with it (music), had they allowed the practical musicians to construct and tune their instruments in their own way, so as to please their ear, it is scarcely possible that they should not have hit on what they wanted, without all the embarrassment of the chromatic and the enharmonic scales of the Greeks."—*Ibid.* Art. Temperament.

OF ORIENTAL MELODY.

Not generally susceptible of harmony. Limited to a certain number. Its character.

THE melody of the East has always been admired, and I believe very justly. The Europeans, however, are at present so much accustomed to harmony, that to their ear this melody will sound less attracting than it would otherwise have been. Indeed, so wide is the difference between the natures of European and Oriental music, that I conceive a great many of the latter would baffle the attempts of the most expert contrapuntist to set a harmony to them, by the existing rules of that science.*

* "We do not say that this *total* innovation (harmony) in the principle of musical pleasure is exceptionable; we rather think it very defective, believing that the thrilling pleasure of music depends more upon the melody or air. We appeal even to instructed musicians whether the heart and affections are not more affected (*and with much more distinct variety of emotion*) by a fine melody, supported, but not obscured, by harmonies judiciously chosen. It appears to us that the effect of harmony, always filled up, is more uniformly the same, and less touching to the soul, than some simple air sung or played by a performer of sensibility and powers of utterance. We do not wonder, then, that the ingenuous Greeks deduced all their rules from this department of music, nor at their being so satisfied with the pleasures it yielded, that they were not solicitous of the additional support of harmony. We see that melody has suffered by the change in every country. There is no

To expect an endless variety in the melody of Hindoostan, would be an injudicious hope, as their authentic melody is limited to a certain number, said to have been composed by professors universally acknowledged to have possessed not only real merit, but also the original genius of composition, beyond the precincts of whose authority it would be criminal to trespass. What the more reputed of the moderns have since done is, that they have adapted them to their own purposes, and formed others by the combination of two or more of them. Thus far they are licensed, but they dare not proceed a step further. Whatever merit an entire modern composition might possess, should it have no resemblance to the established melody of the country, it would be looked upon as spurious. It is implicitly believed, that it is impossible to add to the number of these one single melody of equal merit. So tenacious are the natives of Hindoostan of their ancient practices !

It may here be remarked, that in the art of combining two or more Raginees, the natives are guided by their own rules of modulation, the propriety of which should of course not be judged of by the rules laid down by M. Rousseau, or his commentator D'Alembert ; but by those determined by the native masters, allowing the ear to be the best and most natural judge of that which has its existence merely with the view of affording pleasure to the auditory organ.

The general term for melody in Hindoostan is Rag or Raginee, which is the subject I shall next be led to treat of ;

Scotchman, Irishman, Pole, or Russian, who does not lament that the skill in composing heart-touching airs is degenerated in his respective nation ; and all admire the productions of their muse of the days that are past. They are pleasant and mournful to the soul"—*Ibid.* Art. Temperament.

but before I enter upon that head, I shall offer a few observations which are common to all :

1. Hindoostanee melodies are short, lengthened by repetition and variations.

2. They all partake of the nature of what is denominated by us Rondo, the piece being invariably concluded with the first strain, and sometimes with the first bar, or at least with the first note of that bar.

3. A bar, or measure, or a certain number of measures, are frequently repeated, with slight variation almost *ad lib.*

4. There is as much liberty allowed with respect to pauses, which may be lengthened at pleasure, provided the time be not disturbed.

OF RAGS AND RAGINEES.

Tunes and airs have in themselves some affinity with the affections; as merry tunes, doleful tunes, solemn tunes, tunes inclining men's minds to pity, warlike tunes; so that tunes have a predisposition to the motion of the spirits.—*Bacon.*

The general acceptation of the terms supposed to be incorrect. Reasons offered, why they are limited to season and time. Of the Rag-mala. Absurdity of limiting tunes to seasons. Divisions of Rags and Raginees into classes. Rules for determining the names of the mixed Raginees. Table of compounded Rags. The Rag-mala copiously described.

RAGS and Raginees are generally construed to mean certain musical modes* of Hindoostan. How far this definition is correct, I shall here inquire into.

* *S.* راگ Rag. n. s. m (राग) 1. A mode in music (six in number), music, song, tune; راگ رنگ Rag-rung, n. s. m., music; راگ ساگر Rag-sagar, n. s. m., a song composed of many Rags or musical modes; راگ مالا Rag-mala, n. s. f., the name of a treatise in music—(nothing more than a collection of pictures, exhibiting the traditional history of the primary and subordinate modes and the subject appointed to each).

S. راگني Raginee, n. s. f., a mode in music (wives of Rags, 30 in number).—Hunter's Taylor's Hindoostanee Dictionary, 1808.—Shakespear's Hindoostanee Dictionary, 1817, exactly as the preceding.

The celebrated Dr. Carey of Serampoor, however, in his Bengalee Dictionary, gives the following meaning:

রাগ a tune (this is the only signification applicable).

রাগিণী s. (from রাগ a tune), a female personification of tunes in Hindoo music.

The word "Mode" may be taken in two different significations, the one employing manner of style, and the other a key ;* and strictly speaking, this latter is the sense in which it is usually understood in music.

Mode, in the language of the musicians of this country, is, in my opinion, termed *T'hat,* and not Rag or Raginee ; the signification of which terms should be limited to that given by Dr. Carey. As amongst us there are two modes, the major and the minor, so the natives have a certain number of *T'hats,* to each of which two or more *Rags* or *Raginees* are appropriated. If these signified mode, each should require a different arrangement, which is certainly not the case. Any one may convince himself of this by procuring a performer on the Sitar. This instrument has moveable frets that are shifted from their places, so that when the instrument is properly adjusted, the fingers of the left hand running over them produce those tones only which are proper for the mode to which the frets have been transferred, and no other. Let the Sitar-player be desired to play something in the Raginee Uluya, and after he has done that, tell him to play some other Raginee without altering the frets, and it will be seen that other Raginees may be performed on the same *T'hat.* On the other hand, after he has played Uluya, let him play Lulit, or Bhyrewee, or Cafee, &c., &c., and he will be obliged to alter the *T'hat* or mode by shifting the frets. This proves that the former are all in the same mode or *T'hat.* It is true that a Raginee is not to be considered exactly in the

* Mode, in music. A regular disposition of the air and accompaniments relative to certain principal sounds upon which a piece of music is formed, and which are called the *essential sounds of the mode.* Encyc. Brit.

same situation as a tune is amongst us. It is not strictly a tune according to the acceptation of the word, as its definition given hereafter will shew. A *T'hat* comes nearest to what with us is implied by a mode, and consists in determining the exact relative distances of the several sounds which constitute an octave with respect to each other; while the Raginee disposes of those sounds in a given succession, and determines the principal sounds. The same *T'hat* may be adapted to several Raginees, by a different order of succession; whereas no Raginee can be played but in its own proper *T'hat.* It is likewise not a song, for able performers can adapt the words of a song to any Raginee: nor does a change of time destroy its inherent quality, although it may so far disguise the Raginee before an inexperienced ear as to appear a different one.

After the ancients had made pretty good observations on the firmament of fixed stars, and had as nearly as they could ascertained their respective situations, they thought of reducing them into constellations, under the representations of certain familiar objects, in order to assist the memory to retain them the better and easier. To connect a variety of heterogeneous subjects that have no relation with each other under one common head, in order to preserve a concatenation, has been a practice common amongst the Oriental nations, and subsists to this very day. The Arabian Nights' Entertainments, the Tooteenamah, the Buhardanish, and a variety of works in all the languages of the East, are proofs known to every person who has trod the paths of Oriental literature.

It seems probable, therefore, that the author of the Rags and Raginees, having composed a certain number of tunes, resolved to form some sort of fable in which he might introduce them all in a regular series. To this purpose, he pretended that there were six Rags, or a species of divinity, who presided over as many peculiar tunes or melodies, and that each of them had, agreeably to Hunooman, five, or as Coolnath says, six wives, who also presided each one over her tune. Thus having arbitrarily, and according to his own fancy, distributed his compositions amongst them, he gave the names of those pretended divinities to the tunes.

It is also probable that the Pootrus and Bharjyas are not the composition of the same, but some subsequent genius, who, apprehending that their number would be greatly increased by this additional acquisition, or dreading an innovation in the number established by long usage might not be well received, or that some time or other it might cause a rejection of the supernumerary tunes as not genuine, contrived the story that the Rags and Raginees had begotten children. This opinion is strengthened by its being asserted that forty-eight new modes were added by *Bhurut*.

That this fiction, however, (as well as every other fiction, allegory, and in fact, as it appears to me, the whole of the mythology of the ancient heathens,) pleasingly beguiles us, is acknowledged by Sir William Jones, vol. I, p. 430: "Every branch of knowledge," says he, "in this country, has been embellished by poetical fables, and the inventive talents of the *Greeks* never suggested a more charming allegory than the lovely families of the six *Rágas*, each of whom is a genius or demi-god, wedded to five Raginees or nymphs, and father of eight little genii, called his *Pootrus*, or sons. The fancy of Shakespear and the pencil of *Albano* might have been finely employed in giving speech and form to this assemblage of new aërial beings, who people the fairy-land of Indian imagination: nor have the *Hindu* poets and painters lost the advantages with which so beautiful a subject presented them."

That the name of any one of the Rags or Raginees was arbitrarily assigned by the author to any one of his compositions, is as probable as the often whimsical names given by our country-dance and reel composers to their productions. No person believes that the "Devil's Dream" is a genuine communication from the dreamer. This is further probable from there being very little or no similarity between a Rag and his Raginees. The disparity is sometimes so great, that Hindoo authors disagree with regard to the Rag to which several of the Raginees, Pootrus, or Bharjyas belong. Nay, some of the tunes allowed by one author to be a Rag is emasculated by another to a Raginee, as Dr. Gilchrist justly observes; and on the other hand, a Raginee is classed under the head of Rags. The same uncertainty prevails with respect to their Pootrus and Bharjyas.

If we look to the characters under which the Rags and Raginees are delineated in the Rag-mala, it will be seen that they are altogether metaphorical. As the figures of the signs of the Zodiac are descriptive of the seasons of the year, so these divinities are represented in attitudes and characters most appropriate to the time and season in which the tune was prescribed to the song, although the determining of the time itself is wholly arbitrary.

The songsters of Hindoostan pretend, that any song sung out of the time appropriated for it sounds uncouth. The reason alleged by them is, that the times and seasons allotted to each are those at which the divinities are at leisure to attend at the place where their favorite tune is sung, and to inspire the performer with due warmth in his execution. Sir W. Jones says on this subject, p. 429 : "Whether it had occurred to the Hindoo musicians that the velocity or slowness of sound must depend, in a certain ratio, upon the rarefaction and condensation of the air, so that their motion must be quicker in summer than in spring or autumn, and much quicker than in winter, I cannot assure myself; but am persuaded that their primary modes, in the system ascribed to Pávána, were first arranged according to the number of *Indian* seasons."

Sir W. Jones's observations are very acute and plausible ; they appear quite philosophical ; but to satisfy us of their probability, he should have entered much deeper into the subject, and endeavoured to prove that the nature of the several Rags and Raginees are such as to be really improved by the difference of temperature naturally incident to the varieties of season, even without making allowance for accidental variations, which constantly take place every year. Sir William asserts that the modes ascribed to one system were arranged according to the number of *Indian* seasons, which are six, and his calculations just preceding it are founded on the four seasons of Europe. It seems to me not improbable, that in limiting the season in which each Rag or Raginee should be sung, the composers had their preservation in view, for by this means, they would all necessarily have each one its turn, and for the want of any such regulation, the prettiest ones only would be performed, and the rest neglected and suffered to be forgot. Perhaps this will be considered the more reasonable when we take notice that the same cause which converts all the several parts to one whole conduces likewise to keep every individual part alive, active, and in its turn brought on the stage.

It may probably be with those who are accustomed to hear certain Rags and Raginees at stated hours and seasons, that being reconciled to them from habit, they would not relish tunes so well at what was reckoned improper seasons. Perhaps being a usage of the country, established from time immemorial, and in some measure sanctioned by religious authority, or a dread of being taxed with want of taste, might constrain several to comply with the established custom. But it must be quite indifferent to others unacquainted with these limitations. It would be reckoned extremely ridiculous to call for a particular tune at an improper season. This may indeed shew the ignorance of the person who makes the request in this branch of Hindoostanee music ; but, in my opinion, it can be no imputation against his taste ; for the same tune may sound pleasant or otherwise according to the humour a person may be in, but the time of the day can make no difference. A man deeply in love, for instance, will always relish love ditties, and a huntsman is ever for the chase. Moreover, seasons have more regard to the words of a song than to the tune ; for although the tune should in some measure correspond with the subject, whether gay or grave, &c., yet there are more tunes than one that will or may be made to suit the same set of words. It is also observable that the subject proper for each Rag or Raginee is not determined, and it often happens, through the abuse of unqualified composers, that the words are not seasonable with the tunes.

The Hindoos define Rags to have their origin from words combined in a determinate series, so as to be distinct from each other. Some Rags and Raginees resemble each other in the similarity and succession of their sounds or tones, but differ in the Srootis (see page 29) which gives them a claim to distinction.

Rags and Raginees are divided into three classes (Jati) : first *Sumpoornu,* or those which comprise all the seven notes, in their course, in any determinate succession whatever ; second, *Khadoo,* or such as are composed of six notes ; and third, *Oodoo,* whose extent ranges to but five notes : and hence it is said, that no Rag or Raginee is confined within limits whose extent is less than five notes.

There is likewise another distinction of these with regard to their formation or composition, and this also comprises three classes : first, *Soodh,* or such as are simple and original. This first class is subdivided into two species, viz., *Soodh* and *Muhasoodh : Soodh* are such as are deficient in some of their *Srootis;* and those which retain all their *Srootis* are termed *Muhasoodh. Tooree* is an example of the former, and *Sarung* and *Canhra* of the latter. Second, *Salung.* These are likewise simple, but bear a resemblance to some other, as for example *Sree Rag,* which has the likeness of *Gouree.* Third, *Sunkeernu;* and these are the compound ones. This last class is also subdivided into two species : first, *Sunkeernu,* or such as are compounded of two *Soodhs,* e. g., *Bhyron,* which is formed of *Tooree* and *Canhra ;* and second, *Muhasunkeernu,* or such as consist of two or more of any of the three classes, except two *Soodhs* of course.

There is a diversity of opinion with regard to which of the *Rags* and *Raginees* belong to which class. In general, the *Rags* are believed to be *Soodh,* and the *Raginees, &c., Sunkeernu.* Some suppose even the Rags to be of this last mentioned class. Others reckon these seven *Soodh* : first, *Canhra ;* second, *Sarung ;* third, *Goojree ;* fourth, *Nut ;* fifth, *Mular ;* sixth, *Tooree ;* and seventh, *Gouree.* To the second class, *Salung,* they ascribe the following : first, *Descar ;* second, *Bibhas ;* third, *Lulit ;* fourth, *Rewa ;* fifth, *Bilawal ;* sixth, *Megh ;* seventh, *Soruth* ; eighth, *Dhunasree ;* ninth, *Goura ;* tenth, *Sree Rag ;* eleventh, *Deepuk ;* twelfth, *Cafee ;* and thirteenth, *Kidara.*

The rule for determining the names of the mixed Rags is, agreeably to some authorities, to name the principal one last, and that which is introduced in it first : as *Pooria Dhunasree ;* others more naturally say that that which is introduced in the first part of the song or tune should be mentioned first, and the other or others subjoined to it in regular succession ; *e. g.*, suppose Shyam and Ramculee to be compounded with each other : if Shyam forms the commencement, and Ramculee is afterwards introduced into it, it should be called Shyam Ram ; but if, on the contrary, it commence with Ramculee, and Shyam be afterwards introduced, the whole should be denominated Ram Shyam.

COMPOUND RAGS.

These are Rags compounded from others chiefly by the more modern composers. The word Rag is here used in a general acceptation, and seems here to imply simply "a tune ;" for most of these cannot with propriety be denominated either Rags or Raginees, Pootrus or Bharjyas. I have arranged them alphabetically for easy reference.

Names of Rags.	*Compounded of*
B.	
Bagesree	Dhunasree and Canhra.
Bhempulasee	Dhunasree, Soodh and Poorbee.
Bhoopalee	Gound and Culian; or, according to others, Bilawul and Culian.
Bhyron	Hindol, Soodh, Canhra and Pooria.
Bhyruvee	Buraree, Lulit, Soodh, Sarung, Punchum, and Bilawul; or, agreeably to others, Soodh, Shyam and Bhyron.
Bibhas	Bilawul, Goojree, and Asavuree.
Bichittra	Sreeruvun, Chitee, Gouree, and Buraree.
Bihagra	Kidara, Maroo, and Suruswutee.
Biharee	Maroo and Suncurabhurun.
Bijuya	Tooree, Cumbharee, and Pooria.
Bilawul	Bilawul and Goursarung, or Bilawul and Sarung; or, as others say, Culian and Kidara.
Buhoolee	Ramculee, Goojree, Desear, Bungal, and Punchum; some say Tunc instead of Bungal.
Buhoolgoojree	Desear, Bungal, Ramculee, and Goojree.
Bungal	Dhunasree, Maroo, Gouree, and Lulit; others say Buraree, Gound, and Goojree.
Buraree	Descar, Toree, and Turwun.
Burhuns	Marwa, Rouranee, Chitee, Doorga, and Dhunasree.
Busunt	Deuguree, Nut, Mular, Sarung, and Bilawul.
C.	
Cafee	Suncurabhurun and Gouree.
Camodee	Soorishtuc and Gouree, or, agreeably to others, Sooghraee and Soruthee.
Camod	Gound and Bilawul.
Camod Nut	Camod and Nut.
Caodee	Maroo, Bihagra, and Nut.
Capurgouree	Jutee, Cumbhavutee, Jytsree, Uheeree, Tunc, and Buraree.
Chitee	Sanwunt, Lulit, and Pooria.
Colahul	Bihagra, Culian, and Canhra.
Coocub	Bilawul, Poorbee, Kidara, Deuguree, and Madho.
Coombh	Dhunasree and Soruthee.
Cudum Nut	Dhunasree, Dhuvul, Canhra, Uheeree, Kidara, Soodh, and Mudmadh.
Culaee, or Curaee, or Soogharee	Nutnarayun, Urana, and Bilawul; or, according to others, Bilawul and Canhra.
Culayer	Bilawul, Canhra, Nut, and Mular.
Culian Binod or Culian Camod	Emun and Camod.
Culian Nut	Culian and Nut.
Cumbharee	Sourashtuh and Dhunasree. Composed by Gunesh.
Cumbhavutee	Malsree and Mular.

Names of Rags.	*Compounded of*
Cuntha	Maroo, Kidara, Jytsree and Suncarabhurun.
Curaee, *vide* Culaee.	
Curna Nut	Punchum, Lulit, Bibhas and Goojree.
Curum Punchum	Lulit, Busunt, Hindol and Descar.
D.	
Deepavutee	Deepuk and Suruswutee.
Deepuk	Kidara, Camod, Soodh, Nut and Bagesree.
Desee	Toree and Khutrag.
Descar	Suruswutee, Puruj and Soruth.
Deuguree	Poorbee, Sarung and Soodh. Sung by the Deutas.
Deusakh	Suncurabhurun, Soodh, Mular and Canhra.
Dhoulsree	Bilawulee and Jytsree.
Dhunasree	Toree, Usavuree, and Maroo.
Dhyanjee	Toree, Bibhas, and Suhana.
Diwalee......................	Cumbharee, Malsree and Suruswutee.
Doorga	Malsree, Leelavatee, Gouree and Sarung.
Dukshin Nut	Coocub, Bilawul, Poorbee and Kidara.
E.	
Emun	Kidara, Bilawul and Soodh Culian.
F.	
Furodust	Poorbee, Shyam and Gouree.
G.	
Goojree	Lulita and Ramculee.
Gooneulee	Desee, Toree, Lulit, Usavuree, Descar & Goojree.
Gound	Dhunasree, Mular and Bilawul.
Gcundculee	Goojree and Usavuree.
Goura........................	Gouree, Nut and Turwan.
Gouree	Jujavuntee, Usavuree, Goojree and Soruth; some say, Soohoo and Canhra.
Goursarung	Goura; or, according to others, Gouree and Sarung.
Gumbheer Nut	Canhra and Nut.
Gundhar	Sindhola, Usavuree, Gouree, Deuguree and Bhyron; or, according to some, Khutrag, Usavuree and Desee.
H.	
Hindol	Bilawulee, Lulit, Punchum, Pooria and Bhyron.
Humeer	Kidara, Emun and Soodh Culian. Sung by Goureenath.
Humeer Nut	Humeer and Nut.
Hurkh	Dewsakh, Bilawulee, Sarung, Soodh, Mular and Gound.
J.	
Jujavuntee	Soruth, Dhoulsree and Bilawul; others say, Gouree, Bihagra and Nut.
Jutee Gouree	Lulit and Gouree.
Jytculian	Jytsree and Soodhculian.
Jytsree	Dhoul, Buraree and Descar.

Names of Rags.	*Compounded of*
K.	
Khem	Canhra, Suruswutee and Culian.
Khemculian	Kidara and Humeer; or, as others affirm, Canhra, Suruswutee and Soodhculian.
Khutnug	Maroo, Dhoul, Jytsree and Kidara.
Khutrag	Buraree, Usavuree, Toree, Shyam, Buhoolee and Gundhar. Some say Buhool-Goojree instead of Buhoolee; others, instead of Shyam.
Kidara	Coocba, Poorbee and Bilawul.
Kidar Nut	Kidara and Nut.
Kyrvee	Sarung, Sooha, Goojree and Gouree.
L.	
Leelavutee	Descar, Jytsree and Lulit.
Lulit	Desee, Bibhas and Punchum. Some leave out the last, and others make it comprise of Dewsakh, Bungal, Dhoul and Bibhas.
Luncdhun	Bilharee and Kidara, composed by Hunwunt.
M.	
Madho	Soodh, Mular, Bilawul and Nutnarayun.
Malavatee	Punchum, Camod, Soodhunt and Humeer.
Malgoojree	Ramculee, Shyam, Gundhar and Goojree.
Maligoura	Gouree and Soruth.
Manj	Sarung, Soruth, Bilawul and Mular.
Malcous	Hindol, Busunt, Jujavuntee, Punchum Khutrag, Maroo, Sarung and Sanwuntee.
Malsree	Suncurabhurun, Kidara, Mudmadh and Suruswutee.
Malwa	Gouree, Puraj and Bibhas.
Maroo	Gouree, Puruj and Soruth.
Marwa	Coclut, Canhra and Sooha, composed by Nyrud.
Megh	Culian, Camod, Sanwunt and Busunt.
Mudmadh	Mular, Soodhculian and Mulsree.
Mudmithoon / Madhvee	Nutnarayun, Mular, Soodh, Humeer and Mudmadh, sung by Canh.
Mular	Sarung, Soruth and Bilawul; or, agreeably to others, Nut, Sarung and Meghrag.
Mular-Nut	Mular and Nut.
Mungulashtuk	Jytsree, Canhra, Kidara and Culian. Some add Shyam.
Mungal-Goojree	Ramculee, Shyam, Gundhar and Mungulashtuc. Some say, instead of the last, Buhoolee.
Munohur	Marwa, Turwun and Gouree, or instead of Gouree Biharee.
N.	
Nagdhun	Mular, Kidara and Soohoo.
Nut-Narayun	Suncurabhurun, Mudmadh, Luncdhun and Bilawul.
P.	
Paravutee	Dewculee, Gound, Gouree and Poorbee.
Poorbee	Malwa and Gouree; or, agreeably to others, Gouree, Gound and Deuguree.

Names of Rags.	*Compounded of*
Pooria	Dhoulsree, Tunc, Mungulashtuc and Canhra.
Punchum	Lulit and Busunt. According to some Burareo, Gound and Goojree. Others say, Gundhar, Munohur and Hindol.
Pruluee	Deuguree, Poorbee, Gouree and Gound.
Puruj	Dhunasree, Maroo and Gundhar. Some assert it consists of Maroo, Toree and Usavuree.
Putmunjuree	Maroo, Dhoul, Dhunasree and Cumbharee.
R.	
Rageshwur	Bhyron, Gouree, Kidara, Deuguree, Dewgundhar, Sindhoora, Dhunasree, Canhra and Usavuree.
Rajhuns	Malwa, Sree-Rag and Munohur. Sung by Bhurut.
Rajnarayun Nut	Cumbharee, Pooria and Toree.
Rouránee	Lulit, Leelavutee, Chitee and Punchum.
Ruhus Mungla or Ruhus Mungul	Suncurabhurun, Urana and Soruthee.
Rumbhavutee	Mulsree, Soodh and Mular.
Ruti Bullubh	Nut, Sarung, Bhyron, Lulit and Punchum.
S.	
Sanwunt	Sarung and Mular. According to some Kidara and Camod. Others add also Canhra.
Sanwunt Camod	Kidara and Camod. Some add Soodh. Others say, Sawunt and Camod.
Sarung	Deuguree, Mular and Nut. Others say, Marwa and Mular.
Shiwruti	Burhuns and Sindhw.
Shuhana	Furodust and Canhra.
Sindhoora or Sindhwee	Usavuree and Uheeree.
Soodh-Camod	Soodh and Camod.
Soodh-Culian	Tunc, Camod and Gond.
Soodh-Nut	Bagesree, Pooria and Mudmadh.
Sooghraee *vide* Culaee.	
Soohoo	Malsree, Bilawul and Bibhas. Others substitute Soodh or Bagesree, in the room of Bibhas.
Soruth	Goojree, Punchum, Bhyruvee, Gundhar and Bungal.
Soruthee	Malwa, Emun and Soruth.
Sourashtuc	Gundhar, Goojree, Bungal, Punchum and Bhyruvee.
Sree-Rag	Burhuns, Tunc and Gouree.
Sree ruvun	Sree-Rag, Malsree and Suncurabhurun.
Sree-sumod	Malsree, Soodh, Sree-Rag, Bhempulasee and Tunc.
Stumbh	Malsree, Soodh and Mular.
Sucroun	Soruth, Luncdhun and Bilawul.

Names of Rags.	Compounded of
Suctbulibh	Goonculee, Ramculee, Gundhar, Goojree, Shyam and Gour.
Suncurabhurun	Kidara and Bilawul.
Surd	Bhyron, Sooha and Soodh.
Suruswutee	Nutnarayun, Suncurabhurun and Soodh.
Susirekha	Lulit, Punchum, Tiluk, Sarung and Soohoo.
T.	
Thoomree	Suncurabhurun and Maroo.
Tiluk-Camod	Khutrag and Camod.
Toree	Usavuree and Khutrag. Some add Dhunasree. Others make it consist of Lulit, Dhunasree and Dhoulsree.
Treekshun	Bijuya, Burhuns and Desce.
Trivenee	Nutnarayun, Jytsree and Sunuru.
Tunc	Sree-Rag, Canhra and Bhyron.
Turwun	Descar, Gouree, Poorbee Some, in the room of the last, say Lulit; others Bibhas.
U.	
Ubheeree .... or Uheeree	Culian, Descar, Goojree and Shyam.
Uheer Nut	Uheeree and Nut.
Uheer-Roop	Dhunasree and Tooree.
Unsee	Dhoulsree and Gound.
Urana	Mular and Canhra.

OF THE RAGMALA.*

THE personification of melodies in *Ragmala*, or chaplet of melodies, is what I shall next describe. Custom, which has subsisted from time immemorial, has rendered this an essential branch of knowledge and polite learning. How far these symbolical representations are by native painters made to correspond with what they should represent, I shall leave to the decision of the reader, when he sees one, and compares it with the description which I shall here give of it. I shall, however, remark that the Ragmalas generally offered for sale are sometimes so incorrect, that scarcely one of the representations is strictly in conformity with the

* راگ مالا See Note I, p. 49.

description given in books. As painting is not now exercised in the greatest perfection in Hindoostan, it is probable that drawings intended in the original to represent one object were mistaken for another, and accordingly adopted in the copy. Subsequent copies were made in a similar manner, former errors were perpetuated, and new ones added, till very little resemblance remained between the pictures of the Ragmala and that which should have been represented. The generality of amateurs are more solicitous of possessing a copy of the drawings denominated Ragmala than of ascertaining its accuracy, for which indeed few are competent or will go to the trouble. The painter, if he should even possess skill, as long as he can find purchasers for his work, sees no reason for his being at the pains of reforming the pictures to their original state of purity. I beg leave to quote the opinion of Sir Wm. Jones on the subject of Indian drawings. "Whenever the *Indian* drawing differs from the memorial verse in the *Retnamala,* I have preferred the authority of the writer to that of the painter, who has drawn some terrestrial things with so little similitude, that we must not implicitly rely on his representation of objects." Vol. I, p. 343. On the Antiquity of the Indian Zodiac.

I.—BHYRON.

This rag is personified in the exact representation of Muhadev or Shiv, one of the three principal deities of the Hindoos. He is drawn as a sunyasee or Hindoo mendicant of a comely aspect, having his whole body besmeared with ashes, his hair is clotted into knots, and from amongst them flows the impetuous Gunga. He wears bracelets on his wrists, and his forehead is adorned with a crescent. The monster appear-in the third eye situated between his brows. A hideous serpent is entwined about his shoulders and bosom, and from his neck is pendent a string of skulls instead of flowers. The skin of the huge elephant is negligently thrown over his shoulder, and one of his hands supports a triple dart. Thus equipped, he is mounted on an enormous bull. Sometimes he is represented seated on the elephant's skin, and the bull tied beside him.

I.—*Bhyruvee.*

This is one of the five wives allotted to Bhyron, and is perhaps not only the eldest, but also his best beloved—at least she seems to be the first and most respected.

Her form bespeaks a young and beautiful virgin of a delicate complexion, with beaming eyes ; her hair hangs gracefully down to her waist. A white saree or sheet is thrown over her slender form, and exposes her feet which are tinged red.* A garland of chumpa flowers graces her neck ; she is seated on the summit of a rock ; the cumul (lotus) blooms by her side, and she holds a pair of munjeeras or little cymbals in her hands, with which she keeps time to the song or hymn which she appears to be singing.

* Mr. Wilson, in his translation of the Megha Duta, in a note on verse 212—

O'er every floor the painted footstep treads.

Staining the soles of the feet with a red color derived from *mehndee*, the *Lac, &c.*, is a favorite practice of the Hindu toilet. It is thus elegantly alluded to in the ode to one of the female personifications of music, the Raginee *Asauveree*—

"The rose hath humbly bowed to meet,
"With glowing lips her hallowed feet,
"And lent them all its bloom."

Hindu odes by John David Paterson, Esq., pubished in the new series of Gladwin's *Oriental Miscellany*, Calcutta.

2.—*Buraree.*

This young girl, the beauty of whose countenance is heightened by the contrast of her jetty ringlets, is engaged in dalliance with her lover. The color of her dress is white. Her wrists are adorned with Cungun (bracelets), and her ears with the flowers of the Culpu-turoo.

I cannot account for the apparent incongruity in this and some other Raginees. She is one of the wives of Bhyron, and is here represented as deficient in her conjugal faith towards him. Ovid's advice "'to retaliate in kind" cannot be properly applicable here, as the Hindoos are permitted by law a plurality of wives, but the women are not at liberty to marry twice. But, have not the gods and goddesses been privileged in matters of love from all eternity ?

3.—*Mulhmadh.*

The complexion of this Raginee is of a golden color, and she appears to prefer that to every other tint. Her dress is of the same tinge, and her body is stained with the fragrant die of the saffron. She is engaged in the same manner as the preceding.

It is to be observed for the satisfaction of the European readers that a golden complexion is as much admired by the natives of Hindoostan as a moon-faced beauty, both of which sound uncouth in the idioms of Europe; but it is to be understood that the latter of the two expressions has reference only to the pleasure which the beams of the moon diffuse, and not to its rotundity ; while in the former case respect is only had to the natural beauty of pure gold, and not to its actual hue.

4.—*Sindhvee.*

The sanguinary disposition of this female is displayed in her features. She is clothed in red garments, holds a triple dart in her hand, and a *dopuhuria* flower hangs from her ear. She is enraged at the delay of her lover, and waits, impatient for his arrival.

5.—*Bungal.*

A joginee or female mendicant or devotee. Her face is sprinkled over with ashes; her body is stained with marks of ground sandal; and her forehead streaked with musk. Her clotted hair is tied in a knot; a yellow saree conceals her bosom: she holds a lotus in her right hand, and a triple dart in her left. This Raginee, although the native of a foreign and distant land, appears in the costume properest for a wife of Bhyron.

II.—MALCOUS.

An athletic young man of rosy complexion, and intoxicated with wine. His vestments are blue, and he holds a staff in his hand. A string of large pearls is hung round his neck. He is surrounded by women, whom he addresses with gallant familiarity. The pearls are sometimes exchanged for the heads of such as he has conquered in battle.

It is remarkable that, although wine is prohibited by the religion of several nations, yet votaries to Bacchus are everywhere to be found. Amongst Hindoos, some are not only permitted the use of this intoxicating beverage, but it is even offered in libations by them to the gods; while others abstain from it altogether. By the precept of the faith of Mohummud, its very touch is polluting. The poets, particularly the Moosulmans, however, are very eloquent and lavish of its praises. Scarce a work of fancy either in prose or verse is to be found in which some lines are not dedicated to the altar of the rosy god. Turn up the works of the admirable Hafiz, almost at any page, and you will be convinced of it. The commentators on that work ascribe, it is true, a very different meaning to that word, but any unprejudiced person must find the construction rendered by the commentators on several passages very much strained. Wine used by the natives of Hindoostan, both actually and fictitiously, is always taken to excess, so as to cause deep intoxication.

1.—*Toree.*

This delicate minstrel is clothed in a white saree. Her fair skin is tinged and perfumed with touches of camphor and saffron. She stands in a wild romantic spot playing on the veen. The skill with which she strikes that instrument has so fascinated the deer in the neighbouring groves, that they have forgot their pasture, and stand listening to the notes which she produces. This is one of the effects of music attributed to the ancient musicians, and confirmed even by modern asseveration : *vide* p. 6.

2.—*Gouree.*

This very young brunette has adopted the blossom of the mangoe for her ornament. She is endeavouring to sing her favourite melody, but is so infatuated and intoxicated as to be hardly able to proceed with it.

3.—*Gooncuree.*

The grief which is depicted in the air of this female, the tears which flow fast from her eyes, the scattered wildness of her hair which wantons with the breeze, the sighs which she breathes, and the dejected posture in which she is sitting under the cuu.... cree, with her head leaning forwards, prove the anguish of her heart for the absence of her beloved.

4.—*Cumbhavutee.*

This wanton beauty, neglectful of care, studies her own enjoyment: she is constantly immersed in music and dancing: mirth and pleasure are her constant attendants.*

5.—*Coocubh.*

The revels of the preceding night have rendered her countenance pale, her eyes, though naturally sparkling, are drowsy from want of sleep: the garlands of chumpa flowers with which she had decorated herself lies ecattered about, and her dress is discomposed; but yet she seems to loathe the light of the dawn, and would fain convince her lover that the morn has not yet blushed.

III.—HINDOL.

He is seated in a goldon swing, while a number of nymphs, by whom he is surrounded, amuse him with music and keep time with the rocking of the swing on which he sits, indolently gazing on their charms, enjoying the sweets spontaneously offered to his shrine. His countenance is wan, which seems to indicate that, although an immortal, his

* It is to the commentators that I am indebted for the sole occupation of the goddesses, being pleasure and dress: the fact is,

To sing, to dance,

To dress, and troll the tongue, and roll the eye,

constitutes a very well educated female, according to the customs of Hindoostan. We cannot help, however, being pleased with the simplicity and propriety of taste, which gives to the graceful ornaments of nature so prominent a part in the decoration of feminine beauty.—H. H. Wilson's Megha Duta, p. 76.

constitution is impaired by the early and unceasing career of pleasures and irregularities which he has pursued.

1.—*Ramcuree.*

The complexion of this nymph is pale, her dress is blue, she is decked with jewels, and her forehead is striped with infusion of musk. She has been disappointed in an interview she expected with her lover the preceding night; while he, having had more important business in hand, perhaps a new amour, has just arrived after daylight, and is endeavouring to effect a reconciliation for his late neglect. It is not certain how soon he will obtain his object, for, although we easily forgive those we love, yet the present affair is of a very serious nature. She is not only actuated by jealousy, but is also apprehensive lest her rival wean the affections of her beloved from her.

2.—*Desakh.*

In treatises on the Rags, this Raginee is described as an enraged Amazonian, wielding a naked sword in her hand, with which she has overcome a number of foes and defended her lover who stands by her side; but the general representation in the *Ragmala* is quite ambiguous; there she is drawn in the figure of several athletic young men engaged in various gymnastic exercises, such as wrestling, casting of huge masses of stone, &c. It is quite uncertain what gave rise to this preposterous representation.

3—*Lulit.*

It is not satisfactorily explained why this beautifully fair creature, who is so overwhelmed with grief for the absence of her lover, should decorate herself with all her finery of dress, jewelry and flowers.

4—*Bilawulee.*

The pride of this Raginee consists in the beautiful symmetry of her limbs, and her solicitude to please her beloved is expressed by the pains she takes to adorn herself against his arrival, whom she awaits with anxious expectation and beating heart. She is dressed in rose-coloured vestments.

5—*Putmunjuree.*

O! the pangs of separation: the poignancy of whose sting is known only to those who have felt its wound! May my readers, and particularly those of the fair sex, never experience its fatal power!

The object now before us is oppressed with the deepest anguish. She sheds incessant tears, which give her a sad and solitary relief, the only consolation her tender heart will admit. The flowers hung round her neck no longer laugh in the bloom of freshness, the fever in her mind and body have withered them to sapless leaves, which exhale no more their wonted perfume.

IV.—DEEPUK.

The flame which the ancient musicians are said to have kindled by the performance of this Rag is depicted in his fiery countenance and red vestments. A string of large pearls is thrown round his neck, and he is mounted on a furious elephant accompanied by several women. He is also represented in a different form.

1.—*Desee.*

The excess of passion to which this blooming Raginee is subject induces her to pay a visit to her lover at his abode. She accordingly adds the assistance of art to the natural charms of her person, and puts her resolution into practice.

2.—*Camod.*

What troubles and dangers wlll not love instigate one to undergo! When under its influence what will not youth dare to accomplish! Here we see a nymph forget the natural delicacy of her sex, and venture alone in the desert in the hideousness of night. She quits her soft bed and friendly neighbourhood, and traverses unaccompanied the wilderness infested with ravenous beasts. The chance of an interview with the object of her love she considers well worth the risking of her life and character. A thousand fears now mock her fortitude when she finds herself at the place of assignation *alone,* for he, on whose account she has staked all this, is not yet there! The timidity of her sex then displays itself. She starts at the fall of a leaf, and melts into tears. She has on a short white boddice, and passes unnoticed under cover of a red saree.

3.—*Nut.*

This young maiden prefers the career of glory to that of pleasure. She is adorned with jewels, and has clothed herself in men's attire, and being mounted upon a furious steed, Minerva-like, engages in battle with those of the opposite sex. Her countenance is flushed with the ardours and fatigues of such an undertaking.

4.—*Kidara.*

The subject of this Raginee is a masculine character. The young man in white garments wields a sword in his right hand, and in his left grasps the tusk of an elephant which he has rooted out. A bard standing beside him recites the praises of his valor.

V.—SREE.

A handsome man dressed in white, or some say in red. A string of crystal and ruby beads hung round his neck. He holds a lotus flower in his hand, and is seated upon a carved throne; musicians performing in his presence.

1.—*Malsree.*

Although love holds an exalted rank in the music of Hindoostan, as it does in that of other countries, and instances are not wanting of its existence in a refined state, yet, the beauties of nature are allowed to arrest their share of attention. The fascinating creature before us is an example. She is clad in a flowing yellow robe, and sits under a mangoe tree, in the society of her female companion, enjoying the verdure and luxuriance of the extensive scene before her.

2.—*Marwa.*

Her dress is of gold brocade, and she has a garland of flowers round her neck. She sits in anxious expectation of the arrival of her lover.

3.—*Dhunasree.*

We cannot but sympathise with solitary grief in a beautiful female. There is something so irresistible, that we naturally feel inclined to become acquainted with the circumstance which gave rise to her misfortune, not by a vain curiosity, but with the view of affording her any consolation which may be in our power, and of sympathising with her in her griefs. The misfortunes of the subject now under consideration proceed from the absence of her lover, and that she has long languished is evident from her emaciated frame. Her dress is red, and avoiding the society of her friends, she sits alone under a Moulsree tree, venting her griefs to the woods.

4.—*Busunt.*

Busunt is the spring of Hindoostan, the time of mirth and festivity. The hero of this piece therefore is the voluptuous god Crishnu, who is represented in his usual costume and occupation. His vestment is tinged red. His head is adorned with his favourite plumage, extracted from the tail of the peacock ; in his right hand he holds a bunch of mangoe blossoms, and in the left a prepared leaf of the betel tree. In this manner he stands in a garden surrounded with a number of women as jolly as himself, and all join in the dance, and sing and play a thousand jovial tricks.

5.—*Usavuree.*

The hideousness of this picture is mitigated only by the delicacy of the principal figure. Her dark-brown complexion, the monstrous snake which entwines her arms and legs—her hair tied in a knot on the crown of her head—the wild solitude of the rock environed with waters where she sits, are all beautifully relieved and contrasted with the fine outlines of her features, the white sheet gracefully thrown over her, (which is sometimes changed for a covering of leaves,) and the streaks of dissolved camphor with which she has stained her forehead.

VI.—MEGH.

This is the only Rag that bears a masculine character. He is represented of a dark complexion, his hair is tied in a knot on the crown of his head, and in his hand he balances a sharp-edged sword.

1.—*Tune.*

Various expedients have been resorted to by love-sick maids to allay in some measure the fever raging in their veins. The object of our present inquiry, labouring under its influence, has applied to the crown of her head the leaves of the lotus, which is said to possess refreshing qualities.

2.—*Mular.*

The frequent representation of scenes of separation, and the consequent grief attendant upon it, recalls to one's mind the sad history of ancient Hindoostan! As I review the Ragmala, which I peruse as pictures of real life, I am affected with sadness at the deplorable state in which, in former times, the female sex particularly subsisted. Various sources of abject injustice and oppression still exist; but as they are rendered sacred by their laws, and they have been habituated to them by custom which has prevailed from time immemorial, the poor women acquiesce under them without murmur. Some causes, however, have been removed in the British territories, which must be a source of great comfort to them. The convenience of travelling in these days, even with women, children, and property, must be reckoned as one of the foremost. Such ancient princes of Hindoostan who afforded convenience to travellers are some of the most celebrated amongst them; and the construction of high roads, bridges, tanks, wells, and choukees, for public use and protection, are amongst the most meritorious acts of their religion. The pious and chaste Ram Chundru of Ujodhya is celebrated for his great care in these matters.

This Raginee is delineated of a complexion wan and pale; she is decorated with the white jessamine, and sits sad and solitary, endeavouring to soothe and dissipate her melancholy, with the tones of the Veen, in happier days her delight; but

> "In vain the lute for harmony is strung,
> And round the robe-neglected shoulder hung;
> And faltering accents strive to catch in vain
> Her race's old commemorative strain:
> The falling tear that from reflection springs,
> Corrodes incessantly the silvery strings;
> Recurring woe still pressing on the heart,
> The skilful hand forgets its grateful art;
> And idly wandering strikes no measured tone,
> But wakes a sad wild warbling of its own.
> At times such solace animates her mind,
> As widowed wives in cheerless absence find."

3.—*Goojree.*

The tenor of this picture is not evident. It presents a young female minstrel, of a delicate voice and engaging mien, dressed in yellow short stays and red saree, and adorned with jewels.

4.—*Bhoopalee.*

This is some happy nymph engaged in dalliance with her lover. A white saree is thrown over her body, which is stained with the fragrant saffron. A garland of flowers adorns her bosom. The favoured youth sits by her side, round whose neck her arms are enfolded.

5.—*Descar.*

There is no material difference between this and the preceding delineation. The characters by which we distinguish them are, the string of pearls substituted for the flowers, and the marks with which she has stained herself are of ground sandal.

OF MUSICAL INSTRUMENTS.

Several musical instruments are to be seen in the hands of Apollo's muses, which might give great light to the dispute between the ancient and modern music.—*Addison.*

Their present state susceptible of much improvement. Their classification. Detailed description of the several instruments now in use.

How proud soever the people of Hindoostan may be of their musical instruments, I am of opinion, as I have already observed, that they are susceptible of very important improvements. The defects which have come under my notice are of two sorts; the first regards the materials of which they are made, and the second their construction.

With respect to the first of these defects—the materials of which their musical instruments are made, it appears that very little attention is paid to it, as if it were immaterial what substance was employed for the purpose. This want of choice is influenced by pecuniary considerations, as well as want of ingenuity. It cannot be supposed that such carelessness prevailed during the flourishing period of the Indian empire; but that from the commencement of its decline a check had been opposed to its further refinement is what perhaps all will allow. At present, for reasons offered in a preceding part of the work, it will appear reasonable, that, far from expecting a progressive improvement, we should rather be prepared to anticipate this noble science on the wane in the same portion as the decline of its empire, and the consequent decrease of knowledge and depravity of the people of this once celebrated country. The root of the venerable tree being sapped, its blossoms are no longer supplied with nourishment by the branches which they were designed to decorate, and must soon decay. The security and stability proffered from political motives by the British Government to the native chieftains has, perhaps, materially conduced to render them luxurious and effeminate in a still greater degree than the climate to which those vices are generally attributed ; and these have been the bane of the music of Hindoostan.* In Europe professional men are always employed in the construction of all instruments and engines, or at least their advice is solicited, and suggestions acted upon ; here, the making and fitting up of musical instruments is entrusted entirely to persons who are ignorant not only of the merest elements of music, but who, besides manufacturing musical instruments, are general carpenters and other artificers, who if they even possessed the abilities could not afford to waste their time in experiments for the improvement of musical instruments, the number rather than the quality of which would ensure the greater gain. It is on this account that the better musicians prefer to patch and mend their old instruments rather than construct new ones, of which to find the just proportions, they lack the abilities. Khoosnhal Khan and Oomraw Khan, Veenkars, mentioned before, have in their possession the instrument on which their grandfather Jeewun Shah used to ravish his audience. Some no doubt are not aware that a difference of material produces any difference in the tone of an instrument. There is an

* See page 31, and following.

anecdote of a Rajah, who in token of his approbation presented a favourite player with a silver *Sarungee*, on which he was to perform before him.*

It is problematical whether a violin of the sort just mentioned could produce sounds sufficiently sweet to arrest any attention; but it cannot certainly be denied that a good performer on any instrument, whether musical or other, can do more execution on one of inferior quality than can be produced from one of a far superior quality put into the hands of a person who is only an inferior artist.

Drums and tabors of all sorts are covered with goat's skin, fresh, and in an unprepared state; the body and neck of *Sarungees* are made of wood, one entire piece, excavated, the top covered with skin instead of thin light board; the flutes are pieces of the bamboo cane, formed by nature, and generally bored without regard to just proportion. It is not, however, the musicians that are entirely to blame for making use of such imperfect instruments. A musical instrument of the first class requires so much time and nicety in its construction, besides scientific skill in the maker, that the musicians of Hindoostan cannot now-a-days afford to pay for one; indeed, on this account one is not procurable. What extravagant sums were paid by the Greeks even for their flutes! The more respectable performers in this country, if

* There is a European anecdote similar to the one quoted above. Leonardi da Vinci, the celebrated painter, passed at his time for an excellent violin player, and was even professionally engaged by the Duke of Milan, Ludovico Sforzia. In the sketch of his life, prefixed to his treatise on painting, is this singular statement: "Vinci had a violin of silver made for him, which was shaped in the form of a horse's head, and he surpassed on this instrument all other violin players."

they would be well paid, should rather keep up a large retinue than really superior instrument.

As for the defects which regard their construction, there is one, which exclusive of other minor ones, is found to affect them all. I mean that material radical imperfection which will not admit of a change of keys. They have likewise no method of tuning their instruments to a certain pitch, but are guided in this respect merely by the ear.

If an opinion might be hazarded, why no person has endeavoured to render instruments playable in every key, I should suppose the reason to be this : A drum or tabor, the sound of which is necessarily monotonous, is an ever-attendant and inseparable companion to Indian songs, whether any other instrument be present or not. Its sound is taken as the key-note, and all other instruments that may be present, and the voice, are regulated by it. From this it should appear that as long as the use of the drum or tabor is not laid aside, there will be no necessity for change of keys, and the rythmical nature of Indian music renders a liberal use of the drum more essential, in order to mark the time distinctly, than any other accompaniment.

Musical instruments are divided into four classes—

1. Tut. Such as are strung with wires or gut are thus denominated: The Rubab, the Tumboora, the Sitar, the Sarungee, the Veen, and the Qanoon, &c., belong to this class.

2. Bitut. To this division are referred all those which are covered with skins, as the Mridung, the Dholkee, the Tublas, the Daera, the Duph, the Nuqqara, &c.

3. Ghun. These are instruments of percussion, and used two at a time. The Munjeera, the Jhanjh, the Curtar, &c., (Cymbals, Castanets,) are of this description.

4. Sooghur. Wind instruments are classed under this name. The Surnaee, the Banslee, the Torey, &c., are examples of it.

The grand instrumental music of Hindoostan is the Noubut, and the instruments used in the cabinet are the Mridung, the Dholkee, the Tublas, the Daera, the Duph, the Munjeera, the Curtar, the Sarungee, the Tumboora, the Sitar, the Rubab, the Veen, the Qanoon, and the Banslee. Five of the last are occasionally played solo: the rest are used as accompaniment either to these, or to the voice.

Of the Noubut.

The Noubut is the grandest instrumental music of Hindoostan. It is a concert, and the instruments which comprise a full band of the *Noubut Khanuh* are two pairs of *Nuqqaras,* one pair of large *Noubuts,* one *Quna,* one *Toruy,* one pair of *Jhanjhs,* two *Surna,* two *Nuy,* two *Alghoza,* one *Roshun Choukee Surna,* and one pair *Qulum* flutes, and flageolets.

The effect produced by the joint efforts of expert performers is considerably imposing, and should be witnessed to be properly appreciated. It is heard to advantage from some distance.

THE MRIDUNG, THE DHOLKEE AND THE TUBLAS.

These are drums, and differ from each other in form, construction, and likewise in the manner of playing. The first is the most ancient, and is one of those instruments which accompanied the voice in the more chaste ages; the Dholkee is generally preferred by amateur performers, and is the domestic and homely companion to the music of the uninitiated female; and the last, less solemn than the Mridung, and more adapted to accompany light and trivial compositions, is selected as the fittest counterpart with the Sarungee to the silver tones of the modern meretricious Hindoo dancing girl. It is from hence evident, that the two last are modern licentious inventions, unknown to the ages when music breathed sacred and solemn numbers.

The Mridung is a hollow cylinder of wood, resembling a cask, open at both the ends, which are covered with crude goat's skin of different thicknesses, so as to produce different sounds : one end has likewise a coating of a composition made of rosin, oil, &c., applied to the inside, and is tightened with leather braces like our drums. The Dholkee is similar to this, only the diameter bears a greater proportion to the length, and is a lighter and more delicate instrument. The braces are strings. The difference between both the above and the Tubla is, that the latter are always used two together, the one being the treble and the other the bass, which however may be considered as one instrument, divided from the middle for the sake of convenience.

The method of playing on these instruments is curious. They are struck with the fingers and palms of both hands, and it is surprising what variety of measures, and changes of the same measure, expert players can produce on them. It is allowed to be more difficult to describe the manner of using the blow-pipe than of acquiring its use : the method of playing on these instruments is absolutely indescribable, and is only to be learnt from a master, chiefly by imitation and long practice.

THE DUPH AND THE DAERA.

The first of these is an octagon frame of wood, about three feet in diameter and six inches deep, covered on one side with skin, the stress of which is counterbalanced on the other with a net-work of thin slips of the same. The skin is struck upon, in playing, with the fingers of the right hand, while a tender flexible switch, held perpendicularly over the instrument with the fore-finger of the left, is made to strike on it with the middle finger at stated intervals of the measure.

The Daera, as its name implies, is a circle of wood, metal, or other material, covered on one side, as the preceding. Its diameter is generally about 11 or 12 inches. The right hand fingers are applied in the same manner as in using the Duph, and the thumb of the left is thrust into a string passed through a hole on one side of the circle, so as to form a rest or support for that hand a little above the centre, against which the knuckle of the middle finger is pressed on the inside when a rise in the tone is desired.

Both these instruments are now almost entirely used by amateurs, although the former is sometimes played upon by professional men of the lower order. These instruments may be compared to the Tambour de basque, Tabret or Timbrel of the ancients.

THE MUNJEERA AND THE CURTAR.

These are Cymbals and Castanets, and are of no other use than to mark the time distinctly, which, as I have already several times noticed, is the very life of rythmical music.

THE SARUNGEE.

The Sarungee is the fiddle of Hindoostan. It is strung with four gut strings, and played with a bow, the hairs of which are loose, and tightened with the hand at the time of playing. The two lowest strings are tuned to *Khuruj*, and the others to a perfect fourth. The instrument is held in a position contrary to that in which the violin is used ; that is, in the manner of the bass violin ; and the fingers of the left hand do not press upon the strings, but are held close beside them, while the right hand draws the bow.

Besides the gut-strings, the instrument has a number of metal wires, generally thirteen, of unequal lengths, which go under the gut-strings. These wires are tuned to the mode proper to the Raginee intended to be played. The bow can never touch or approach them, so they are of use only to reverberate with the sound of the gut-strings. This proves that the musicians of Hindoostan are aware of the fact that sound propagated on one string will communicate vibration to another that is in unison with it, or the difference of whose tone is exactly an octave.

THE TUMBOORA.

The Tumboora or Tanpoora is another very ancient instrument, and the simplest of all those of the guitar kind. It somewhat resembles that instrument, but has a very long neck without frets. The body is generally made of about the two-thirds of the dry shell of a gourd, the top covered with a thin board. It is strung with three or four wire strings, one brass and the rest steel. The lowest is tuned to the key note, and the others to its quint and octave above. These are struck alternately, the instrument reclining on the shoulder. Its use is calculated, as the name indicates, to fill up all pauses and vacuities in the song, and likewise to keep the songster from straying from the tone which he originally adopted.

THE SITAR.

This is likewise a modern instrument, and was invented by Umeer Khosro of Delhi. It resembles the last mentioned instrument, but is made a good deal smaller, and has movable frets of silver, brass, or other material, which are fastened with catgut or silk. Seventeen frets are generally used, and as they are movable, they answer every purpose required. The shifting of these to their proper places requires a delicate ear.

This instrument derives its name from si سه signifying in Persian *three*, and tar تار *a string*, as that number is commonly used. More modern performers have made several additions.

Of the three wires, one is steel, and the others brass. These last are tuned in unison, and are called Khuruj from their sound, and the other is a perfect fourth to it. The fingers of the left hand slide over the frets on the finger-board, and stop the notes in the same manner as on the guitar, and the wires are struck with the fore-finger of the right, to which is fitted a kind of plectrum or instrument called a *Mizrab*,* made of a piece of wire curiously twisted, to facilitate the various motions of the finger.

The Sitar is very much admired, is used both by professional men and amateurs, and is really a very pleasing toned instrument in the hands of an expert performer.

THE RUBAB.

This instrument is strung with gut-strings, and in shape and tone resembles a Spanish guitar. It is played with a plectrum of horn held between the fore-finger and thumb

* From the Arabic verb ضرب to strike.

of the right hand, while the fingers of the left stop the strings on the fingerboard. I have heard some performers on this, who are said to excel, and their performance certainly deserved praise, for the delight with which they inspired their hearers. The Puthans are remarkably fond of this instrument, which is very common at Rampoor.

THE VEEN.

The *Veen* is one of the most ancient of the musical instruments of Hindoostan. It was played upon by the minstrel Mooni Narud, to whom the credit of its invention is allowed. It is the instrument of the greatest capacity and power; and a really superior *Veen* in the hands of an expert performer is perhaps little inferior to a fine-toned piano, and indeed, for Hindoostanee music, the best devised, and calculated to be adapted to all practical modifications.

Although the *Veen* has a fingerboard and frets, it is not strictly confined in its intonation, as a guitar, a pianoforte, or an organ is; for it is so delicate an instrument, that the slightest difference in the pressure of the finger, or of its distance from the frets, will cause a sensible variation in the tone, of which a good performer avails himself. Hence results that beautiful nicety of just intonation in every mode which charms the musical ear. To convey a correct idea of this beauty, we need only observe that the superiority of the violin over most other instruments is to be derived from this source.

The *Veen* is strung with seven metal wires, three steel and four brass; but as is the case with the Sitar and the Rubab, the melody is generally played on one of the steel wires, and the rest are chiefly for accompaniment; several fingers of the right hand striking simultaneously on several of the wires : each of the fingers to be thus employed is armed with a plectrum usually made with the large scales of fishes, and fastened on with springs, or tied down with thread.

THE BANSULEE, OR BUNSEE.

The flute was formerly a very favourite instrument, and is said to have produced wonderful effects in the hands of the god Crishnu. There are few professional performers on this instrument now.

OF THE VARIOUS SPECIES

OF

VOCAL COMPOSITIONS OF HINDOOSTAN.

Twenty different species described.

THE most ancient sorts of composition are, 1st, the *Geet*; 2nd, the *Took*; 3rd, the *Chhund*; 4th, the *Prubund*; 5th, the *Dharoo*; 6th, the *Dhooa*; and 7th, the *Mun*. These are chiefly in the Sanscrit, and difficult both of comprehension and execution. The first four I have heard; but much of these is not known in these days.

The various species of the more modern compositions are the following :—

1. The *Dhoorpud*. This may properly be considered as the heroic song of Hindoostan. The subject is frequently the recital of some of the memorable actions of their heroes, or other didactic theme. It also engrosses love matters, as well as trifling and frivolous subjects. The style is very masculine, and almost entirely devoid of studied ornamental flourishes. Manly negligence and ease seems to pervade the whole, and the few turns that are allowed are always short and peculiar. This sort of composi-

tion has its origin from the time of Rajah Man of Gualiar, who is considered as the father of Dhoorpud singers. The Dhoorpud has four *Tooks* or strains,—the 1st is called *Sthul, Sthaee*, or *Bedha;* the 2nd, *Untura;* the 3rd, *Ubhog;* and the last, *Bhog*. Others term the two last *Ubhag*. *Dhoorpuds*, in which the names of flowers are introduced, in such manner that the meaning will admit of two different constructions, are called *Phoolpund;* and two *Dhoorpuds* which correspond with each other in time, syllable, and accent, are denominated *Joogool*.

2. *Kheal*. In the *Kheal* the subject generally is a love tale, and the person supposed to utter it, a female. The style is extremely graceful, and replete with studied elegance and embellishments. It is chiefly in the language spoken in the district of Khyrabad, and consists of two *Tooks*. Sooltan Hoosyn Shurqee of Jounpoor is the inventor of this class of song. A species of this, consisting of only one *Took*, is called *Chootcula;* another, termed *Burwee*, comprises two *Tooks*, and is in the Poorbee tongue.

Although the pathetic is found in almost all species of Hindoostanee musical as well as poetical compositions, yet the *Kheal* is perhaps its more immediate sphere. The style of the *Dhoorpud* is too masculine to suit the tender delicacy of female expression, and the *Tuppa* is more conformable to the character of a maid, who inhabits the shores of the Ravi, (and has its connexion with a particular tale,) than with the beauties of Hindoostan; while the *Ghuzuls* and *Rekhtus* are quite exotic, transplanted and reared on the Indian soil since the Mahomedan conquest. To a person who understands the language sufficiently, it is enough to hear a few good *Kheals*, to be convinced of the beauties of

Hindoostanee songs, both with regard to the pathos of the poetry and delicacy of the melody.

3. *Tuppa.* Songs of this species are the admiration of Hindoostan. It has been brought to its present degree of perfection by the famous Shoree, who in some measure may be considered its founder. Tuppas were formerly sung in very rude style by the camel-drivers of the Punjab, and it was he who modelled it into the elegance it is now sung. *Tuppas* have two *Tooks,* and are generally sung in the language spoken at Punjab, or mixed jargon of that and Hindee. They recite the loves of Heer and Ranjha, equally renowned for their attachment and misfortunes, and allude to some circumstance in the history of their lives.

4. *Thoomree.* This is an impure dialect of the Vrujbhasha. The measure is lively and so peculiar, that it is not mistaken by one who has heard a few songs of this class. It is useless to waste words in description, which must after all prove inadequate, of a subject which will impress the mind more sensibly when attention is bestowed on a few songs.

5. *Rag-Sagur,* or the ocean of *Rags.* It is a species of Rondo, which commences with a particular *Rag.* Each successive strain is sung in a different *Rag,* and at the end of each, the first strain is repeated.

6. *Holee* or *Horee,* consists of four *Tooks* or strains like *Dhoorpud,* and the style is peculiar to itself.

If the songs of Hindoostan were classed by subjects, perhaps that which recites the amours of Chrishnu would be the most voluminous. The age of that voluptuary forms a very important era in the history of India, and it is not to be wondered at that it should so materially influence their song.

Every nation has celebrated the valorous deeds of its heroes in song, and so have the natives of Hindoostan done. Numerous compositions are in existence, which recite the victories and virtues of their ancient princes and heroes. The joys of love, however, have everywhere been more numerously sung ; and so has Crishnu, who is represented as the unrivalled Damon, Paris, and Adonis of Hindoostan ; all the excellencies of these are united in him. Equally amorous in his own turn, and beloved by all the fair without exception. He is emphatically styled " Mohun," or the enchanter. His person was so graceful, that every woman who once beheld him, became instantly enamoured of it. His pipe possessed such irresistible attractive charms, that none who ever heard it could attend to any thing else, however serious, incumbent, or necessary. It diffused a sort of phrenzy along with its tone, the influence of which could not be withstood by any woman of Vruj. Neither the usual cares of the household, the desire of arraying so natural to the female sex, nor the threats of the enraged husband ; no, not even the attention due to a hungry and crying infant could for a moment detain her from following the impulse occasioned by the sound of Crishnu's flute.

I have observed above, that songs which have love for their theme, are more numerous amongst all nations. In Hindoostan there is one other motive for their being esteemed—being the acts of the *god Crishnu*, they are considered as pious hymns. The old sing them as acts of devotion, the young derive pleasure from their contents ; by the pious they are held sacred ; while the profane find in them many things which they glory either to have themselves performed, or should have been glad to have had it in their power to achieve. The wise man has folly enough to be beguiled by them, and the fool possesses sufficient taste to relish their beauties. All, in short, agree in admiring songs of this class, how different soever their motives might be for this predilection in its favor.

The scenes of Crishnu's frolics were the villages of Gocool and Muthoora, on the opposite banks of the Jumna or Yamoona, and the wilds of Vrindabun. No milkmaid could here pass without being attacked by the amorous Crishnu. All Hindoo women went a wâtering to the Jumna with pitchers on their heads or under their arms, and never returned without at least an amorous embrace or a kiss.

These are recited in the *holees.* One song of this class describes a maiden reproaching Crishnu with his audaciousness in taking liberties with her; another admires his comeliness and extraordinary address. One with beating heart warns her female friends to be cautious how they venture to the river-side alone; another with tears in her eyes states her doleful tale, how she has been roughly treated and shamefully abused by the god. In this a forsaken girl bemoans her fate, and imprecates her rivals; in that other she declares the excess of her passion, and fondly confines the god in her arms. One declares her resolution of bearing no longer with his insults and oppressions; another congratulates her friend's arrival at a village like Gocool, where love revels. The forcible seizure of milk or a kiss forms the theme of one song; while in another you hear them bribe his stay with both. Some adore him as a god, others esteem him as a lover, and a few treat him as an impudent fellow.

7. *Jut.* A few hemistichs, each in a different dialect and *Rag.*

8. *Tirvut* and *Turana.* No words are adapted to these. It being considered necessary, however, to utter something for the easier and more perfect vocalization of this species of music, the following set of words has been adopted for this purpose, without regard to the order of succession here set down.

درآ درآ تا داني

There is a tale connected with these words, which is in almost every one's mouth, and therefore not necessary to be inserted here.

9. *Surgum*—Is sung with the notes contained in the Hindee scale [*Surgum*], as the name implies. It is literally what we call Solfa-ing or Solmization, although it is not now invariably used with the same view.

10. *Bishnoopud.* This a species of Hindoo hymns. It was founded by *Shoordas,* a blind poet and musician, and is of a moral tendency.

11. *Chutoorung*—Is four strains: 1, Kheal; 2, Turana; 3, Surgum; and 4, Tirvut. It is of modern invention.

12. *Ghuzul* and *Rekhtu.* These are in the Ordoo and Persain languages, and differ from each other, according to some, merely in the subject they treat of. The former has for its theme a description of the beauties of the beloved object, minutely enumerated, such as the green beard, moles, ringlets, size, shape, &c., &c., as well as his cruelties and indifference, and the pain endured by the lover; whilst in the Rekhtu he eulogizes the beauty of the beloved in general terms, and evinces his own intention of persevering in his love, and bearing with all the difficulties to which he might be exposed in the accomplishment of his desires. They consist mostly of from five to ten or a dozen couplets. One

species of these is termed *Charbyt*, and contains only four couplets, as its name indicates.

13. *Dadra* and *Nucta*—Are of various lengths, and generally in the dialect spoken in the districts of Bundelkhund and Bughelkund. The subject is almost universally mean—the petition of the fond woman for the acquisition of the most trifling favors.

14. *Gurca.* War songs in praise of valour. This is generally in the tongue spoken by the Rajpoots. It is the profession of a class of songsters denominated Dharees. Those in the language of Vruj and Gualiar are called *Sadra.* One species of this, in very lengthened couplets, is termed *Bugud.* Those in the Charnee tongue are denominated *Bur.*

15. *Palna.* Cradle songs or hymns. The subject is appropriate. Childhood and blessings for longevity, &c.

16. *Sohla* is sung on marriages.

17. *Moulood.* One or two hemistichs in praise of the Almighty, or of Mahommud. It is chiefly in the Arabic.

18. *Stooti.* In praise of superiors.

19. *Qoul, Qulbana* and *Kool* are in Arabic. These are sung by Quvvals.

20. *Zicree.* The subject of these is morality, and is sung in the dialect of Goojrat. It was originally introduced in Hindoostan by Qazee Muhmood.

OF THE PECULIARITIES

OF

MANNERS AND CUSTOMS IN HINDOOSTAN,

TO WHICH

ALLUSIONS ARE MADE IN THEIR SONG.

When she spoke,
Sweet words, like dropping honey, she did shed;
And 'twixt the pearls and rubies softly brake,
A silver sound, that heavenly music seem'd to make.—*Fairy Queen.*

The winds were hushed, no leaf so small
At all was seen to stir,
Whilst turning to the water's fall
The small birds sung to her.—*Drayton's Cynthia.*

I saw a pleasant grove,
With chaunt of tuneful birds resounding love.—*Milton.*

Earth smiles with flow'rs renewing, laughs the sky,
And bids to lays of love their tuneful notes apply.—*Dryden.*

Its characteristic nature. Reasons assigned for several of them, which now no longer exist, and examples produced.

It will perhaps be desirable to expatiate a little on such parts of the prevailing manners and customs of ancient Hindoostan as influence their music. The songs of a nation, as well as its poetry, go a great way towards developing its domestic practices, rites, and ceremonies, as also its habits of life. Those of Hindoostan are very characteristic, and it is perhaps, as is justly observed, owing to this happy union of melody and poetry, when judiciously adapted to each other, that we can reconcile ourselves to the extraordinary power music is said to have anciently possessed over the human soul, not only in Hindoostan, but likewise over the occidental nations, and probably over the whole world.

The allowed insignificancy of the female sex in the idea of a Hindoo, the contempt with which they are generally beheld, have very considerable effects on their poetry. A transient observation should likewise be made on the Arabians and Persians, as their music is generally understood and cultivated in this country. The Hindee Ghuzuls are in imitation and on the model of the Persian.

In Arabic poetry the man is invariably in love with the woman who is the object beloved. In Persia he is represented, contrary to the dictates of nature, as in love with his own sex. This is evident in all lyric poems of that country. Their pieces abound with the praises of the youthful cup-bearer, the beauty of his green beard, and the comeliness of his mien. In Hindoostan the fair sex* are the first to woo, and the man yields after much courting. In compositions

* "We must here make an allowance for *Indian* prejudices, which always assigns the active part of amorous intercourse to the female, and make the mistress seek the lover, not the lover his mistress."—Note on verse 255, Translation of Megha Duta.

I have endeavoured to assign a reason in the next paragraph after the following, which seems to me to obviate the necessity of any allowance being made for the passage on which Mr. Wilson has given this note, or of calling it a prejudice. The original text of Calidas appears to me quite natural, consistently with the customs of his country.

of this country, therefore, love and desire, hope and despair, and in short every demonstration of the tender passion, is first felt in the female bosom, and evinced by her pathetic exclamations.

If we should trace the origin of this disparity in the poetry of these nations, it will perhaps appear that the women in Arabia are less subject to be wounded by Cupid's darts, and are similar to the lukewarm beauties of Cabool. The peculiar custom of Persia is evidently the reason that their pieces abound with themes of the cast just noticed. The poor neglected women in vain expose their charms—in vain add the assistance of art to the comeliness of their persons—in vain has nature bestowed such charms, and been so lavish in her gifts to beings whom it does not much benefit. Alas! lovely creature, adorn not thy head with those precious gems, nor thy person with rich brocades; for neither these nor thy jetty ringlets, hanging gracefully down thy back, nor the reviving perfume, which thou carriest about thee, shall have any influence on the icy heart of the beloved object of thy cares—his warmth is reserved for another, he fancys superior beauties in the yet unsprung beard of his beloved Saqee, which, if it claim any attention, it is purely that it approaches to and resembles thy softness.

In Hindoostan I can see no other motive but that the men being permitted, by law and the custom of the country, a plurality of wives, the women should grow fond by neglect. Having from the total want of education no means of mental amusement, they consider the society of their husbands as their supremest felicity; and as he has to bestow a portion of his time on every individual wife, it may be fairly presumed that no one of them can be cloyed with him. From this permission of polygamy she is the more solicitous to engage and secure his affections by ardent demonstrations of fondness. A precept of Hindoo law should likewise be remembered, which prohibits the women to engage in the bonds of Hymen more than once during their lives. How far this precept of flagrant injustice is relished by the females, I shall leave the fair sex to determine.

To comprehend the songs of this country, and to relish their beauties, we must not figure to ourselves Hindoostan in the state in which it is at present, but must transport ourselves back to those earlier ages to which allusions are made by them : to those times, when these regions enjoyed not the tranquillity at present subsisting in its parts, but when they were possessed by petty chieftains, arbitrary in their respective dominions—when no highroads existed, but communication between one village and another was maintained by narrow footpaths, and rude mountains and junguls formed the natural barrier of the different chiefs, guarded by almost impossible woods and wild beasts—when navigation by river was as impracticable as travelling by land—when a journey even to a few leagues was rendered hazardous by robbers and marauders, who infested the despicable roads of themselves formidable, and rendered more so by frequent interruptions from rivulets and morrasses, and from ravines and nallas, which during the rains presented by their rapidity and intricacies very powerful obstacles—when topography was almost unknown, and the advice of a stranger adventitiously met was to be cautiously embraced, as robbers lurked about the roads in various disguises to seize on their prey by force or stratagem : to the time, in short, when parting even for a journey to an adjoining village, was accompanied by mutual tears, and prayers for safe return.

A distant tour such as in these days is looked upon with indifference, was formerly contemplated and consulted on for a year or two before undertaken; and when a man who had accomplished his purpose returned home in safety, after encountering all the hardships incident to it, the wonderful recital of his adventures, the skill with which he conducted himself in the presence of princes, his valour and intrepidity in times of danger, his cunning and foresight in preventing or avoiding the toils of the evil-minded, and all these exaggerated by the vanity of the traveller, formed the theme of admiration to the village, and the subject of pride to his relatives, not soon likely to be forgot.

It is observed by the author of "An Inquiry into the Life and Writings of Homer," page 26, "that it has not been given by the gods to one and the same country to produce rich crops and warlike men, neither indeed does it seem to be given to one and the same kingdom, to be thoroughly civilized, and afford proper subjects for poetry." It is this which renders Hindoostanee songs flat and unpalatable, unless we transport ourselves back to their barbarous and heroic ages. Their abhorrence of innovation induces them to retain their ancient ways of thinking, or at least to imitate their manner of thinking in times of yore, notwithstanding the changes introduced by time. Indeed, from what has been observed in this and the preceding paragraph, although I heartily rejoice at the effects of the British government in India, I should really be sorry that their poetry should be tinctured with the rules and regulations in force at present, and their poetical and fictitious lovers reach their homes in the security which the government allows.

Hindoo women are married at so tender an age, that it is indeed very seldom that they feel any influence of love till some years after marriage: there are therefore consequently very few pieces to be found wherein a maiden (by which I mean an unmarried woman) is concerned.

It is customary in Hindoostan for the parents and their sons, with their daughters-in-law, and maiden daughter, to live together, and in the event of the young men going abroad in quest of employment, to leave their wives behind. What induced them to do this in former times was the difficulties and dangers attendant on the roads, which rendered it impossible to perform a journey of any extent in company with females, who would not only be liable to the greatest abuse even immediately in the neighbourhood, but also to be torn from the arms of their husbands to grace the beds of any chieftain who might chance to take a fancy to them, or might be induced to do it through mere wantonness and caprice.

Let us figure to ourselves an amiable and fond woman in the bloom of her age, wasting her years in sighs for her absent and beloved husband, in whom are centered all her hopes of life—let us behold her at public festivals, where themes to which her heart is familiar are sung in the most pathetic language enforced by the charms of melody—let us accompany her to the riverside, which she daily visits to procure water for the use of the household, and where she witnesses a thousand tender interviews—let us turn our eyes to her domestic scenes, we see her happier sisters-in-law adorning and ornamenting themselves, and sporting in all the gaiety natural to their age, and she striving to stifle her grief, and appear cheerful. Perhaps she hears news of her husband intention shortly to return: she revives as the drooping flower refreshed by sudden and timely rain. If this be in the winter, she laments his absence during the long cold nights of that season, and calls him cruel for not having thought of home earlier. Winter past, she trembles at the idea of the scorching rays of the sun, which will assail him on his journey. But when the rains set in, those months which are the most delightful* of all in Hindoostan to those whose hearts are not afflicted by separation, then it is that she feels her existence insupportable. Cheering hope, which beguiled her during the former seasons, no longer affords its balmy aid, and she despairs of his arrival this year. Every cloud, every flash of lightning sends forth a dart to her tender bosom, and every drop of rain adds fresh poignancy to the wound in her agonizing heart. If she endeavours by domestic toils to wean her thoughts for a moment from her absent lover, the Coel, and particularly the Pupeeha, reminds her of him by her constant and reiterated interrogations of *Pee-cuhan—Pee-cuhan*?

* "The commencement of the rainy season, being peculiarly delightful in Hindoostan, from the contrast it affords to the sultry weather immediately preceding, and also rendering the roads pleasant and practicable, is usually selected for travelling. Hence frequent allusions occur in the poets to the expected return of such persons as are at this time absent from their family and home."—Note on line 20 of the Translation of the Megha Duta, by H. H. Wilson, Esq.

> " Sprang from such gathering shades to happier sight."
>
> The meaning of Calidas seems to be somewhat different.
>
> मेघालोके भवति सुखिनोऽप्यन्यथावृत्तिचेतः ।
> कण्ठाश्लेषप्रणयिनि जने किंपुनर्दूरसंस्थे ॥

And a hundred Hindoostanee songs will prove that after the rains are set n, it is no season for travelling.

These, however, are not the only birds which are addressed by the females of Hindoostan, by the title of Byree or enemy; the peacock,* the chatak, and several others are said to add to their affliction, and remind them of their absent lovers. Superstition lends her aid to afflict or comfort them, by attaching importance to the throbbing of the eyes or pulsations of the limbs.†

The husband remaining from home for several years together, his wife, if she had been married very young, when she attains the years of maturity, begins to feel the power of love, and readily finds a youth on whom she fixes her affections,‡ having perhaps little more knowledge of her absent husband than from hearsay. In such a state of things, the lover can seldom be admitted at home on account of the smallness of the house, and the number of relatives. She sees herself therefore reduced to the necessity of

* "Or can the peacock's animated hail,
The bird with lucid eyes, to lure thee fail?"

"The wild peacock is exceedingly abundant in many parts of *Hindoostan*, and is especially found in marshy places; the habits of this bird are in a great measure aquatic, and the setting in of the rains is the season in which they pair; the peacock is therefore always introduced in the description of cloudy or rainy weather, together with the *cranes* and *chatakas.*"—Cloud Messenger, pp. 29, 1, 148.

† "O'er her left limbs shall glad pulsations play."

"Palpitation in the left limbs, and a throbbing in the left eye, are here described as auspicious omens when occurring in the females: in the male, the right side is the auspicious side, corresponding with the ideas of the *Greeks*, described by Potter, *q. v.*"—*Ibid.*

‡ An objection very frequently started by Europeans against Hindoo poetry and songs is, that they are generally too licentious and voluptuous. To such I would recommend the perusal of the note by Mr. Wilson on line 468 of his translation of the Megha Duta. It is too long to quote.

visiting* him at his, to effect which, it requires a great deal of circumspection and evasive art. The female sex being generally more fond, affords a fertile source of dread from the influence of rivals. It is undeniable that such practices are immoral; but such is the fact, and nature, unrestrained by education, (and the women of Hindoostan are perfectly ignorant of all knowledge, but the art of pleasing,) will positively have its headlong course. Taking all matters into consideration, the poor women of this country should be an object of our compassion rather than of our contempt. The stimulus given to India by British example, and capital employed for the education of native females, is not amongst the least of her beneficial operations. The time will come when their worth shall be duly appreciated by the daughters of India; and then, should this work chance to be perused by them, they will sigh at the follies of their ancestors, smile at their own good fortune, and perhaps think kindly on him who has endeavoured to palliate their weakness, and bring them nearer on a level with the more blessed fair sex of other regions.

The tenor of Hindoostanee love-ditties, therefore, generally, is one or more of the following themes:

1. Beseeching the lover to be propitious.
2. Lamentations for the absence of the object beloved.
3. Imprecating of rivals.
4. Complaints of inability to meet the lover from the

* "The pearls that bursting zones have taught to roam,
Speak of fond maids, and wanderers from home."

"I have already mentioned that the *Hindoos* always send the lady to seek her lover, and they usually add a very reasonable degree of ardour and impatience."—Note on line 466, Wilson's Megha Duta.

watchfulness of the mother and sisters-in-law, and the tinkl ing of little* bells worn as ornaments round the waist and ancles, called payel, bichhooa, &c.

5. Fretting, and making use of invectives against the mother and sisters-in-law, as being obstacles in the way of her love.

6. Exclamation to female friends termed Sukhees, and supplicating their assistance ; and

7. Sukhees reminding their friends of the appointment made, and exhorting them to persevere in their love.

* " My fair awakens from her tinkling zone."

" A girdle of small bells (क्षुद्रघण्टिका) is a favourite Hindoo ornament ; also silver circles at the ancles and wrists, which emit a ringing noise as the wearer moves."—Wilson's Megha Dutta, pp. 85, 1, 514.

The use of this ornament was probably first imposed by jealous husbands to check clandestine visits, should the wives be so inclined; the sound emitted by them rendering them more liable to detection : until women using them being regarded more chaste, others were obliged to comply with the fashion to avoid aspersion of character. Thus did the Hindoos endeavour to fetter their wives, and secure their affections by such inadequate means ; neglecting their moral instruction, which is the only safe barrier.

BRIEF ACCOUNT

OF

THE MOST CELEBRATED MUSICIANS OF HINDOOSTAN.

"A happy genius is the gift of nature."—*Dryden.*

"Invention is a kind of muse, which, being possessed of the other advantages common to her sisters, and being warmed by the fire of Appollo, is raised higher than the rest."—*Ibid.*

THE invention of all arts and sciences, as I mentioned in the early part of this treatise, has always been attributed by heathen nations to beings of superior order, of celestial orgin, to demi-gods. These, however, were undoubtedly not the inventors of those arts and sciences which are attributed to them, but merely the compilers and collectors of the fruits of the industry and invention of ingenious men, who preceded them for centuries ; but as the compiler centered in his own person the aggregate sum of knowledge then existing, he of course possessed a greater fund than any other individual of that particular profession which he chose to investigate, and was of course, from his aggregate knowledge of what others possessed only in parts, enabled to make comparisons of the several details, and form rules for the whole, consistent, precisely defined, and universal. It should likewise be remembered that

> By improving what was done before,
> Invention labours less, but judgment more.—*Roscommon.*

These compilers of sciences, if they were powerful and wise princes, persons reputed for religious sanctity, austerity of manners, of extraordinary benevolence, virtue, wisdom, or genius, could not but be looked upon, by so superstitious and polytheistical a nation as the Hindoos, as an emanation from the Supreme Being, an *Uvutar;* and their excessive fondness for fable and mythology would soon prompt them to adopt allegories, for which the genius of this people seems to have been nothing inferior to that of the Egyptians.

The Hindoos, although an idolatrous, were never so luxurious and vicious a nation as their conquerors, the Mahomedans; most of the vices existing in this country having been introduced after the conquest. The songs of the aborigines of Hindoostan will bear comparison with those of any other country for purity and chasteness of diction, and elevation and tenderness of sentiment.

By a rule of the Mahomedan law, the women of all Cafirs or unbelievers, to which class the Hindoos belong, are to them Hulal, or lawful, without marriage; and since the acquisition of the country to the latter, all manner of excesses and debauchery reached their acme. The vice of drunkenness was, I am persuaded, unknown, at least of the stimulating and inflammatory class. The opium, Bhung, and Dhatoora, (the two latter of which were chiefly used by the Hindoos,) are rather stupefying and sedative than irritative. There is no term, I believe, in Sungscrit, or tongues derived from it, for a slave or eunuch. The fear of the loss of caste, in the want of sound religion and refined morality, acted as a very wholesome check against promiscuous and unguarded indulgence of passion, except amongst the very lowest classes of society and outcastes.

A great many of the songs of this country abound with the praises of drunkenness. These are certainly not of Hindoo origin, for the Hindoos never drank wine or spirits; and although the Mahomedan religion prohibits the use of wine, the very touch of which is reckoned polluting, very few of their monarchs and nobles have refrained from indulging themselves freely with this beverage. They know no medium; it was, and now is, drank by such as make use of it to excess. They never dilute their liquor with water, and in times of their prosperity, it was contrived to be made so pure and strong that it could not be drank; in which case, roast meat was a constant companion to liquor, in which they dipped the bits of roast, as we do in sauce. It was made strengthening and nutritive by the addition of all sorts of flesh of quadrupeds and birds into the still previous to distillation. The liquor is used even now by the more wealthy Mahomedans, and is called *Ma ool luhum.*

The conquest of Hindoostan by the Mahomedan princes forms a most important epoch in the history of its music. From this time we may date the decline of all arts and sciences purely Hindoo, for the Mahomedans were no great patrons to learning, and the more bigotted of them were not only great iconoclasts, but discouragers of the learning of the country. The progress of the theory of music once arrested, its decline was speedy; although the practice, which contributed to the entertainment of the princes and nobles, continued until the time of Mohummud Shah, after whose reign history is pregnant with facts replete with dismal scenes. But the practice of so fleeting and perishable a science as that of a succession of sounds, without a knowledge of the theory to keep it alive, or any mode to record it on paper, dies with the professor.

Amongst the most ancient musicians of this country, who are reckoned inventors, compilers, and masters of the science, we find the most prominent to be Sumeshwur, Bhurut, Hunooman, the goddesses Parvutee, Suruswutee, and Doorga, Vayoo, Shesh, Narud (the Mooni or devotee), Coolnath, Cushyup (another Mooni), Haha, Hoohoo, Ravun, Disha, and Urjoon. The first three and Coolnath have left treatises.

The most renowned of the Nayuks have been Gopal, a native of the Dukhun, who flourished during the reign of Sooltan Ula ood deen, and his contemporary Umeer Khosrow* of Dehli, Sooltan Hoosyn Shurque of Jounpoor, Rajah Man, Qilladar of Gualiar, founder of the Dhoorpud, Byjoo, Bhoonnoo, Pandvee, Buksoo, and Lohung. The four following lived at the time of Rajah Man of Gualiar,—Jurjoo, Bhugwan, Dhondhee, and Daloo.

The *Gundharbs* and *Gooncars,* that is, such as were eminent singers, but were not acquainted with the theory of music, are

* It is related that when Gopal visited the court of Delhi, he sung that species of composition called *Geet,* the beauty of which style, enunciated by the powerful and harmonious voice of so able a performer, could not meet with competition. At this the monarch caused Umeer Khosrow to remain hid under his throne, whence he could hear the musician unknown to him. The latter endeavoured to remember the style, and on a subsequent day, sung Qoul and Turuna in imitation of it, which surprised Gopal, and fraudulently deprived him of a portion of his due honor.

very numerous; and the following are chiefly those who had the honor of performing in the presence of Julul ood deen Mohummud Ucbur, King of Delhi. Tansen was originally with Rajah Ram, and was sent to court at the special request of the king; Soojan Khan, Soorgyan Khan of Futehpoor, Chand Khan and Sooruj Khan (brothers), Tanturung Khan, the son of Tansen Mudun Ray Baba Ramdas, and his son Soordas, a blind moral poet and musician, the founder of the Vishnoopud, who sung

> As the wakeful bird
> Sings darkling, and in shadiest covert hid,
> Tunes her nocturnal note,

Baj Bahadoor, Chundoo, Daood, Is-haq, Shekh Khizur, Shekh Bechoo, Husun Khan, Soorut Sen, and his brother Lala Debee, Neelam Prucash and Meerza Aquil, and the Veen players Feeroz Khan and Noubat Khan.

In more modern times, Sudarung and Udharung, Noor Khan, Lad Khan and Pyar Khan, Janee and Gholam Rusool, Shucker and Mukhun, Teetoo and Meethoo, Mohummud Khan and Chhujjoo Khan, and Shoree, the founder of the Tuppa, stand in high repute; and several practical musicians of both sexes are even now to be met with, who, although ignorant of the theory of music, may, for extent, sweetness, pliability, and perfect command of the voice, rival some of the first-rate minstrels of Europe. Mohummud Khan and Serho Baee, amongst others whom I have heard, are living examples of superior vocal powers; and Khoosh-hal Khan and Oomrao Khan, Veen players, of instrumental execution. Good performers on other instruments are more numerous.

ON THE MUSICAL MODES OF THE HINDOOS.

BY

SIR WILLIAM JONES.

ON

THE MUSICAL MODES

OF

THE HINDOOS:

Written in 1784, and since much enlarged,

BY THE PRESIDENT.

MUSIC belongs, as a *science*, to an interesting part of natural philosophy, which, by mathematical deductions from constant phenomena, explains the causes and properties of sound, limits the number of mixed, or *harmonic*, sounds to a certain series, which perpetually recurs, and fixes the ratio, which they bear to each other or to one leading term; but, considered as an *art*, it combines the sounds, which philosophy distinguishes, in such a manner as to gratify our ears, or effect our imaginations; or, by uniting both objects, to captivate the fancy, while it pleases the sense; and speaking, as it were, the language of beautiful nature, to raise correspondent ideas and emotions in the mind of the hearer: it then, and then only, becomes what we call a *fine art*, allied very nearly to verse, painting, and rhetoric; but subordinate in its functions to pathetic poetry, and inferior in its power to genuine eloquence.

Thus it is the province of the *philosopher* to discover the true direction and divergence of sound propagated by the successive compressions and expansions of air, as the vibrating body advances and recedes; to show why sounds themselves may excite a tremulous motion in particular bodies, as in the known experiment of instruments tuned in unison, to demonstrate the law, by which all the particles of air; when it undulates with great quickness, are continually accelerated and retarded; to compare the number of pulses in agitated air with that of the vibrations which cause them; to compute the velocities and intervals of those pulses in atmospheres of different density and elasticity; to account, as well as he can, for the affections, which music produces; and, generally, to investigate the causes of the many wonderful appearances, which it exhibits: but the *artist*, without considering, and even without knowing, any of the sublime theorems in the philosophy of sound, may attain his end by a happy selection of *melodies* and *accents* adapted to passionate verse, and of *times* conformable to regular metre; and, above all, by *modulation*, or the choice and variation of those *modes*, as they are called, of which, as they are contrived and arranged by the *Hindoos*, it is my design, and shall be my endeavour, to give you a general notion with all the perspicuity that the subject will admit.

Although we must assign the first rank, transcendently and beyond all comparison to that powerful music which may be denominated the sister of poetry and eloquence, yet the lower art of pleasing the sense by a succession of agreeable sounds not only has merit and even charms, but may, I persuade myself, be applied on a variety of occasions to salutary purposes. Whether, indeed, the sensation of hearing be caused, as many suspect, by the vibrations of an elastic ether flowing over the auditory nerves and propelled along their solid capillaments, or whether the fibres of our nerves which seem indefinitely divisible, have, like the strings of a lute, peculiar vibrations proportioned to their length and degree of tension, we have not sufficient evidence to decide; but we are very sure, that the whole nervous system is affected in a singular manner by combinations of sound, and that melody alone will often relieve the mind, when it is oppressed by intense application to business or study. The old musician, who rather figuratively, we may suppose, than with philosophical seriousness, *declared the soul itself to be nothing but harmony*, provoked the sprightly remark of CICERO, that *he drew his philosophy from the art, which he professed;* but if, without departing from his own art, he had merely described the human frame as the noblest and sweetest of musical instruments, endued with a natural disposition to resonance and sympathy, alternately affecting and affected by the soul, which pervades it, his description might, perhaps, have been physically just; and certainly ought not to have been hastily ridiculed. That any medical purpose may be fully answered by music, I dare not assert; but after food, when the operations of digestion and absorption give so much employment to the vessels, that a temporary state of mental repose must be found, especially in hot climates, essential to health, it seems reasonable to believe, that a few agreeable airs, either heard or played without effort, must have all the good effects of sleep and none of its disadvantages; *putting the soul in tune*, as MILTON says, for any subsequent exertion; an experiment which has often been successfully made by myself, and which any one who pleases may easily repeat. Of what I am going to add, I cannot give equal evidence; but hardly know how to disbelieve the testimony of men, who had no system of their own to support, and could have no interest in deceiving me. First, I have been assured by a credible eye-witness, that two wild antelopes used often to come from their woods to the place where a more savage beast, SIRA JUDDAULAH, entertained himself with concerts, and that they listened to the strains with an appearance of pleasure, till the monster, in whose soul there was no music, shot one of them to display his archery: secondly, a learned native of this country told me, that he had frequently seen the most venomous and malignant snakes leave their holes, upon hearing tunes on a flute, which, as he supposed, gave them peculiar delight; and, thirdly, an intelligent Persian, who repeated his story again and again, and permitted me to write it down from his lips, declared, he had more than once been present, when a celebrated lutanist, MIRZA MOHAMMED, surnamed BULBUL, was playing to a large company in a grove near *Shiraz,* where he distinctly saw the nightingales trying to vie with the musician, sometimes warbling on the trees, sometimes fluttering from branch to branch, as if they wished to approach the instrument, whence the melody proceeded, and at length dropping on the ground in a kind of ecstasy, from which they were soon raised, he assured me, by a change of the mode.

The astonishing effects ascribed to music by the old *Greeks,* and in our days, by the *Chinese, Persians,* and *Indians,* have probably been exaggerated and embellished; nor, if such effects had been really produced, could they be imputed, I think, to the mere influence of sounds, however combined or modified: it may, therefore, be suspected (not that the accounts are wholly fictitious, but) that such wonders were performed by music in its largest sense, as it is now described by the *Hindoos,* that is, by the union of *voices, instruments,* and *action*; for such is the complex idea conveyed by the word

Sangita, the simple meaning of which is no more than *Symphony;* but most of the *Indian* books on this art consist accordingly of three parts, *gāna, vādya, nrĭtya,* or *song, percussion,* and *dancing;* the first of which comprises the measures of poetry, the second extends to instrumental music of all sorts, and the third includes the whole compass of theatrical representation. Now it may easily be conceived that such an alliance, with the potent auxiliaries of distinct articulation, graceful gesture, and well adapted scenery, must have a strong general effect, and may, from particular associations, operate so forcibly on very sensible minds, as to excite copious tears, change the colour and countenance, heat or chill the blood, make the heart palpitate with violence, or even compel the hearer to start from his seat with the look, speech, and actions of a man in a phrensy: the effect must be yet stronger, if the subject be *religious,* as that of the old *Indian* dramas, both great and small (I mean both regular plays in many acts and shorter dramatic pieces on *divine love)* seems in general to have been.

In this way only can we attempt to account for the indubitable effects of the *great airs* and impassioned *recitative* in the modern *Italian* dramas, where three beautiful arts, like the Graces united in a dance, are together exhibited in a state of excellence, which the ancient world could not have surpassed, and probably could not have equalled: an heroic opera of METASTASIO, set by PERGOLESI, or by some artist of his incomparable school, and represented at *Naples,* displays at once the perfection of human genius, awakens all the affections, and captivates the imagination at the same instant through all the senses.

When such aids as a perfect theatre would afford are not accessible, the power of music must in proportion be less; but it will ever be very considerable, if the words of the song be fine in themselves, and not only well translated into the language of melody, with a complete union of musical and rhetorical accents, but clearly pronounced by an accomplished singer, who feels what he sings, and fully understood by a hearer, who has passions to be moved; especially if the composer has availed himself in his *translation* (for such may his composition very justly be called) of all those advantages with which nature, ever sedulous to promote our innocent gratifications, abundantly supplies him. The first of those natural advantages is the variety of *modes*, or *manners*, in which the seven harmonic sounds are perceived to move in succession, as each of them takes the lead, and consequently bears a new relation to the six others. Next to the phenomenon of seven sounds perpetually circulating in a geometrical progression, according to the length of the strings or the number of their vibrations, every ear must be sensible, that two of the seven intervals in the complete series, or octave, whether we consider it as placed in a circular form, or in a right line with the first sound repeated, are much shorter than the five other intervals; and on these two phenomena the modes of the *Hindoos* (who seem ignorant of our complicated harmony) are principally constructed. The longer intervals we shall call *tones*, and the shorter (in compliance with custom) *semitones*, without mentioning their exact ratios; and it is evident that, as the *places* of the semitones admit *seven* variations relative to one fundamental sound, there are as many modes, which may be called *primary;* but we must not confound them with our modern modes, which result from the system of accords now established in *Europe*; they may rather be compared with those of the *Roman* Church, where some valuable remnants of old *Grecian* music are preserved in the sweet, majestic, simple, and affecting strains of the Plain Song. Now, since each of the tones may be divided, we find *twelve* semitones in the whole series; and, since each semitone may, in its turn, become the leader of a series formed after the model of every primary mode, we have *seven* times *twelve*, or *eighty-four* modes in all, of which *seventy-seven* may be named *secondary;* and we shall see accordingly that the *Persian* and the *Hindoos* (at least in their most popular system) have exactly *eight-four* modes, though distinguished by different appellations, and arranged in different classes: but, since many of them are unpleasing to the ear, others difficult in execution, and few sufficiently marked by a character of sentiment and expression, which the higher music always requires, the genius of the *Indians* has enabled them to retain the *number* of modes which nature seems to have indicated, and to give each of them a character of its own by a happy and beautiful contrivance. Why any one series of sounds, the ratios of which are ascertained by observation and expressible by figures, should have a peculiar effect on the organ of hearing and by the auditory nerves, on the mind, will then only be known by mortals, when they shall know why each of the seven colours in the rainbow, where a proportion, analogous to that of musical sounds, most wonderfully prevails, has a certain specific effect on our eyes; why the shades of green and blue, for instance, are soft and soothing, while those of red and yellow distress and dazzle the sight: but, without striving to account for the phenomena, let us be satisfied with knowing, that some of the *modes* have distinct perceptible properties, and may be applied to the expression of various mental emotions; a fact which ought well to be considered by those performers, who would reduce them all to a dull uniformity, and sacrifice the true beauties of their art to an injudicious temperament.

The ancient *Greeks*, among whom this delightful art was long in the hands of poets, and of mathematicians who had much less to do with it, ascribe almost all its magic to the diversity of their *Modes*, but have left us little more than the names of them, without such discriminations as might have enabled us to compare them with our own, and apply them to practice; their writers addressed themselves to *Greeks*, who could not but know their national music; and most of those writers were professed men of science, who thought more of calculating ratios than of inventing melody; so that, whenever we speak of the soft *Eolian* mode, of the tender *Lydian*, the voluptuous *Ionic*, the manly *Dorian*, or the animating *Phrygian*, we use mere phrases, I believe, without clear ideas. For all that is known concerning the music of *Greece*, let me refer those who have no inclination to read the dry works of the *Greeks* themselves, to a little tract of the learned WALLIS, which he printed as an Appendix to the Harmonics of PTOLEMY; to the Dictionary of Music by ROUSSEAU, whose pen, formed to elucidate all the arts, had the property of spreading light before it on the darkest subjects, as if he had written with phosphorus on the sides of a cavern; and, lastly, to the dissertation of DR. BURNEY, who, passing slightly over all that is obscure, explains with perspicuity whatever is explicable, and gives dignity to the character of a modern musician by uniting it with that of a scholar and philosopher.

The unexampled felicity of our nation, who diffuse the blessings of a mild government over the finest part of *India*, would enable us to attain a perfect knowledge of the Oriental music, which is known and practised in these *British* dominions, not by mercenary performers only, but even by *Mussalmans* and *Hindoos* of eminent rank and learning. A native of *Cāshān*, lately resident at *Murshedābād*, had a complete acquaintance with the *Persian* theory and practice; and the best artists in *Hindoostān* would cheerfully attend our concerts. We have an easy access to approved *Asiatic* treatises on musical composition, and need not lament with CHARDIN, that he neglected to procure at *Isfāhun* the explanation of a small tract on that subject, which he carried to *Europe*. We may here examine the best instruments of *Asia*, may be masters of them, if we please, or at least may compare them with ours; the concurrent labours, or rather amusements, of several in our own body, may facilitate the attainment of correct ideas on a subject so delightfully interesting; and a free communication from time to time of their respective discoveries would conduct them more surely and speedily, as well as more agreeably, to their desired end. Such would be the advantages of union, or, to borrow a term from the art before us, of *harmonious accord*, in all our pursuits, and above all in that of knowledge.

On *Persian* Music, which is not the subject of this paper, it would be improper to enlarge: the whole system of it is explained in a celebrated collection of tracts on pure and mixed mathematics, entitled *Durratu'ltāj*, and composed by a very learned man, so generally called *Allāmi Shīrāzi*, or the *great philosopher* of *Shīrāz*, that his proper name is almost forgotten; but, as the modern *Persians* had access, I believe to PTOLEMY'S harmonics, their mathematical writers on music treat it rather as a science than as an art, and seem, like the *Greeks*, to be more intent on splitting tones into quarters and eighth parts, of which they compute the ratios to show their arithmetic, than on displaying the principles of modulation, as it may affect the passions. I apply the same observation to a short, masterly tract of the famed ABUSINA, and suspect that it is applicable to an elegant essay in *Persian*, called *Shamsu'láswát*, of which I have not had courage to read more than the preface. It will be sufficient to subjoin on this head that the *Persians* distribute their *eighty-four* modes, according to an idea of locality, into twelve *rooms*, twenty-four *recesses*, and fourty-eight *angles* or *corners:* in the beautiful tale, known by the title of the *Four Dervises*, originally written in *Persia* with great purity and elegance, we find the description of a concert, where four singers, with as many different instruments, are presented "*modulating* "in twelve *makáms* or *perdahs*, twenty-four *shôbahs*, and "forty-eight *gushas*, and beginning a mirthful song of *Hafiz*, "vernal delight in the *perdah* named *rást* or direct." All the twelve *perdahs*, with their appropriated *shôbahs*, are enumerated by AMIN, a writer and musician of *Hindoostan*, who mentions an opinion of the learned, that only *seven* primary modes were in use before the reign of PARVÍZ, whose musical entertainments are magnificently described by the incomparable NIZÁMI: the modes are chiefly denominated, like those of the *Greeks* and *Hindoos*, from different regions or towns; as among the *perdahs*, we see *Hijáz*, *Irák*, *Isfahán:* and, among the *shôbahs*, or secondary modes, *Zabul*, *Nishapur*, and the like. In a *Sanscrit* book, which shall soon be particularly mentioned, I find the scale of a mode, named *Hijéja,* specified in the following verse :—

Máns' agraha sa nyásò' c'hilò hijéjastu sáyáhnè.

The name of this mode is not *Indian* ; and, if I am right in believing it a corruption of *Hijàz,* which could hardly be written otherwise in the *Nágari* letters, we must conclude that it was imported from *Persia ;* we have discovered then a *Persian* or *Arabian* mode with this diaposon—

D, E, F♯, G♯, A, B, C♯, D ;

where the first semitone appears between the *fourth* and *fifth* notes, and the second between the *seventh* and *eighth ;* as in the natural scale Fa, sol, la, si, ut, re, mi, fa : but the C♯, and G♯, or ga and ni of the *Indian* author, are variously *changed,* and probably the series may be formed in a manner not very different (though certainly there is a diversity) from our major mode of D. This melody must necessarily end with the *fifth* note, from the tonic, and begin with the tonic itself; and it would be a gross violation of musical decorum in *India,* to sing it at any time except at the close of day ; these rules are comprised in the verse above cited ; but the species of octave is arranged according to Mr. Fowke's remarks on the *Víná,* compared with the fixed *Swaragráma,* or gamut, of all the Hindoo musicians.

Let us proceed to the *Indian* system, which is minutely explained in a great number of *Sanscrit* books by authors, who leave arithmetic and geometry to their astronomers, and properly discourse on music as an art confined to the pleasures of imagination. The *Pandits* of this province unanimously prefer the *Dámódara* to any of the popular *Sangítas ;* but I have not been able to procure a good copy of it, and am perfectly satisfied with the *Nárayan*, which I received from *Benáres*, and in which the *Dámódar* is frequently quoted. The *Persian* book, entitled *A present from* INDIA, was composed, under the patronage of AAZEM SHÁW, by the very diligent and ingenious MIRZA KHAN, and contains a minute account of *Hindoo* literature in all or most of its branches ; he possesses to have extracted his elaborate chapter on music with the assistance of *Pandits* from the *Rágárnava*, or Sea of Passions, the *Rágadarpana*, or Mirror of Modes, the *Sabhávinóda*, or Delight of Assemblies, and some other approved treatises in *Sanscrit*. The *Sangítadarpana*, which he also names among his authorities, has been translated into *Persian ;* but my experience justifies me in pronouncing that the *Moghols* have no idea of accurate translation, and give that name to a mixture of gloss and text with a flimsy paraphrase of them both ; they are wholly unable, yet always pretend, to write *Sanscrit* words in *Arabic* letters ; that a man, who knows the *Hindoos* only from *Persian* books, does not know the Hindoos ; and that an *European*, who follows the muddy rivulets of *Mussalman* writers on *India*, instead of drinking from the pure fountain of *Hindoo* learning, will be in perpetual danger of misleading himself and others. From the just severity of this censure I except neither ABÚLFAZL, nor his brother FAIZÍ, nor MOHSANI FÁNÍ, nor MIRZA KHÁN himself ; and I speak of all four after an attentive perusal of their works. A tract on music in the idiom of *Meat'hurà*, with several essays in pure *Hindoostanee*, lately passed through my hands ; and I possess a dissertation on the same art in the soft dialect of *Panjab*, or *Panchanada*, where the national melody has, I am told, a peculiar and striking character ; but I am very little acquainted with those dialects, and persuade myself that nothing has been written in them, which may not be found more copiously and beautifully expressed in the *language*, as the *Hindoos* perpetually call it, *of the gods*, that is, of their ancient bards, philosophers and legislators.

The most valuable work that I have seen, and perhaps the most valuable that exists, on the subject of Indian Music, is named *Rágávibódha*, or *the Doctrine of Musical Modes ;* and it ought here to be mentioned very particularly, because none of the *pandits*, in our provinces, nor any of those from Casí or Cashmir, to whom I have shown it, appear to have known that it was extant ; and it may be considered as a treasure in the history of the art, which the zeal of Colonel POLIER has brought into light, and perhaps has preserved from destruction. He had purchased, among other curiosities, a volume containing a number of separate essays on music in prose and verse, and in a great variety of idioms : besides tracts in *Arabic*, *Hindi* and *Persian*, it included a short essay in *Latin* by ALSTEDIUS, with an interlineary *Persian* translation, in which the passages quoted from LUCRETIUS and VIRGIL made a singular appearance ; but the brightest gem in the string was the Rágavibódha, which the Colonel permitted my *Nágri* writer to transcribe, and the transcript was diligently collated with the original by my *pandit* and myself. It seems a very ancient composition, but is less old unquestionably than the *Ratnacára* by SARNGA DEVA, which is more than once mentioned in it, and a copy of which MR. BURROW procured in his journey to *Heridwar* : the name of the author was Sóma, and he appears to have been a practical musician as well as a great scholar and an elegant poet ; for the whole book, without excepting the strains noted in letters, which fill the fifth and last chapter of it, consists of masterly couplets in the melodious metre called *Aryà;* the *first, third,* and *fourth* chapters explain the doctrine of musical sounds, their division and succession, the variations of scales by temperament, and the enumeration of modes on a system totally different from those which will presently be mentioned; and the *second* chapter contains a minute description of different *Vīnās* with rules for playing on them. This book alone would enable me, were I master of my time, to compose a treatise on the music of *India,* with assistance in the practical part from an *European* professor and a native player on the *Víná;* but I have leisure only to present you with an essay, and even that, I am conscious, must be very superficial; it may be sometimes, but, I trust, not often, erroneous; and I have spared no pains to secure myself from error.

In the literature of the *Hindoos* all nature is animated and personified; every fine art is declared to have been revealed from heaven; and all knowledge, divine and human, is traced to its source in the *Vēdas;* among which the *Sāmavēda* was intended to be *sung,* whence the reader, or singer of it, is called *Udgátri* or *Sámaga:* in Colonel POLIER's copy of it, the strains are noted in figures, which it may not be impossible to decipher. On account of this distinction, say the *Brāhmens,* the *Supreme preserving power,* in the form of *Crishna,* having enumerated in the *Gìtà* various orders of beings, to the chief of which he compares himself, pronounces, that "*among the* Védas *he was the* Sáman." From that *Véda* was accordingly derived the *Upavēda* of the *Gandharbas,* or musicians in INDRA'S heaven; so that the divine art was communicated to our species by BRAHMA himself or by his *active power* SERASWATI, the goddess of Speech, and their mythological son *Náred,* who was in truth an ancient lawgiver and astronomer, invented the *Víná,* called also *Cach'hapi,* or *Testudo;* a very remarkable fact, which may be added to the other proofs of a resemblance between that *Indian* god, and the MERCURY of the *Latians.* Among inspired mortals, the first musician is believed to have been the sage BHERAT, who was the inventor, they say, of *Nátacs* or dramas; represented with songs and dances, and author of a musical system, which bears his name. If we can rely on MIRZAKHÁN, there are four principal *Matas,* or systems; the first of which is ascribed to ISWARA, or OSIRIS; the second to BHERAT; the third to HANUMAT, or PÁVAN, the Pan of *India,* supposed to be the son of PAVANA, the regent of air; and the fourth to CALLI NATH, a *Rishi,* or *Indian* philosopher, eminently skilled in music, theoretical and practical: all four are mentioned by SOMA; and it is the *third* of them, which must be very ancient, and seems to have been extremely popular, that I propose to explain after a few introductory remarks; but I may here observe with SOMA, who exhibits a system of his own, and with the author of the *Náráyan,* who mentions a great many others, that almost every kingdom and province had a peculiar style of melody, and very different names for the modes, as well as a different arrangement and enumeration of them.

The two phenomena, which have already been stated as the foundation of musical modes, could not long have escaped the attention of the *Hindoos,* and their flexible language readily supplied them with names for the seven *Swaras* or sounds, which they dispose in the following order, *shádja,* pronounced *sharja, rishabha, gándhára, madhyama, panchama, dhaivata*, *nishāda* ; but the first of them is emphatically named *swara*, or the *sound*, from the important office which it bears in the scale ; and hence, by taking the seven *initial letters* or syllables of those words, they contrived a notation for their airs, and at the same time exhibited a gamut, at least as convenient as that of GUIDO : they call it *Swaragrāma* or *septaca*, and express it in this form :

Sa, ri, ga, ma, pa, dha, ni,

three of which syllables are, by a singular concurrence, exactly the same, though not all in the same places, with three of those invented by DAVID MOSTARE, as a substitute for the troublesome gamut used in his time, and which he arranges thus :

Bo, ce, di, ga, lo, ma, ni.

As to the notation of melody, since every *Indian* consonant include by its nature the short vowel *a*, five of the sounds are denoted by single consonants, and the two others have different short vowels taken from their full names ; by substituting long vowels, the *time* of each note is doubled, and other marks are used for a farther elongation of them ; the octaves above and below the mean scale, the connection and acceleration of notes ; the graces of execution or manners of fingering the instrument, are expressed very clearly by small circles and ellipses, by little chains, by curves, by straight lines horizontal or perpendicular, and by crescents, all in various positions : the close of a strain is distinguished by a lotus-flower ; but the time and measure are determined by the prosody of the verse, and by the comparative length of each syllable, with which every note or assemblage of notes respectively corresponds. If I understand the native musicians, they have not only the *chromatic* but even the second or new, *enharmonic,* genus; for they unanimously reckon twenty-two *s'rutis,* or quarters and thirds of a tone, in their octave: they do not pretend that those minute intervals are mathematically equal, but consider them as equal in practice, and allot them to the several notes in the following order; to *sa, ma,* and *pa,* four; to *ri,* and *dha,* three; to *ga,* and *ni,* two; giving very smooth and significant names to each *s'ruti.* Their original scale, therefore, stands thus,

Sa, ri, ga, ma, pa, dha, ni, sa.

4s' 3s' 2s' 4s' 4s' 3s' 2s'

The semitones accordingly are placed as in our diatonic scale: the intervals between the fourth and fifth, and between the first and second, are major tones; but that between the fifth and sixth, which is minor in our scale, appears to be major in theirs; and the two scales are made to coincide by taking a *s'ruti* from *pa,* and adding it to *dha,* or, in the language of *Indian* artists, by raising *Servaretnà* to the class of *Sántā* and her sisters; for every *s'ruti* they consider as a little nymph, and the nymphs of *Panchama,* or the *fifth* note, are *Mālińí, Chapalá, Lolā,* and *Servaretnà,* while *Sántā* and her two sisters regularly belong to *Dhaivata:* such at least is the system of COHALA, one of the ancient bards, who has left a treatise on music.

SOMA seems to admit that a quarter or third of a tone cannot be separately and distinctly heard from the *Vinà;* but he takes for granted that its effect is very perceptible in their arrangement of modes; and their sixth, I imagine, is almost universally diminished by one *s'ruti;* for he only mentions two modes, in which all the seven notes are *unaltered.* I tried in vain to discover any difference in practice between the *Indian* scale and that of our own; but, knowing my ear to be very insufficiently exercised, I requested a *German* professor of music to accompany with his violin a *Hindoo* lutanist, who sung *by note* some popular airs on the loves of CRISHNA and RADHA ; he assured me that the scales were the same ; and Mr. SHORE afterwards informed me, that, when the voice of a native singer was in tune with his harpsicord, he found the *Hindoo* series of seven notes to ascend, like ours, by a sharp third.

For the construction and character of the *Vinà*, I must refer you to the very accurate and valuable paper of Mr. FOWKE in the first volume of your Transactions ; and I now exhibit a scale of its fingerboard, which I received from him with the drawing of the instrument, and on the correctness of which you may confidently depend : the regular *Indian* gamut answers, I believe, pretty nearly to our major mode :

Ut, re, mi, fa, sol, la, si, ut ;

and, when the same syllables are applied to the notes, which compose our minor mode, they are distinguished by epithets expressing the change which they suffer. It may be necessary to add, before we come to the *Rágas*, or modes, of the *Hindoos*, that the twenty-one *múrch'hanas*, which Mr. SHORE'S native musician confounded with the two and twenty *s'rutis*, appear to be no more than *seven* species of diapason multiplied by *three*, according to the difference of pitch in the compass of three octaves.

Rága, which I translate a mode, properly signifies a *passion* or *affection* of the mind ; each mode being intended, according to BHERAT'S definition of it, to move one or another of our simple or mixed affections ; and we learn accordingly from the *Náráyan*, that, in the days of CRISHNA, there were

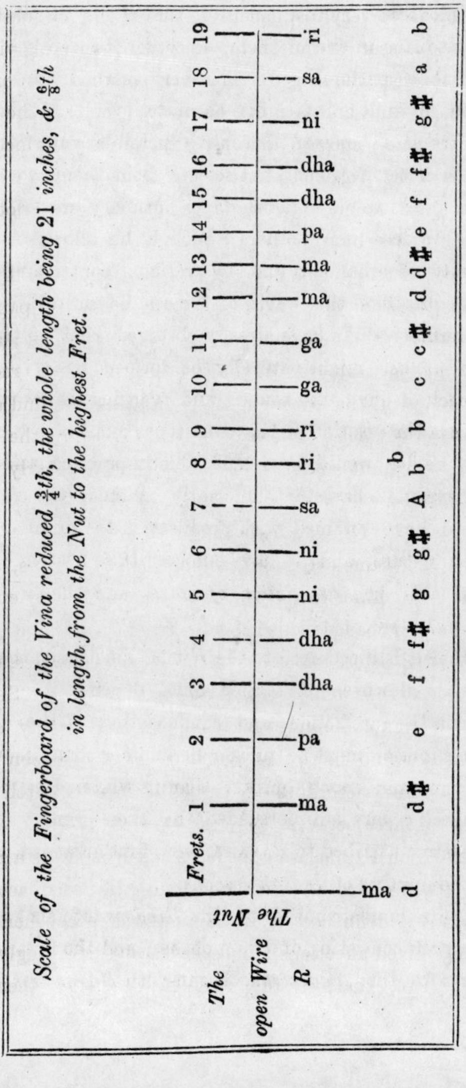

Scale of the Fingerboard of the Vina reduced $\frac{3}{4}$th, the whole length being 21 inches, & $\frac{6}{8}$th in length from the Nut to the highest Fret.

sixteen thousand modes, each of the *Gopis* at *Mat'hurà* choosing to sing in one of them, in order to captivate the heart of their pastoral god. The very learned Sóma, who mixes no mythology with his accurate system of *Rágas*, enumerates *nine hundred and sixty* possible variations by the means of temperament, but selects from them as applicable to practice only *twenty-three* primary modes, from which he deduces many others; though he allows that by a diversity of ornament and by various contrivances, the Rágas might, like the waves of the sea, be multiplied to an infinite number. We have already observed that *eighty-four modes* or *manners* might naturally be formed by giving the lead to each of our *twelve* sounds, and varying in *seven* different ways the position of the semitones; but, since many of those modes would be insufferable in practice, and some would have no character sufficiently marked, the *Indians* appear to have retained with predilection the number indicated by nature, and to have enforced their system by two powerful aids, the *association of ideas,* and the *mutilation of the regular scales.*

Whether it had occurred to the *Hindoo* musicians, that the velocity or slowness of sounds must depend, in a certain ratio, upon the rarefaction and condensation of the air, so that their motion must be quicker in summer than in spring or autumn, and much quicker than in winter, I cannot assure myself; but am persuaded that their primary modes, in the system ascribed to Pavana, were first arranged according to the number of *Indian* seasons.

The year is distributed by the *Hindoos* into six *ritus*, or seasons, each consisting of two months; and the first season, according to the *Amarcósha,* began with *Márgasírsha,* near the time of the winter solstice, to which month accordingly we see *Crishna* compared in the *Gita*; but the old lunar year began, I believe, with *A'swina*, or near the autumnal equinox, when the moon was at the full in the first mansion: hence the musical season, which takes the lead, includes the months of *A'swin* and *Cártic*, and bears the name of *Sarad*, corresponding with part of our autumn; the next in order are *Hemanta* and *Sisira*, derived from words which signify *frost* and *dew*; then come *Vasantà*, or spring, called also *Surabhi* or fragrant, and *Pushpasamaya*, or the flower time; *Grîshma*, or heat; and *Vershá*, or the season of rain. By appropriating a different mode to each of the different seasons, the artists of *India* connected certain strains with certain ideas, and were able to recal the memory of autumnal merriment at the close of the harvest, or of separation and melancholy (very different from our ideas at *Calcutta*), during the cold months; of reviving hilarity on the appearance of blossoms, and complete vernal delight in the month of *Madhu* or *honey*; of languor during the dry heats, and of refreshment by the first rains, which cause in this climate a second spring. Yet further: since the lunar year, by which festivals and superstitious duties are constantly regulated, proceeds concurrently with the solar year, to which the seasons are necessarily referred, *devotion* comes also to the aid of music, and all the *powers of nature*, which are allegorically worshipped as gods and goddesses on their several holidays, contribute to the influence of song on minds naturally susceptible of religious emotions. Hence it was, I imagine, that PAVAN, or the inventor of his musical system, reduced the number of original modes from *seven* to *six*; but even this was not enough for his purpose; and he had recourse to the *five* principal divisions of the day, which are the *morning*, *noon*, and *evening*, called *trisandhya*, with the two intervals between them, or the *forenoon* and *afternoon:* by adding *two* divisions, or intervals of the night, and by leaving one species of melody without any such restriction, Sóma reckons *eight* variations in respect of time; and the system of Pavan retains that number also in the second order of derivative modes. Every branch of knowledge in this country has been embellished by poetical fables; and the inventive talents of the *Greeks* never suggested a more charming allegory than the lovely families of the six *Rágas*, named, in the order of seasons above exhibited, Bhairava, Ma'lava, Sri-ra'ga, Hindola, or Vasanta, Di'paca, and Me'gha; each of whom is a Genius, or Demi-god, wedded to five *Ráginis*, or Nymphs, and father of *eight* little Genii, called his *Putras*, or Sons: the fancy of Shakspeare and the pencil of Albano might have been finely employed in giving speech and form to this assemblage of new aërial beings, who people the fairy-land of *Indian* imagination; nor have the *Hindoo* poets and painters lost the advantages, with which so beautiful a subject presented them. A whole chapter of the *Náráyan* contains descriptions of the *Rágas* and their consorts, extracted chiefly from the *Dámódar*, the *Caláncura*, the *Retnamálá*, the *Chandricà*, and a metrical tract on music ascribed to the God Nared himself, from which, as among so many beauties a particular selection would be very perplexing, I present you with the first that occurs, and have no doubt that you will think the *Sanscrit* language equal to *Italian* in softness and elegance:

Lilá vihárēnā vanāntarālē,
Chinvan prasúnāni vadhū sahāyah,
Vilasi vēsódita divya múrtih,
Srîrága ēsha praťhitah priťhivyám.

"The demi-god SRÍRÁGA, famed over all this earth, sweetly "sports with his nymphs, gathering fresh blossoms in the "bosom of yon grove; and his divine lineaments are dis-"tinguished through his graceful vesture."

These and similar images, but wonderfully diversified, are expressed in a variety of measures, and represented by delicate pencils in the *Rágamálàs*, which all of us have examined, and among which the most beautiful are in the possession of Mr. R. JOHNSON and Mr. HAY. A noble work might be composed by any musician and scholar, who enjoyed leisure and disregarded expence, if he would exhibit a perfect system of *Indian* music from *Sanscrit* authorities, with the old melodies of SO'MA applied to the songs of JAYADE'VA, embellished with descriptions of all the modes accurately translated, and with Mr. HAY'S *Rágamálà*, delineated and engraved by the scholars of CIPRIANI and BARTOLOZZI.

Let us proceed to the second artifice of the *Hindoo* musicians, in giving their modes a distinct character and a very agreeable diversity of expression. A curious passage from PLUTARCH'S treatise on Music is translated and explained by Dr. BURNEY, and stands as the text of the most interesting chapter in his dissertation; since I cannot procure the original, I exhibit a paraphrase of his translation, on the correctness of which I can rely; but I have avoided, as much as possible, the technical words of the Greeks, which it might be necessary to explain at some length. "We are "informed," says PLUTARCH, "by ARISTOXENUS, that musicians "ascribe to OLYPMUS of *Mysia* the invention of *enharmonic* "melody, and conjecture that, when he was playing diat-"onically on his flute, and frequently passed from the highest "of four sounds to the lowest but one, or conversely, skipping "over the second in descent, or the third in ascent, of that "series, he perceived a singular beauty of expression, which "induced him to dispose the whole series of seven or eight "sounds by similar skips, and to frame by the same analogy "his *Dorian* mode, omitting every sound *peculiar* to the "diatonic and chromatic melodies then in use, but without "adding any that have since been made essential to the *new* "enharmonic: in this genus, they say, he composed the "Nome, or strain, called *Spondean*, because it was used in "temples at the time of religious *libations*. Those, it seems, "were the *first* enharmonic melodies; and are still retained "by some who play on the flute in the antique style without "any division of a semi-tone; for it was after the age of "OLYMPUS that the quarter of a tone was admitted into "the *Lydian* and *Phrygian* modes; and it was he, therefore, "who, by introducing an exquisite melody before unknown "in Greece, became the author and parent of the most beau-"tiful and affecting music."

This method then of adding to the character and effect of a mode by diminishing the number of its primitive sounds was introduced by a *Greek* of the lower *Asia*, who flourished, according to the learned and accurate writer of the travels of ANACHARSIS, about the middle of the *thirteenth* century before CHRIST; but it must have been older still among the *Hindoos*, if the system, to which I now return, was actually invented in the age of RÁMA.

Since it appears from the *Nárāyan*, that *thirty-six* modes are in general use, and the rest very rarely applied to practice, I shall exhibit only the scales of the six *Rágas* and thirty *Rāginis*, according to So'MA, the authors quoted in the *Nárāyan*, and the book explained by *Pandits* to MIRZA KHA'N; on whose credit I must rely for that of *Cacubhā*, which I cannot find in my *Sanscrit* treatises on music: had I depended on him for information of greater consequence, he would have led me into a very serious mistake; for he asserts, what I now find erroneous, that the *graha* is the first note of every mode, with which every song that is composed in it, must invariably begin *and end.* Three distinguished sounds in each mode are called *graha, nyása, ans'a,* and the writer of the *Nárāyan* defines them in the two following couplets;

Graha swarah sa ityuctó yó gitādau samarpitah,
Nyāsa swarastu sa próctó yó gitádi samāpticah:
Yó vyactivyanjacò gánè, yasya servē' nugá minah,
Yasya servatra bāhulyam vády ansó pi nrīpótamah.

"The note called *graha* is placed at the beginning, and "that named *nyāsa,* at the end, of a song; that note, which "displays the peculiar melody, and to which all the others "are subordinate, that which is always of the greatest use, "is like a sovereign, though a mere *ans'a* or portion."

"By the word *vādi,*" says the commentator, "he means the "note, which announces and ascertains the *Rága*, and which "may be considered as the parent and origin of the *graha* "and *nyása*:" this clearly shows, I think, that the *ans'a* must be the tonic; and we shall find that the two other notes are generally its third and fifth, or the mediant and the dominant. In the poem entitled *Mágha* there is a musical simile, which may illustrate and confirm our idea :

> *Analpatwát pradhánatwád ans'asyévê taraswaráh,*
> *Vijigíshórnripatayah prayánti pericháratám.*

"From the greatness, from the transcendent qualities, of "that Hero, eager for conquest, other kings march in subor-"dination to him, as other notes are subordinate to the "*ans'a.*"

If the *ans'a* be the tonic, or modal note, of the *Hindoos,* we may confidently exhibit the scales of the Indian modes, according to SO'MA, denoting by an asterisk the omission of a note.

BHAIRAVA :	*dha,*	*ni,*	*sa,*	*ri,*	*ga,*	*ma,*	*pa.*
Varáti :	*sa,*	*ri,*	*ga,*	*ma,*	*pa,*	*dha,*	*ni.*
Mediyamádi :	*ma,*	*pa,*	*,*	*ni,*	*sa,*	*,*	*ga.*
Bhairavi :	*sa,*	*ri,*	*ga,*	*ma,*	*pa,*	*dha,*	*ni.*
Saindhavi :	*sa,*	*ri,*	*,*	*ma,*	*pa,*	*dha,*	*.
Bengáli :	*sa,*	*ri,*	*ga,*	*ma,*	*pa,*	*dha,*	*ni.*
MÁLAVA :	*ni,*	*sa,*	*ri,*	*ga,*	*ma,*	*pa,*	*dha.*
Tódi :	*ga,*	*ma,*	*pa,*	*dha,*	*ni,*	*sa,*	*ri.*
Gaudi :	*ni,*	*sa,*	*ri,*	*,*	*ma,*	*pa,*	*.
Góndácri :	*sa,*	*ri,*	*ga,*	*ma,*	*pa,*	*,*	*ni.*
Sust'hávats.			not in SO'MA.				
Cacubhà :			not in SO'MA.				
SRIRÁGA :	*ni,*	*sa,*	*ri,*	*ga,*	*ma,*	*pa,*	*dha.*
Málavas'ri :	*sa,*	*,*	*ga,*	*ma,*	*pa,*	*,*	*ni.*
Márvai :	*ga,*	*ma,*	*pa,*	*,*	*ni,*	*sa,*	*,
Dhanyási :	*sa,*	*,*	*ga,*	*ma,*	*pa,*	*,*	*ni.*
Vasanti :	*sa,*	*ri,*	*ga,*	*ma,*	*,*	*dha,*	*ni.*
Asáverti :	*ma,*	*pa,*	*dha,*	*ni,*	*sa,*	*ri,*	*ga.*

HINDOLA:	*ma,*	*,	*dha,*	*ni,*	*sa,*	*,	*ga.*
Rámacri:	*sa,*	*ri,*	*ga,*	*ma,*	*pa,*	*dha,*	*ni.*
Dés'ácshi:	*ga,*	*ma,*	*pa,*	*dha,*	*,	*sa,*	*ri.*
Lelità:	*sa,*	*ri,*	*ga,*	*ma,*	*,	*dha,*	*ni.*
Vélávali:	*dha,*	*ni,*	*sa,*	*,	*ga,*	*ma,*	*.
Patamanjari:				*not in* SO'MA.			
DIPACA:				not in SO'MA.			
Désí:	*ri,*	*,	*ma,*	*pa,*	*dha,*	*ni,*	*sa.*
Cámbódi:	*sa,*	*ri,*	*ga,*	*ma,*	*pa,*	*dha,*	*.
Nettà:	*sa,*	*ri,*	*ga,*	*ma,*	*pa,*	*dha,*	*ni.*
Cédári:	*ni,*	*sa,*	*ri,*	*ga,*	*ma,*	*pa,*	*dha.*
Carnáti:	*ni,*	*sa,*	*,	*ga,*	*ma,*	*pa,*	*.
ME'GHA:				not in SO'MA.			
Taccà:	*sa,*	*ri,*	*ga,*	*ma,*	*pa,*	*dha,*	*ni.*
Mellári:	*dha,*	*,	*sa,*	*ri,*	*,	*ma,*	*pa.*
Gurjarí:	*ri,*	*ga,*	*ma,*	*,	*dha,*	*ni,*	*sa.*
Bhúpáli:	*ga,*	*,	*pa,*	*dha,*	*,	*sa,*	*ri.*
Désacri:	*sa,*	*ri,*	*ga,*	*ma,*	*pa,*	*dha,*	*ni.*

It is impossible that I should have erred much, if at all, in the preceding table, because the regularity of the *Sanscrit* metre has in general enabled me to correct the manuscript: but I have some doubt as to *Vélavali*, of which *pa* is declared to be the *ans'a* or tonic, though it is said in the same line, that both *pa* and *ri* may be omitted: I, therefore, have supposed *dha* to be the true reading, both MIRZA KHAN and the *Nárayan* exhibiting that note as the leader of the mode. The notes printed in *Italic* letters are variously charged by temperament or by shakes and other graces; but, even if I were able to give you in words a distinct notion of those changes, the account of each mode would be insufferably tedious, and scarce intelligible without the assistance of a masterly performer on the *Indian* lyre. According to the best authorities adduced in the *Nárâyan,* the thirty-six modes are, in some provinces, arranged in these forms :

BHAIRAVA :	*dha,*	*ni,*	*sa,*	*ri,*	*ga,*	*ma,*	*pa.*
Varáti :	*sa,*	*ri,*	*ga,*	*ma,*	*pa,*	*dha,*	*ni.*
Medhyamádi	*ni,*	*sa,*	*,*	*ga,*	*ma,*	*pa,*	*dha.*
Bhairavì :	*sa,*	*,*	*ga,*	*ma,*	*,*	*dha,*	*ni.*
Saindhavì :	*pa,*	*dha,*	*ni,*	*sa,*	*ri,*	*ga,*	*ma.*
Bengâlì :	*sa,*	*ri,*	*ga,*	*ma,*	*pa,*	*dha,*	*ni.*
MÁLAVA :	*ma,*	*,*	*daa,*	*ni,*	*sa,*	*ri,*	*ga.*
Tôdì :	*ma,*	*pa,*	*dha,*	*ni,*	*sa,*	*ri,*	*ga.*
Gaúdì :	*ni,*	*sa,*	*ri,*	*ga,*	*ma,*	*,*	*dha.*
Gôndacrì :	*sa,*	*,*	*ga,*	*ma,*	*pa,*	*,*	*ni.*
Susťhâvotì :	*dha,*	*ni,*	*sa,*	*ri,*	*ga,*	*ma,*	*.*
Cacubbà :	not in the *Nârâyan.*						
SRÍRÁGA :	*sa,*	*ri,*	*ga,*	*ma,*	*pa,*	*dha,*	*ni.*
Málavasrì :	*sa,*	*ri,*	*ga,*	*ma,*	*pa,*	*dha,*	*ni.*
Mâravì :	*sa,*	*,*	*ga,*	*ma,*	*pa,*	*dha,*	*ni.*
Dhanyâsì :	*sa,*	*ri,*	*ga,*	*ma,*	*pa,*	*dha,*	*ni.*
Vasantì :	*sa,*	*ri,*	*ga,*	*ma,*	*pa,*	*dha,*	*ni.*
Asâverì :	*ri,*	*ga,*	*ma,*	*pa,*	*dha,*	*ni,*	*sa.*
HINDO'LA :	*sa,*	*,*	*ga,*	*ma,*	*,*	*dha,*	*ni.*
Rámacrì :	*sa,*	*ri,*	*ga,*	*ma,*	*pa,*	*dha,*	*ni.*
Dêsâcsbì :	*ga,*	*ma,*	*pa,*	*dha,*	*ni,*	*sa,*	*.*
Lelità :	*sa,*	*,*	*ga,*	*ma,*	*pa,*	*,*	*ni.*
Vêlâvalì :	*dha,*	*ni,*	*sa,*	*ri,*	*ga,*	*ma,*	*pa.*
Patamanjarì :	*pa,*	*dha,*	*ni,*	*sa,*	*ri,*	*ga,*	*ma.*
DIPACA :	omitted.						
Dêsì :	*ni,*	*sa,*	*ri,*	*ga,*	*ma,*	*pa,*	*dha.*
Câmbôdì :	*sa,*	*ri,*	*ga,*	*ma,*	*pa,*	*dha,*	*ni.*
Nettâ :	*sa,*	*ri,*	*ga,*	*ma,*	*pa,*	*dha,*	*ni.*
Cedârì :	omitted.						
Carnâtì :	*ni,*	*sa,*	*ri,*	*ga,*	*ma,*	*pa,*	*dha.*

ME'GHA :	*dha,*	*ni,*	*sa,*	*ri,*	*ga,*	*ma,*	*pa.*
Taccà :			(a mixed mode.)				
Mellári :	*dha,*	*ni,*	*,	*ri,*	*ga,*	*ma,*	*.
Gurjarì :			omitted in the *Nārāyan.*				
Bhúpālì :	*sa,*	*ri,*	*ga,*	*,	*pa,*	*dha,*	*.
Dēsacrì :	*ni,*	*sa,*	*,	*ga,*	*ma,*	*pa,*	*.

Among the scales just enumerated we may safely fix on that of SRÍRÁGA for our own major modes, since its form and character are thus described in a *Sanscrit* couplet :

Játinyásagraha grāmāns' ēshu shádjō' lpapanchamah,
Sringāravírayōrjnēyah Srîrâgò gítacōvidaih.

" Musicians know *Srírāga* to have *sa* for its principal note "and the first of its scale, with *pa* diminished, and to be used " for expressing heroic love and valour." Now the diminution of *pa* by one *s'ruti* gives us the modern *European* scale,

ut, re, mi, fa, sol, la, si, ut,

with a minor tone, or, as the *Indians* would express it, with three *s'rutis*, between the fifth and sixth notes.

On the formulas exhibited by MÍRZAKHÁN, I have less reliance ; but, since he professes to give them from *Sanscrit* authorities, it seemed proper to transcribe them :

BHAIRAVA :	*dha,*	*ni,*	*sa,*	*,	*ga,*	*ma,*	*.
Varáti :	*sa,*	*ri,*	*ga,*	*ma,*	*pa,*	*dha,*	*ni.*
Medhyamádi :	*ma,*	*pa,*	*dha,*	*ni,*	*sa,*	*ri,*	*ga.*
Bhairavì :	*ma,*	*pa,*	*dha,*	*ni,*	*sa,*	*ri,*	*ga.*
Saindhavì :	*sa,*	*ri,*	*ga,*	*ma,*	*pa,*	*dha,*	*ni.*
Bengálì :	*sa,*	*ri,*	*ga,*	*ma,*	*pa,*	*dha,*	*ni.*
MÁLAVA :	*sa,*	*ri,*	*ga,*	*ma,*	*pa,*	*dha,*	*ni.*
Tōdì :	*sa,*	*ri,*	*ga,*	*ma,*	*pa,*	*dha,*	*ni.*
Gaúdì :	*sa,*	*,	*ga,*	*ma,*	*,	*dha,*	*ni.*
Gōndacrì :	*ni,*	*sa,*	*,	*ga,*	*ma,*	*pa,*	*.
Sust'hávatì :	*dha,*	*ni,*	*sa,*	*ri,*	*ga,*	*ma,*	*.
Cacubbà :	*dha,*	*ni*	*sa,*	*ri,*	*ga,*	*ma,*	*pa.*

SRI'RA'GA :	*sa,*	*ri,*	*ga,*	*ma,*	*pa,*	*dha,*	*ni.*
Málavasrì :	*sa,*	*ri,*	*ga,*	*ma,*	*pa,*	*dha,*	*ni.*
Máravì :	*sa,*	*,*	*pa,*	*ga,*	*ma,*	*dha,*	*ni.*
Dhanyásì :	*sa,*	*pa,*	*dha,*	*ni,*	*ri,*	*ga,*	*.*
Vasantì :	*sa,*	*ri,*	*ga,*	*ma,*	*pa,*	*dha,*	*ni.*
Asáverì :	*dha,*	*ni,*	*sa,*	*,*	*,*	*ma,*	*pa.*
HINDO'LA :	*sa,*	*,*	*ga,*	*ma,*	*pa,*	*,*	*ni.*
Rámacrì :	*sa,*	*,*	*ga,*	*ma,*	*pa,*	*,*	*ni.*
Dêsăcshì :	*ga,*	*ma,*	*pa,*	*dha,*	*ni,*	*sa,*	*.*
Lelità :	*dha,*	*ni,*	*sa,*	*,*	*ga,*	*ma,*	*.*
Vêlávalì :	*dha,*	*ni,*	*sa,*	*ri,*	*ga,*	*ma,*	*pa.*
Patamanjarì :	*pa,*	*dha,*	*ni,*	*sa,*	*ri,*	*ga,*	*ma.*
DIPACA :	*sa,*	*ri,*	*ga,*	*ma,*	*pa,*	*dha,*	*ni.*
Dêsí :	*ri,*	*ga,*	*ma,*	*,*	*dha,*	*ni,*	*sa.*
Cambŏdi :	*dha,*	*ni,*	*sa,*	*ri,*	*ga,*	*ma,*	*pa.*
Nettà :	*sa,*	*ni,*	*dha,*	*pa,*	*ma,*	*ga,*	*ri.*
Cêdări :	*ni,*	*sa,*	*,*	*ga,*	*ma,*	*pa,*	*.*
Carnati :	*ni,*	*sa,*	*ri,*	*ga,*	*ma,*	*pa,*	*dha.*
ME'GHA :	*dha,*	*ni,*	*sa,*	*ri,*	*ga,*	*,*	*.*
Taccà :	*sa,*	*ri,*	*ga,*	*ma,*	*pa,*	*dha,*	*ni.*
Mellări :	*dha,*	*ni,*	*,*	*ri,*	*ga,*	*ma,*	*.*
Gurjarí :	*ri,*	*ga,*	*ma,*	*pa,*	*dha,*	*ni,*	*sa.*
Bhúpáli :	*sa,*	*ga,*	*ma,*	*dha,*	*ni,*	*pa,*	*ri.*
Dêsacri :	*sa,*	*ri,*	*ga,*	*ma,*	*pa,*	*dha,*	*ni.*

It may reasonably be suspected that the *Moghol* writer could not have shown the distinction, which must necessarily have been made, between the different modes, to which he assigns the same formula; and, as to his inversions of the notes in some of the *Răginis*, I can only say, that no such changes appear in the *Sanscrit* books which I have inspected. I leave our scholars and musicians to find, among the scales here exhibited, the *Dorian* mode of OLYMPUS; but it cannot escape notice, that the Chinese scale C, D, E, *, G, A, *, corresponds very nearly with *ga, ma, pa*, *, *ni, sa*, *, or the Máravì of SO'MA: we have long known in *Bengal*, from the information of a *Scotch* gentleman skilled in music, that the wild but charming melodies of the ancient highlanders were formed by a similar mutilation of the natural scale. By such mutilations, and by various alterations of the notes, in tuning the *Vina*, the number of modes might be augmented indefinitely; and CALLINÁT'HA admits *ninety* into his system, allowing *six* nymphs, instead of *five*, to each of his musical deities: for *Dípaca*, which is generally considered as a lost mode (though MÍRZÁKHÁN exhibits the notes of it), he substitutes *Punchama*; for *Hindóla*, he gives us *Vasanta*, or the Spring; and for *Málava, Natanáráyan* or CHRISHNA, the Dancer; all with scales rather different from those of Pavan. The system of ISWARA, which may have had some affinity with the old *Egyptian* music invented or improved by OSIRIS, nearly resembles that of HANUMAT; but the names and scales are a little varied: in all the systems, the names of the modes are significant, and some of them as fanciful as those of the fairies in the Midsummer Night's Dream. Forty-eight new modes were added by BHERAT, who *marrys* a nymph, thence called Bhâryá, to each Putra, or Son, of a Rága; thus admitting, in his musical school, a *hundred* and *thirty-two manners* of arranging the series of notes.

Had the *Indian* empire continued in full energy for the last two thousand years, religion would, no doubt, have given permanence to systems of music invented, as the *Hindoos* believe, by their gods, and adapted to mystical poetry; but such have been the revolutions of their government since the time of ALEXANDER, that although the *San-*

scrit books have preserved the theory of their musical composition, the practice of it seems almost wholly lost (as all the *Pandits* and *Rājas* confess) in *Gaur* and *Magarha*, or the provinces of *Bengal* and *Behar*. When I first read the songs of *Jayadêva*, who has prefixed to each of them the name of the mode in which it was anciently sung, I had hopes of procuring the original music; but the *Pandits* of the south referred me to those of the west, and the Bráhmens of the west would have sent me to those of the north; while they—I mean those of *Népál* and *Caṣhmír*—declared that they had no ancient music, but imagined, that the notes to the *Gítagóvinda* must exist, if anywhere, in one of the southern provinces, where the Poet was born: from all this I collect, that the art, which flourished in *India* many centuries ago, has faded for want of due culture, though some scanty remnants of it may, perhaps, be preserved in the pastoral roundelays of *Mat'hurā* on the loves and sports of the *Indian* APOLLO. We must not, therefore, be surprised, if modern performers on the *Víná* have little or no *modulation*, or *change of mode*, to which passionate music owes nearly all its enchantment: but that the old musicians of *India*, having fixed on a leading mode to express the *general* character of the song, which they were *translating into the musical language*, varied that mode, by certain rules, according to the variation of sentiment or passion in the poetical phrases, and always returned to it at the close of the air, many reasons induce me to believe; though I cannot but admit, that their modulation must have been greatly confined by the restriction of certain modes to certain seasons and hours, unless those restrictions belonged merely to the principal mode. The scale of the *Víná*, we find, comprised both our *European* modes, and, if some of the notes can be raised a semi-tone by a stronger pressure on the frets, a delicate and experienced singer might produce the effect of minute enharmonic intervals: the construction of the inscrument, therefore, seems to favor my conjecture; and an excellent judge of the subject informs us, that, "the open wires are "from time to time struck in a manner that prepares the "ear for a change of modulation, to which the uncommonly "full and fine tones of those notes greatly contribute." We may add, that the *Hindoo* poets never fail to change the *metre*, which is their *mode*, according to the change of subject or sentiment in the same piece; and I could produce instances of *poetical modulation* (if such a phrase may be used) at least equal to the most affecting modulations of our greatest composers: now the musician must naturally have emulated the poet, as every translator endeavours to resemble his original; and, since each of the *Indian* modes is appropriated to a certain affection of the mind, it is hardly possible, that, where the passion is varied, a skilful musician could avoid a variation of the mode. The rules for modulation seem to be contained in the chapters on *mixed modes*, for an intermixture of *Mellárí* with *Tódí* and *Saindhaví* means, I suppose, a transition, however short, from one to another: but the question must remain undecided, unless we can find in the *Sangítas* a clearer account of modulation than I am able to produce, or unless we can procure a copy of the *Gítagóvinda* with the music, to which it was set, before the time of CALIDAS, in some notation, that may be easily deciphered. It is obvious, that I have not been speaking of a modulation regulated by harmony, with which the *Hindoos*, I believe, were unacquainted; though, like the *Greeks*, they distinguish the *consonant* and *dissonant* sounds : I mean only such a transition from one series of notes to another, as we see described by the *Greek* musicians, who were ignorant of *harmony* in the modern sense of the word, and, perhaps, if they had known it ever so perfectly, would have applied it solely to the support of melody, which alone speaks the language of passion and sentiment.

It would give me pleasure to close this essay with several specimens of old *Indian* airs from the fifth chapter of So'MA ; but I have leisure only to present you with one of them in our own characters accompanied with the original notes. I selected the mode of *Vasanti,* because it was adapted by JAYADÉVA himself to the most beautiful of his odes, and because the number of notes in SÓMA, compared with that of the syllables in the *Sanscrit* stanza, may lead us to guess, that the strain itself was applied by the musician to the very words of the poet. The words are :

Lalita lavanga latá perisílana cómala malaya samíré,
Madhucara nicara carambita cócila cújita cunja cutíré
Viharati heriŕiha sarasa vasanté.
Nrĭtyati yuvati janéna saman sac'hi virahi Janasya durantè.

"While the soft gale of *Malaya* wafts perfume from the "beautiful clove-plant, and the recess of each flowery arbour "sweetly resounds with the strains of the *Cócila,* mingled "with the murmurs of the honey-making swarms, Heri "dances, O lovely friend, with a company of damsels in this "vernal season ; a season full of delights, but painful to "separated lovers."

I have noted SÓMA's air in the major mode of A, or *sa,* which, from its gaiety and brilliancy, well expresses the general hilarity of the song ; but the sentiment, often under

ANCIENT SANSCRIT NOTATION.

VASANTA.

वसन्तः

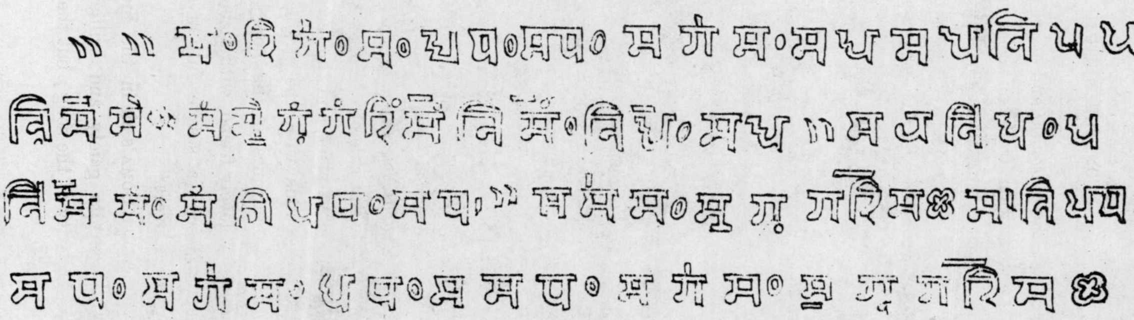

pain, even in a season of delights, from the remembrance of pleasures no longer attainable, would require in our music a change to the minor mode; and the air might be disposed in the form of a rondeau ending with the second line, or even with the third, where the sense is equally full, if it should be thought proper to express by another modulation that *imitative melody,* which the poet has manifestly attempted: the measure is very rapid, and the air should be gay, or even quick, in exact proportion to it.

AN OLD INDIAN AIR.

The preceding is a strain in the mode of HINDÓLA, beginning and ending with the fifth note *sa*, but wanting *pa*, and *ri*, or the second and sixth : I could easily have found words for it in the *Gítagóvinda*, but the united charms of poetry and music would lead me too far; and I must now with reluctance bid farewell to a subject, which I despair of having leisure to resume.

ANECDOTES OF INDIAN MUSIC.

BY

SIR W. OUSELEY.

(*From "The Oriental Collections" Vol. I.*)

ANECDOTES OF INDIAN MUSIC.

BY

SIR W. OUSELEY.

WHEN I first resolved to apply myself to the study of the fine arts, as cultivated among the Persians, I solicited fr●m various correspondents settled in the East the communication of such books and original information on those subjects as their situation might enable them to procure, whilst I availed myself of every opportunity that offered in this country to increase my collection of Oriental manuscripts.

With two fine copies of Sadi's *Gulistan* and *Boston*, which once belonged to the celebrated *Chardin**, I have lately been so fortunate as to pruchase a short, but very curious, essay on *Persian* Music, which from many circumstances I am willing to persuade myself was brought to Europe by that ingenious Orientalist, and is the same manuscript of which he laments that he had not procured the explanation while at *Isfahan*.† But as my design in the present essay relates

* From his notes, written in a most minute hand, and in the French and Latin languages, on several pages of the *Gulistan*, the Second Number of this work shall be enriched with extracts.

† Chardin, (Quarto Edition, 1735) Vol. III, P. 158.

Sir William Jones, in his Dissertation on the Musical Modes of the Hindus, mentions a Persian treatise entitled "*Durratu ltaj*, composed by a very learned man, so generally called *Allami Shirazi*, or *the great philosopher* of *Shiraz*, that his proper name is almost forgotten." *Asiatic Researches*, Vol. III.—An ingenious friend has communicated the title of the Essay on Music comprised in that collection.

only to the music of Hindustan, I shall proceed to mention, that among several books sent to me from that country, some, though written in the Persian language, profess to be translated from the Sanscrit, and treat of the musical modes, the *Raugs* and *Rauginees* of the *Hindus*. From these, however, so little has been borrowed in the course of the following remarks, that if any thing curious or entertaining should be found in them, the thanks of the reader will be principally due to my brother Mr. Gore Ouseley, whom a residence of several years in india has rendered perfectly acquainted with the theory and practice of *Hindu* Music.

By him were communicated the Indian airs, and drawings of musical instrument : I can only boast of having compiled from his letters : of having deciphered (not without difficulty) the notation of the Ramgully, and translated a few passages from a Persian manuscript treatise on music, which I shall mention hereafter, and for the perusal of which I am indebted to the politeness of Sir George Staunton.

On the subject of those ancient and extraordinary melodies, which the Hindus call *Raugs*, and *Rauginees*, (راگ and راگني) the popular traditions are as numerous and romantic, as the powers ascribed to them are miraculous. Of the six *Raugs*, the five first owe their origin to the God *Mahadeo*, who produced them from his five heads. *Parbuttee*, his wife, constructed the sixth ; and the thirty

رساله موسقي از كتاب دره‌التاج تصنيف عالم عامل و فاصل كامل اعني كلامه شيرازي

which, from certain circumstances, he once believed to be the composition of *Sadi*.

We find an Essay on Music among the Works of another celebrated poet, *Jami*.

Rauginees were composed by *Brimha.* Thus, of celestial invention, these melodies are of a peculiar genus: and of the three ancient genera of the *Greeks* resemble most the *enharmonic;* the more modern compositions are of that species termed *Diatonic.* A specimen of these is given in the *Hindovee* air, *Gul buddun thoo hum see,* in the annexed plate; of which the words (too trifling to deserve translation) are thus written in the original language:

اي كلبدن تون همسين كاهي حدا هواري
دو چار سهلن ملكي كچه تهمت كياري
اري‌لا و ميرا سجن كا كني جدا كداري

In the same plate I have given the notes of a *Hindu Jungle Tuppa* and of a *Bengalee* tune; of which the following are the words:

Nock erbesor Jeelee Mille
Poteer gulla doorea Koonja
Choola dauntee hassia Naaloo
Rangonee gwalia naalo

A considerable difficulty is found in setting to music the Raugs and Rauginees, as our system does not supply notes or signs sufficiently expressive of the almost imperceptible elevations and depressions of the voice in these melodies; of which the time is broken and irregular, the modulations frequent and very wild. Whatever magic was in the touch when Orpheus swept his lyre, or Timotheus filled his softly breathing flute, the effects said to have been produced by two of the six *Raugs,* are even more extraordinary than any of those ascribed to the modes of the ancients. *Mia Tonsine,* a wonderful musician in the time of King *Akber,* sung one of the *Night Raugs,* at mid-day: the powers of his music were such that it instantly became night, and the darkness extended in a circle round the palace as far as the sound of his voice could be heard.

There is a tradition, that whoever shall attempt to sing the *Raug Dheepuck* is to be destroyed by fire. The Emperor *Akber* ordered *Naik Gopaul*, a celebrated musician, to sing that *Raug:* he endeavoured to excuse himself, but in vain; the Emperor insisted on obedience: he therefore requested permission to go home, and bid farewell to his family and friends. It was winter when he returned, after an absence of six months. Before he began to sing he placed himself in the waters of the Jumna till they reached his neck. As soon as he had performed a strain or two, the river gradually became hot; at length began to boil; and the agonies of the unhappy musician were nearly insupportable. Suspending for a moment the melody thus cruelly extorted, he sued for mercy from the Monarch, but sued in vain. *Akber* wished to prove more strongly the powers of this Raug: *Naik Gopaul* renewed the fatal song: flames burst with violence from his body, which, though immersed in the waters of the *Jumna*, was consumed to ashes!

These, and other anecdotes of the same nature, are related by many of the Hindus, and implicitly believed by some.

The effect produced by the *Maig Mullaar Raug* was immediate rain. And it is told, that a singing girl once, by exerting the powers of her voice in this Raug, drew down from the clouds timely and refreshing showers on the parched rice-crops of Bengal, and thereby averted the horrors of famine from the *Paradise of Regions.** An European, in

* An Arabic title given to the province of Bengal by Aurungzeeb. See Jones' Perf. Gram. p. 82.

that country, inquiring after those whose musical performance might produce similar effects, is gravely told, "that the art is now almost lost; but that there are still musicians possessed of those wonderful powers in the west of India." But if one inquires in the West, they say, "that if any such performers remain they are to be found only in Bengal."

Of the present music and the sensations it excites one can speak with greater accuracy. "Many of the Hindu melodies" (to use the words of an excellent musician) "possess the plaintive simplicity of the Scotch and Irish, and others a wild originality pleasing beyond description."

Counterpoint seems not to have entered, at any time, into the system of Indian Music. It is not alluded to in the manuscript treatises which I have hitherto persued, nor have I discovered that any of our ingenious Orientalists speak of it as being known in Hindustan. The books, however, which treat of the music of that country are numerous and curious. Sir William Jones mentions the works of *Amin*, a musician; the *Damodara*, the *Narayan*, the *Ragarnava*, (or sea of passions); the *Sabhavinoda*, (or delight of assemblies); the *Ragavibodha*, (or doctrine of musical modes); the *Ratnacara*, and many other *Sanscrit* and *Hindustani* treatises. There is besides the *Raugaderpun*, (or mirror of Raugs) translated into Persian by *Fakur Ullah* from an Hindovee Book on the Science of Music, called *Muncuttuhub*, compiled by order of *Man Sing, Rajah of Gualier*. The *Sungeet Durpon* (or mirror of melody) is also a Persian translation from the *Sanscrit*. To these I am enabled to add, by the kindness of the learned Baronet whom I have before mentioned, the title of another Hindovee work translated by *Deenanaut*, the son of *Bausdheo*, into the Persian language on the first of the month *Ramjan*, in the year of the Hegira 1137, of our æra 1724.

رساله علم موسقي ترمين پوبهي پار جاتک که براني در يانتن راگ رآگني و نواختن سازمي آيه

"An Essay on the Science of Music, translated from the book *Paurjauthuck:* the object of which is to teach the understanding of the *Raugs* and *Rauginees,* and the playing upon musical instruments."

From this work, while I refer the reader to the learned observations of Sir William Jones, and other ingenious members of the Asiatic Society, on the musical modes, and the instruments of the *Hindus,* I shall here briefly state that they have a gamut, consisting of seven notes, like our own, which being repeated in three several Ast, hans,* or octaves, form in all a scale of twenty-one natural notes. The seven notes which form the gamut are expressed, *Sa, ra, ga, ma, pa, da, na,* or *Sa, ri, ga, ma, pa, dha, ni*——And, when written at length, stand thus:

کهرج Kau, redge
رکهب Rekhub
کندهار Gundhaur
مدهم Mud, dhum
پنچم Punchum
دهوت Dhawoth
نکهاد Neekhaudh——

* From the *Sanscrit* words *ashta* or *asthan, (signifying eight)* and *ara* (the *spoke of a wheel,* or any thing resembling it,) a very learned Orientalist is of opinion that the Hebrew *Ashtaroth,* and the Persian *Sitarah,* (formerly *Astarah)* (a star with eight rays) are most probably derived. The Persian numeral هشت is evidently the same as the *Sanscrit.* See Mr. Wilford's Essay on Egypt and the Nile—Asiatic Res. Vol. III.

Of these seven words, (the first excepted) the initial letters are used in writing music to represent the notes. Instead of the initial of the first or lowest, (*Kauredge*) that of the word سر (sur) is used, which signifies emphatically the *note,* —being, as it were, the foundation of the others, "and named" (says Sir William Jones*) "*Swara,* or the *sound,* from the important office which it bears in the scale."—The use of *Sur* or *Swara* instead of *Kauredge* prevents a possibility of mistaking the initial of the latter for that of *Gundhaur;* a circumstance which might otherwise happen, the characters being alike in form. But it is not the initial letter only of each note that we find used in writing music: *Rekhub* is often thus described ري *Dhawoth* دھ and *Neekhaudh* ني;—when the gamut may be expressed according to the form given by Sir William Jones: *sa ri ga ma pa dha ni.*—And in a manuscript before me the first note is always fully described سر (sur).

In each of the three octaves, wherein these seven notes are repeated, there are twenty-two *Srutis* or *soorts,* (DIESES) by which the Major and Minor tones are most curiously distinguished:

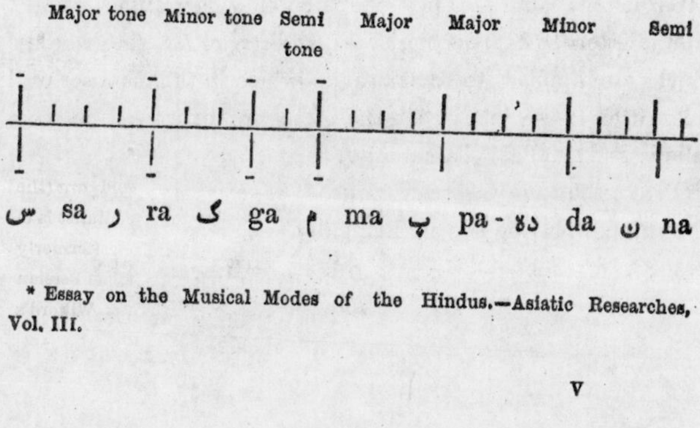

* Essay on the Musical Modes of the Hindus.—Asiatic Researches, Vol. III.

The following words are found written at length, either preceding, under or over the notes according to the necessary variations. I have given their pronunciation and signification :

استاد *Istaud*, slow.

رو *Ro*, quick.

گشت *Gusht*, quaver.

جنبان *Jumbaun*, shake.

کشید *Kasheed*, lengthen, or continue the sound.

طرح *Thurrah*, double, but not so quick as to be confounded into one.

طیهپ *Teep* } Either of these words marks the note to be raised an octave.
کپالي *Kopaúlee* }

Sometimes one note is affected by two of those words ; as *Thurrah* and *Kasheed* placed over or under the note *Dhowoth* in the *Ramgully*, of which I have given the notation : and in the manuscript before me those words are written in red ink, while the characters which represent the notes are in black.

I shall endeavour to explain the notation of the tune, given in the annexed plate, in the following manner, using capital letters to express the notes, and *italics* for the words which are applied to them, and which in the manuscript are written in red ink, but in the plate are expressed in an oblique and smaller character.

(Before the tune we read *Canoon e newaktun Ramgully*, The rule for playing the air Ramgully.)

SA	SA	GA	SA	DHA	KPY
Istaud	*Ro*	*Ro*	*Ro*	*Ró*	*Istaud*

Or. Coll: 1797. No1.

قانون نواختن راگني آمد

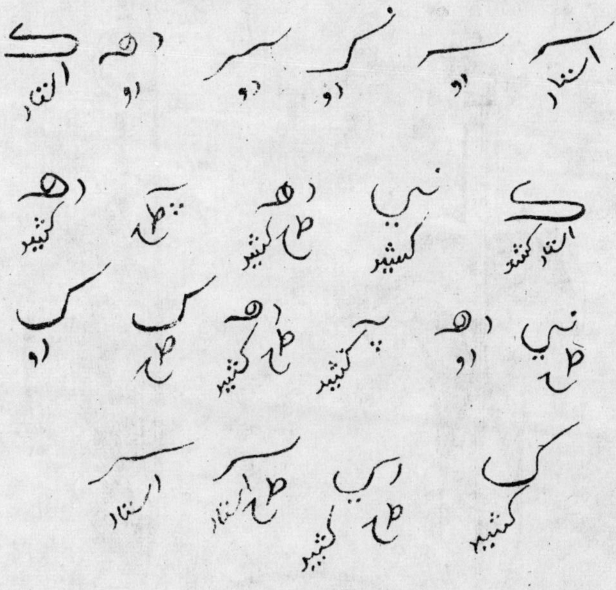

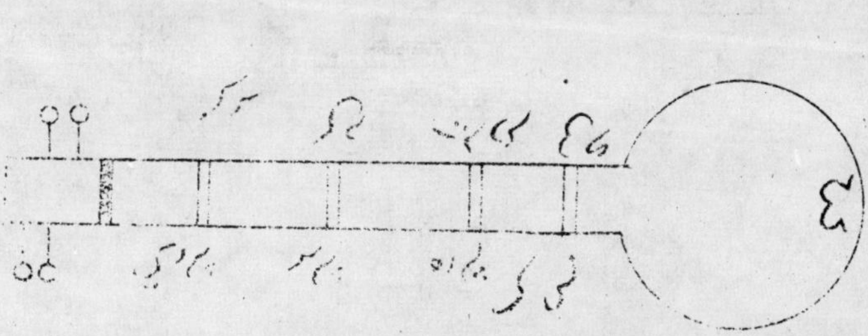

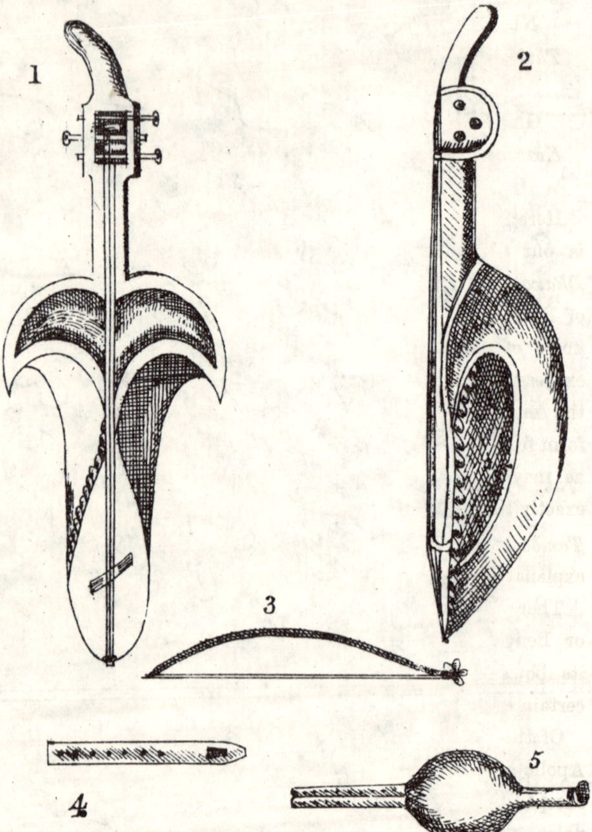
1
2
3
4
5

KPY	NI	DHA	PA	DHA
Istaud gusht	*Kasheed*	*Thurrah kasheed*	*Thurrah*	*Kasheed*

NI	DHA	PA	MA	GA	GA
Thurrah	*Ro*	*Kasheed*	*Thurrah Kasheed*	*Thurrah*	*Ro*

GA	RI	SA	SA
Kasheed	*Thurrah Kasheed*	*Thurrah Kasheed*	*Istaud*

Here SA signifies sur, (which itself, as I before remarked, is put for the first note *Kauredge*) ; GA, *Gundhaur ;* DHA, *Dhawoth*, &c., but the reader will perceive the introduction of KPY in the above scheme, not enumerated among the notes of the Gamut. I have used those three letters to express *Kopalee* (signifying the octave of the note) which in the manuscript is described by an Arabic *Cas* of a different form from the character which represents the note *Gundhaur*, as may be seen in the engraving, where I have given, copied exactly from the drawing in the manuscript, a figure of the *Tambooreh* طنبورة with the notes applied to the finger-board, explanatory of its scale.

There are annexed also, representations of the *Serinda*, or Bengal violin, in full (fig. 1.) and profile (fig. 2.,) with its bow, (fig. 3.) The strings of this instrument are of a certain kind of silk.

Of the *Baaseree*, (fig. 4.,) or pipe of *Krishnah*, the Hindu Apollo : one perforated bamboo similar to our Flageolet, except that each hole is not so exactly divided by notes, but many by half notes : its tone is soft and plaintive, and so easily filled that some blow it with their nostrils.

Of the *Toomeree,* (fig. 5.,) an instrument more common in the Deckan than in Bengal: it is formed a Gourd or *Cuddos* nut, and two small perforated bamboos, with reeds in each, like those of the bag-pipe.

In a future Number* of this Publication the subject of Indian Music shall be continued ; the notes given of a tune set [from] the voice of the singing girls of *Cashmere,* and some passages from an original manuscript in Persian, on the Music of that province.

ON THE GRA'MAS OR MUSICAL SCALES OF THE HINDUS.

BY

J. D. PATERSON, Esq.

(From Asiatic Researches, Vol. 9.)

ON

THE GRA'MAS OR MUSICAL SCALES

OF THE HINDUS.

BY

J. D. PATERSON, Esq.

When music was first reduced to a science, it is probable, that it was confined to the few scientific men, whose education and studies fitted them to understand its principles; and that the first efforts of the science were displayed in hymns to the deities: each being addressed in a peculiar mode, rhythmus, and expression.

According to Plato,* the *Egyptians* were restricted by their laws to certain fixed melodies, which they were not permitted to alter; he says, that the lawgivers of *Egypt* appear to have laid it down as a principle, that "young men in cities should be accustomed to beautiful figures and beautiful melodies, and that it was one of their institutions to *exhibit in their temples* what these were, and what the qualities which they possessed; and besides these it was not lawful either for painters or other artificers to introduce any that were new, or even to think of any other than those belonging to their country." He adds, "nor is it lawful at present to do this either in these particulars or in the whole of music. If you observe, therefore, you will find, that paintings and sculptures there, which were executed ten thousand

* On Legislation. Dialogue 2nd

years ago, as if they were not of such great antiquity, are neither more beautiful nor more deformed than the paintings or carvings of the present day, but are fashioned by just the same art."

When CLINIAS observes, that he spoke of a wonderful circumstance, he replies, "It is, however, a circumstance pertaining to law and politics in a transcendent degree, you will likewise find other things there of a trifling nature, *but this respecting music is true and deserves attention*, because the legislator could firmly give laws about things of this kind and with confidence introduce such melodies as possessed a natural rectitude: *but this must be the work of a God*, or of some divine person ; just as they say there, that their melodies, which have been preserved for such a length of time, are the *Poems* of *Isis*."

PLATO considers this restriction as proper and necessary to prevent the introduction of sensual licentiousness and effiminacy. There appears to have been some such idea of restriction, amongst the ancient *Hindus*, by the confinement of their music to thirty-six melodies : *viz.*, the six *Ragas* and thirty *Raginis:* the forty-eight *Putrus* are melodies, which seem to have been introduced in after times, when the discipline, alluded to by PLATO, had begun to be relaxed.

But the *Indian Ragas* and *Raginis* are fixed respectively to particular seasons of the year and times of the night or day. This is a circumstance particularly deserving remark, as it is probably peculiar to the *Hindu* music.

It is likely, that these melodies were in former times appropriated to the service of different deities. In such case the *Ragas* or *Raginis* would derive their appropriation to particular times and seasons, from the times and seasons allotted by the *Hindu* ritual for the performance of the services to which they were respectively appropriated. This appears probable: but whatever might have been the original cause of this apparent singularity, it has become so completely engrafted on the ideas of music amongst the natives of *India*, that they cannot at this day divest their minds of the prejudice. The Muslemans have universally adopted it; and a performer, who should sing a *Raga* out of its appropriated season, or an hour sooner or later than the time appointed, would be considered as an ignorant pretender to the character of a musician. This restraint upon their music, which *Europeans* would think insupportable, the *Indian* considers as absolutely necessary to give a true relish to the melody. The origin of this custom seems lost in antiquity. No *Hindu*, with whom I have conversed, has been able to account for it. We may, therefore, suppose it probable, that it originated, as I have observed before, in the religious restraints to which music appears to have been subjected, when first reduced to fixed principles as a science.

Music must have been cultivated in very early ages by the *Hindus;* as the abridged names of the seven notes, *viz.*, *sa, ri, ga, ma, pa, dha, ni,* are said to occur in the *Sama Veda;* and in their present order. Their names at length are as follow:

Shadja pronounced *Sarja* or *Kharja.*

Rishabha pronounced *Rikhabh.*

Gand'hara.

Madhyama.

Panchama.

Dhaivata.

Nishada pronounced *Nikhad.*

Hence we find, that the above-mentioned abbreviated names of these notes, which are used in what we call *Solfaing* or *Solmization*, are the first syllables of their names, *viz.*, *Sa, ri, ga, ma, pa, dha, ni.* The complete scale is called *Swaragráma* or assemblage of tones ; it is likewise called *Septac* or *heptachord*, as containing, or consisting of, seven notes.

The *Hindus* place the seven notes under the protection of seven *Ad'hisht'hâtrǐ Dévatás*, or superintending divinities, as follow :

Shadja, under the protection of AGNI.
Rǐshabha, of BRAHMA.
Gándhára, of SARASVATÍ.
Madhyama, of MAHÁDEVA.
Panchama, of SRÍ or LACSHMÍ.
Dhaivatâ, of GAN'E'S'A.
Nishâda, of SÚRYA.

Of these notes, there are four descriptions : 1st the *Bâdi*, which is the *Ansâ* or key note ; and is described as the *Rajah* on whom all the rest depend ; the 2nd is *Sanbadi* which is considered as the *Mantri* or principal minister of the Rajah ; the 3rd are *Anubâdi*, described as subjects attached to their Lord ; 4th *Bibâdi*, mentioned as inimical to him.*

The *Hindus* divide the octave into twenty-two intervals, which are called *S'ruti*, by allotting four *S'ruti* to represent the interval which we call a major tone, three to describe a minor tone, and two the semi-tone : not as being mathematically just, but as means of representing to the eye, and to the understanding, the supposed relations which these intervals

* The three last distinctions seem to correspond to the *Homophonia*, *Paraphonia*, and *Antiphonia*, of the Greeks. GAUDENTIUS in his Harmonic Introduction, explains *Paraphonia*, a mean between consonance and dissonance ; where the sound, to the ear, appears consonant. H. T.

bear to each other; merely to shew, that a semi-tone is half a major tone, and that the minor tone is a medium between the major and semi-tone, being less than the former and greater than the latter. Mathematical calculation is out of the question.

Perhaps they were induced to make this division of the octave, by considering the minor tone as not divisible by two without a fraction; and therefore made the whole number three, to represent it: for, if we divide the octave into twelve semi-tones, this will give twenty-four quarter tones or *S'ruti*; but by allowing three to represent each of the two minor tones, instead of four, there will remain only twenty-two, the number of *S'ruti* admitted.

The *S'rutis* are personified as so many nymphs; and, in the *Sangita Rutnácara*, are thus named and arranged.*

To *Shadja* or *Sa* . . . 4	*Tibra*, *Cumudvati*, *Mundá*, *Chandovya*
To *Rishabha* or *Ri* 3	*Dayávati*, *Renjani*, *Reticá*
To *Gándhára* or *Ga* 2	*Rudri*, *Cródhá*
To *Madhyama* or *Ma* 4	*Bájricá*, *Prasarani*, *Priti*, *Márjani*
To *Panchama* or *Pa* 4	*Cirti*, *Ractá*, *Dipari*, *Alápini*
To *Dhaivata* or *Dha* . . . 3	*Madanti*, *Róhini*, *Ramya*
To *Nisháda* or *Ni* . . . 2	*Upta*, *Cábiri*

* The names, exhibited in the *Sangita Dâmôdara*, are quite different. They seldom occur except in the writings of authors treating on music. H. T. C.

The *Hindus* have three *Grámas* or scales: *viz.*, *Shadja-Gráma*, *Madhyama-Gráma*, and *Gándhára-Gráma*. The foregoing arrangement of the *S'ruti* is that of the *Shadja-Gráma*, which consists of two disjunct, but perfectly similar, *Tetrachords*, separated by a major tone. The *Madhyama-Gráma* is formed from this by a transposition of the major tone between *Pa* and *Dha*, and of the minor tone between *Dha* and *Ni;* thus the technical language of *Hindu* music, *Dha* takes one *S'ruti* from *Pa*, and becomes thus possessed of four, leaving three to *Pa*.

The two *Grámas* may be thus represented.

Shadja Gráma (*Tetrachord.* Sa–Ma; *Tetrachord.* Pa–Sa)

	Sa	Ri	Ga	Ma	Pa	Dha	Ni	Sa
Shadja Gráma	1. 2. 3. 4	1. 2. 3.	1. 2	1. 2. 3. 4.	1. 2. 3. 4.	1. 2. 3.	1. 2.	
	Major Tone - 4.	Minor Tone - 3.	Semi Tone - 2.	Major Tone - 4.	Major Tone - 4.	Minor Tone - 3.	Semi Tone - 2.	

	Sa	Ri	Ga	Ma	Pa	Dha	Ni	Sa
Madhyama Gráma.	1. 2. 3. 4.	1. 2. 3.	1. 2.	1. 2. 3. 4.	1. 2. 3.	1. 2. 3. 4.	1. 2.	
	Major Tone, - 4.	Minor Tone, - 3.	Semi Tone, - 2.	Major Tone, - 4.	Minor Tone, - 3.	Major Tone, - 4.	Semi Tone, - 2.	

HINDOVEE.

A HINDU JUNGLE TUPPAH.

BENGALEE.

When the change of key requires a different modulation, the changes in the disposition of the *S'ruti* are called *Vicrit*: they reckon twelve such.

When a note is to be rendered graver or deeper, they say that such a note takes one or more *S'ruti* from the note immediately below it, as in the example of the change from the *Shadja Gráma* to the *Madhyama Grama*, where *Dha* is made one *S'ruti* flatter than in the former scale.

If a note is to be raised, the expression is, that such a note gives one or more *S'ruti* to the note immediately below it; which operation renders the note proportionally sharper, as its distance from the note immediately below it is consequently increased; and to that immediately above it, the distance is in the same proportion diminished.

The *Gandhara Grama* is formed from the *Madhyama Grama;* and in the construction of it, the *Sangita Darpana* points out three changes in the scale.

1*st.* *Gand'hara* takes one *S'ruti* from *Rishabha*, and becomes of three *i. e.*, by rendering the third note *Ga* flat, the interval between *Ri* and *Ga* is reduced to a semi-tone, and that between *Ga* and *Ma* becomes a minor tone.

2*nd.* *Panchama* loses one *S'ruti* to *Gandhara.*

I am at a loss to know how this can take place: I rather suspect an error in the text, and would propose to substitute *Dha* the sixth note instead of *Gandhara.* The three *S'ruti* of *Panchama* make the interval between the 5th and 6th: by losing one, it is reduced to a semi-tone; but it cannot lose this one to *Gandhara*, which is the third note. There are but two methods of reducing this interval to a semi-tone: one by raising the fifth note; the other by rendering the sixth flat. But here the interval between the 4th and 5th remains unaltered. It must in this case be done by making *Dha* the 6th note flat; or, in the language of *Hindu* music, by giving one of *Panchama's S'rutis* to *Dhaivata.*

3rd. *Suddhaswara* gives one *S'ruti* to *Nishada.* Here *Nishada* is rendered one *S'ruti* flat. *Suddhaswara* is not the name of a note; but is explained to me to be a term applied to a note possessing its full compliment of *S'rutis.* It may, therefore, be applied, in this case, to *Dhaivata;* for, although it may give one *S'ruti* to *Nishada,* yet it gains one from *Panchama,* and still retains four complete *S'rutis.*

If these conjectures are admitted, and we compare it with the *Madhyama Grama* (to which these changes evidently refer), it will stand thus :—

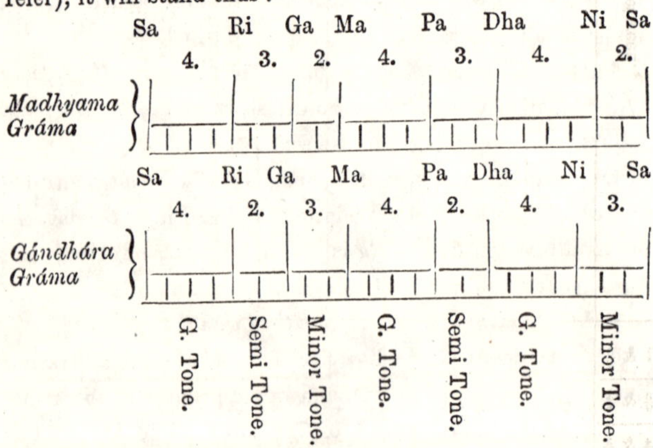

That the *Hindus* probably, by this division of the octave, meant nothing more than what I have before supposed, may appear from the following table, in which the intervals, between each note and the note above it, are taken from Mr. MALCOLM'S series of the octave in the two modes (as given by Mr. CHAMBERS, under the article scale). This I have done, in order to compare those intervals with the *S'ruti* of the *Hindus*, and to show the difference.

Malcolm's series of the octave.	Malcolm's series of the octave.
$\frac{3}{9}$ $\frac{4}{5}$ $\frac{3}{4}$ $\frac{2}{3}$ $\frac{3}{5}$ $\frac{8}{15}$ $\frac{1}{2}$	$\frac{3}{9}$ $\frac{5}{6}$ $\frac{4}{4}$ $\frac{2}{3}$ $\frac{5}{8}$ $\frac{5}{9}$ $\frac{1}{2}$
Major Mode or *Madhyama Gráma.*	Minor Mode or *Gándhára Gráma.*

The difference between.	Proportion of the intervals between each note, and the note above it.	What they ought to be if the scale was divided into 22 parts or the whole string into 44.	What they are as stated by the Hindus.		The difference between.	Proportion of the intervals between each note, and the note above it.	What they ought to be if the scale was divided into 22 parts or the whole string into 44.	What they are as stated by the Hindus.
1 & $\frac{8}{9}$	$\frac{1}{9}$	$4\frac{8}{9}$	4		1 & $\frac{8}{9}$	$\frac{1}{9}$	$4\frac{8}{9}$	4
$\frac{8}{9}$ & $\frac{4}{5}$	$\frac{4}{45}$	$3\frac{41}{45}$	3		$\frac{8}{9}$ & $\frac{5}{6}$	$\frac{1}{18}$	$2\frac{4}{9}$	2
$\frac{4}{5}$ & $\frac{3}{4}$	$\frac{1}{20}$	$2\frac{1}{5}$	2		$\frac{5}{6}$ & $\frac{3}{4}$	$\frac{1}{12}$	$3\frac{2}{3}$	3
$\frac{3}{4}$ & $\frac{2}{3}$	$\frac{1}{12}$	$3\frac{2}{3}$	4		$\frac{3}{4}$ & $\frac{2}{3}$	$\frac{1}{12}$	$3\frac{2}{3}$	4
$\frac{2}{3}$ & $\frac{3}{5}$	$\frac{1}{15}$	$2\frac{14}{15}$	3		$\frac{2}{3}$ & $\frac{5}{8}$	$\frac{1}{24}$	$1\frac{5}{6}$	2
$\frac{3}{5}$ & $\frac{8}{15}$	$\frac{5}{75}$	$2\frac{14}{15}$	4		$\frac{5}{8}$ & $\frac{5}{9}$	$\frac{5}{72}$	$1\frac{1}{13}$	4
$\frac{8}{15}$ & $\frac{1}{2}$	$\frac{1}{30}$	$1\frac{7}{15}$	2		$\frac{5}{9}$ & $\frac{1}{2}$	$\frac{1}{18}$	$2\frac{4}{9}$	2

If we revert to the *Shadja Grama*, we shall find it composed of two disjunct, but perfectly similar *Tetrachords*, separated by a major tone: both *Tetrachords* are expressed by the name numbers 4. 3. 2; and, if we reject the fractions of the first *Tetrachord* in the foregoing table, we have the same number: and, as they considered the 2nd *Tetrachord* as perfectly similar to the first, they probably made use of the same numbers to express that similitude.

There are three kinds of characteristic melody for the structure of *Ragas*, either by the use of all, or the exclusion of one, or two, particular notes. Those *Ragas*, in which the whole seven notes are employed, are called *Humir huran*. Those, which exclude one particular note, and only use the remaining six, are called *Cad'hir*. Those, which exclude two particular notes, and only reserve five, are called *Orav*. There is a passage in *Dr. Burney's* history of music, and one, in the British Encyclopædia (speaking of the *Guglia Rotta*,* or the broken pillar lying in the *Campus Martius* at *Rome*,) by which it appears, that there is on this pillar or obelisk the figure of a musical instrument with two strings and with a neck; that, by the means of its neck, this instrument was capable, with only two strings, of producing a great number of notes; that these two strings, if tuned fourths to each other, would furnish that series of sounds called by the ancients *Heptachord*, which consists of a conjunct *Tetrachord* as B. C. D. E; F. G. A; if tuned in fifths, they would produce *an octave*, or two *disjunct Tetrachords*.

This may possibly explain the principle of the construction of the *Shadja Grama* of the *Hindus*; and there is a similar

* A fragment of an *Egyptian* obelisk of the highest antiquity, which had been brought to *Rome* unde *Augustus*. It is covered with Hieroglyphics.

instrument still in use, called *Dwitantri,* which I have often seen and heard; and, as far as I remember, it is tuned in fifths. It consists of a wooden body, hollowed out and covered with parchment; it has a neck and two strings, and is struck with a plectrum.

The *Madhyama Grâma* is evidently our major modes; and, if I am right, that of *Gandhara* is our minor mode.

The extent of the *Hindu* scale is three *Septacas;* which are thus fancifully described: the lowest or first *Septaca,* called *Mundra-sthâna,* is derived or produced from the navel, extending upwards to the chest; the second *Madhya-sthána,* from the chest to the throat; the third *Târa-sthâna,* from the throat to the brain.

The scale is denominated *Grâma,* (literally village,) because there is in it the assemblage of all the notes, *S'rutis* and *Múrchhanás,* arranged in their proper places, as mankind assemble in towns and villages, and there assume their different degrees and stations.

In considering the names given to the three *Grâmas,* it appears to me, that the *Shadja Gráma* takes its name from the lowest note in that scale, as being the foundation of the first *Tetrachord;* the second *Tetrachord* being apparently formed from the first by fifths: in which case the 6th must necessarily be more *acute* than in the *Diatonic* scale; and the interval between the 5th and 6th is therefore represented by four *S'rutis* to signify, that *Dha* bears the same proportion to *Pa,* that *Ri* does to *Sa.* The intervals of the *Shadja Grâma* may be represented as follow:—

	$\frac{8}{9}$		$\frac{4}{5}$		$\frac{3}{4}$		$\frac{2}{3}$		$\frac{16}{27}$		$\frac{8}{15}$		$\frac{1}{2}$	
Sa		*ri*		*ga*		*ma*		*pa*		*dha*		*ni*		*sa*

The modulation of the *Madhyama Gráma* probably took its rise from making *Madhyama* the 5th note in the scale; in which case you will have

Ni sa ri ga ma pa dha.

OR

Si ut re me fa sol la.

This is precisely the diatonic scale of the *Greeks;* and here it became necessary to render *Dha* a comma lower in the scale, which the *Hindus* express by making *Dha* receive one *S'ruti* from *Pa.* The alteration, thus suggested, they adopted; and with it formed their 2nd scale from the *Shadja Grắma,* giving it the name of *Madhyama,* probably to denote its origin.

The *Gándhắra Grắma* appears to have a similar origin; by making *Gắndhára* the 5th. This will produce

Dha ni sa ri ga ma pa.

OR

La si ut ri mi fa sol.

Which is the natural minor mode *La:* but keeping *Sa* as their first note, the *Vicrits,* or changes before mentioned, became necessary, to give it the same modulation; and it was probably called *Gắndhắra Grắma* to denote its origin.

Of the notes and *S'rutis* I have spoken above, I shall now endeavour to explain what these *Múrchhanas* are; or rather what I conceive them to be. Each *Gráma* is said to contain seven *Múrchhanas:* hence they reckon twenty-one in all.

Sir W. Jones says they appear to be no more than seven pieces of diapason multiplied by three, according to the difference of pitch in the compass of three octaves.* But the *Múrchhanas* are described to be the seven notes, each arranged in its proper station in the scale, which renders them fit to be applied in the composition of the *Ragas*, &c. It appears to me therefore, that they are the intervals of each *Gráma*, which I would arrange as follows.

The *Shadja Gráma* is composed of two disjunct but perfectly similar *Tetrachords*, separated by a major tone, and both *Tetrachords* have a major third; the *Múrchhanas* of this *Gráma* I suppose to be

1st. from Sa to Ri	}	1st. 2nd.
2nd.—— Sa to Ga	}	1st. 3rd.
3rd. —— Sa to Ma	}	1st. 4th.
4th. from Pa to Dha	}	2nd. 2nd.
5th. —— Pa to Ni	}	2nd. 3rd.
6th. —— Pa to Sa	}	2nd. 4th.
7th. —— Pa to Sa		8 octave.

The *Múrchhanas* of *Madhyama Gráma* :

2nd. from Sa to Ri.
3rd. —— Sa to Ga, greater third.
4th. —— Sa to Ma.
5th. —— Sa to Pa.
6th. —— Sa to Dha, greater sixth.
7th. —— Sa to Ni.
8th. —— Sa to Sa.

* In citing a passage from the Epic Poem on the death of SISUPALA, which is entitled *Mágha*, Sir W. JONES translated *Múrchhaṇa* "musical interval." (See As. Res. Vol. 1st p. 265.) He afterwards gave a different interpretation of it, (Vol. 3rd. p. 71,) as stated in the text. In his version of that passage, Sir W. JONES mistook the meaning of the term *S'ruti*, (which is there translated ear, instead of quarter tone,) but he has rightly explained it in his treatise on the musical modes of the Hindus. H. T. C.

Múrchhaná of *Găndhára Gráma:*

Sa to Ri.
Sa to Ga, minor third.
Sa to Ma.
Sa to Pa.
Sa to Dha, minor sixth.
Sa to Ni.
Sa to Sa.

The *Múrchhanás* are all personified, and distinguished by names,* viz.

Those of the *Shadja Gráma* are :—

1st. *Uttara mundá.*
2nd. *Uttarayita.*
3rd. *Rechaní.*
4th. *Sud haprajaya.*
5th. *Sancita.*
6th. *Chacranta.*

Those of *Madhyama Gráma*, are :—

1st. *Saubiri.*
2nd. *Harina.*
3rd. *Culopantá.*
4th. *Sudha Mad'hya.*
5th. *Marghi.*
6th. *Purvi.*
7th. *Rishica.*

* This list is apparently from the *Sangita-Ratnacara*. The personified *Múrchhanás* have other names in the *Sangita-Damodara*. H. T. C.

Those of *Gandhara Gráma*, are :—

1st. *Mandrá.*

2nd. *Vis'álá.*

3rd. *Sumuc'hi.*

4th. *Chitra.*

5th. *Rohini or Chitravati.*

6th. *Suc'ha.*

7th. *Alapa.*

The use of these *Múrchhánas* is, in my opinion, to teach the learner to rise an octave by tones and semitones; and to descend again by the same notes; and to rise and fall by greater intervals, directly, by omitting the intermediate notes; in short the practice of solmisation.

ON

THE VINA OR INDIAN LYRE.

BY

FRANCIS FOWKE, Esq.

(From "Asiatic Researches," Vol. I.)

THE VINA

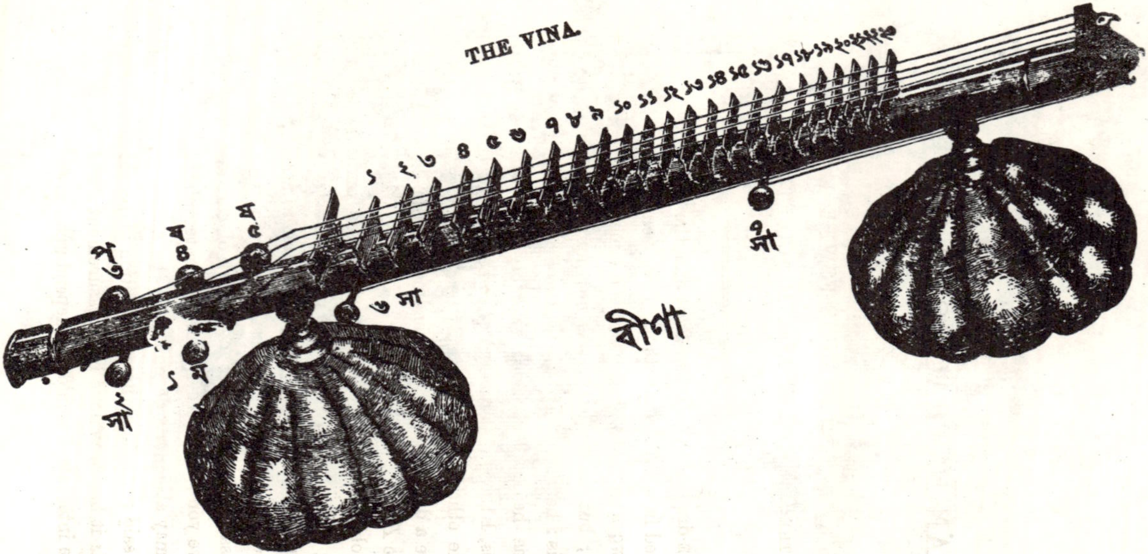

AN EXTRACT OF A LETTER

ON THE VINA

FROM FRANCIS FOWKE, ESQ.,

TO THE PRESIDENT ASIATIC SOCIETY OF BENGAL.

THE drawings of *Jeewan Shah* and the *Been* will be despatched in a small boat to-morrow, you wished to have had the two attendant musicians in the same drawing with *Jeewan Shah;* but the draftsman was not equal to the perspective of this: he would have run all the figures one into the other: and as he has succeeded telerably well with the principal figures, I thought it was better to be sure of that, especially as the other figures can easily be added by a *European* artist. I have a double pleasure in sending you the enclosed account of the *Been.*

In obliging you, I look forward to the instructive amusement I shall share with the public at large in the result of your researches into this subject of *Indian* music; and I am exceedingly happy, by furnishing you with facts, highly necessary indeed, but the mere work of care and observation, to give you greater leisure for the contemplation of the whole You may absolutely depend upon the accuracy of all that I have said respecting the construction and scale of this instrument: it has been done by measurement: and with regard to the intervals, I would not depend upon my ear, but had the

Been tuned to the harpsichord, and compared the instruments carefully, note by note, more than once. What I myself am aware of, will certainly not escape your penetration, that there may be a little of the bias of hypothesis, or an opinion pretty strongly established, in what I have said of the confined modulation of the *Indian* music.

But it is easy to separate my experiments and conjectures; and my prejudices cannot mislead you; though they may possibly suggest a useful hint, as half errors often do.

The *Been* is a fretted instrument of the guitar kind. The finger-board is $21\frac{6}{8}$ths inches long. A little beyond each end of the finger-board are two large gourds, and beyond these are the pegs and tail-piece which hold the wires.

The whole length of the instrument is three feet seven inches. The first gourd is fixed at ten inches from the top, and the second is about two feet $11\frac{1}{2}$. The gourds are very large, about fourteen inches diameter, and have a round piece cut out of the bottom, about five inches diameter. The finger-board is about two inches wide. The wires are seven in nnmber, and consist of two steel ones, very close together, in the right side; four brass ones on the finger-board; and one brass one on the left side.

They are tuned in the following manner :—

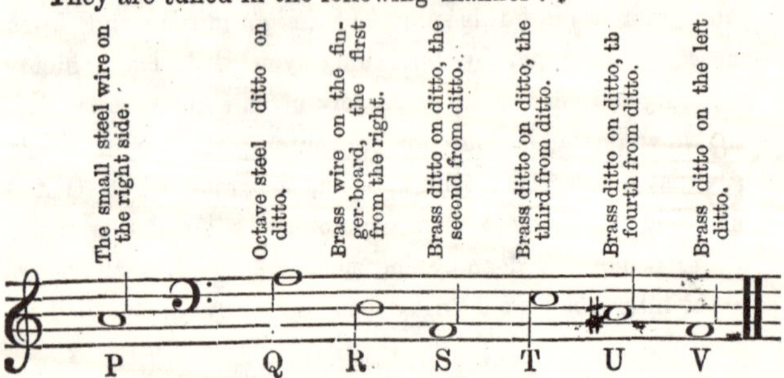

The great singularity of this instrument is the height of the frets; that nearest the nut is one inch $\frac{1}{8}$, and that at the other extremity about $\frac{7}{8}$ths of an inch, and the decrease is pretty gradual. By this means the finger never touches the finger-board itself. The frets are fixed on with wax by the performer himself, which he does entirely by ear. This was asserted by *Pear Cawn* the brother of *Jeewan Shah,* who was ill at the time, but *Pear Cawn* is a performer very little, if at all, inferior to *Jeewan Shah.* The frets of *Pear Cawn's* instrument were tolerably exact. Any little difference is easily corrected by the pressure of the finger. Indeed, the performers are fond, on any note that is at all long, of pressing the string very hard, and letting it return immediately to its natural tension, which produces a sound something like the close shake on the violin; but not with so agreeable an effect; for it appears sometimes to alter the sound half a tone.

The frets are nineteen in number. The notes that they give will appear on the following scale. I have added below the names which the performer himself gives to the notes in his own language. It is very observable, that the semitones change their names on the same semitone as in the *European* scale.

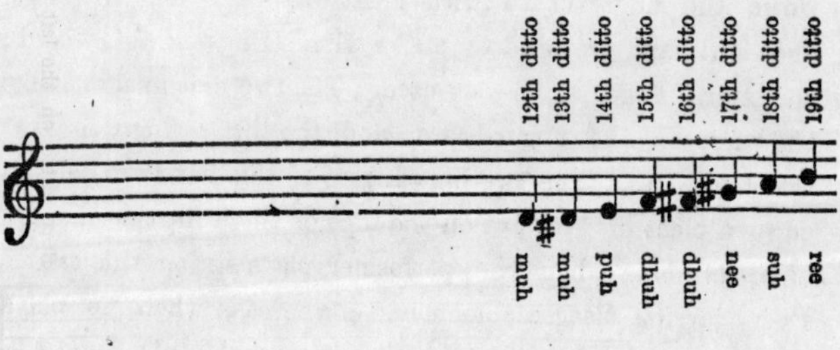

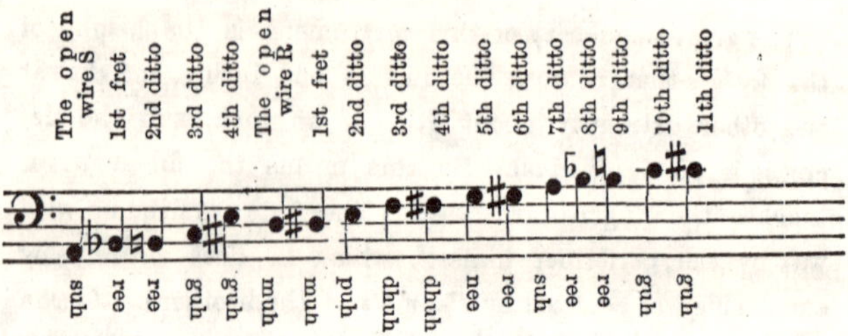

On the wires R and S, which are those principally used, there is an extent of two octaves, a whole note with all the half notes complete in the first octave, but the g ♮ and b b wanting in the second. The performer's apology for this was, that he could easily get those notes by pressing the string a little hard upon the frets f ♯ and a ♮, which is very true from the height of the frets: but he asserted that this was no defect in his particular instrument, but that all *Beens* were made so. The wires T U, are seldom used, except open.

The *Been* is held over the left shoulder, the upper gourd resting on that shoulder, and the lower one on the right knee.

The frets are stopped with the left hand; the first and second fingers are principally used. The little finger of the hand is sometimes used to strike the note V.

The third finger is seldom used, the hand shifting up and down the finger-board with great rapidity. The fingers of the right hand are used to strike the strings of this hand; the third finger is never used. The two first fingers strike the wires on the finger-board, and the little finger strikes the two wires. The two first fingers of this hand are defended by a piece of wire put on the tops of them in the manner of a thimble; when the performer plays strong, this causes a very jarring disagreeable sound; whereas, when he plays softly, the tone of the instrument is remarkably pleasing.

The style of music on this instrument is in general that of great execution. I could hardly ever discover any regular air or subject. The music seems to consist of a number of detached passages, some very regular in their assent and descent; and those that are played softly, are most of them both uncommon and pleasing.

The open wires are struck, from time to time, in a manner that, I think, prepares the ear for a change of modulation, to which the uncommonly full and fine tones of these notes greatly contribute; but the ear is, I think, always disappointed; and if there is ever any transition from the principal key, I am inclined to think it is very short. Were there any other circumstances, respecting the *Indian* music, which lead to suppose that it has, at some period, been much superior to the present practice, the style, scale and antiquity of this instrument, would, I think, greatly confirm the supposition.

SUNGEET.

BY

FRANCIS GLADWIN, Esq.

(From the "Ayeen Akbery," Vol. III.)

SUNGEET

BY

FRANCIS GLADWIN, ESQ

SUNGEET is the art of vocal and instrumental music; together with that of dancing.

The rules thereof are comprised in seven books, *viz.*, First, *Soor*, the nature of sound, which is of two kinds; *Annahut*, a sound without any earthly cause, and which they consider to have existed from all eternity after the following manner. ...en a man closes the orifices of his ears with his fingers, he perceives an inward noise, to which they give this name. They say this proceeds from *Brahma*, and that it cannot be heard without stopping the ears, till a man is in the state of *Muckut*, when it becomes part of his nature. *Akut*, a sound which proceeds from a cause which, like speech, they consider to be an accident of air, occasioned by percussion. They say that Providence has given every man twenty-two nerves, extending from the belly to the crown of the head, through eighteen of which the air paffs from the navel upwards; and according as these nerves are employed forcibly or weakly, in such degree, is the sound uttered.

The air does pass through the fifth, sixth, eighteenth and nineteenth nerves, consequently they are mute: but the sound uttered through the others, they divide into seven kinds, in the following order: 1, *Surj*, is like the voice of the peacock, and which is produced by the fourth nerve. 2, *Righbeh*, is like the voice of the *Peepeeheh*, a bird resembling the *Sar,* which sings in the rainy season. It is in compass from the seventh to the tenth nerve. 3, *Gandhar,* is like the bleating of a goat, and reaches from the ninth to the thirteenth nerve. 4, *Mudhem,* is like the voice of the crane, and reaches from the thirteenth to the sixteenth nerve. 5, *Punchem,* is like the voice of the bird called the *Koyil,* and reaches to the seventh nerve. 6, *Dehwat,* is like the voice of the lizard and reaches from the eighth to the twenty-second. 7, *Nikhad,* is like the noise of the elephant, and reaches from the twenty-second to the third.

An air which contains all these seven *Soors,* they call *Sumpoorun.* If it has six, *Khadow.* If five, *Owduh* ; and no air has fewer. But the Tan (or symphony) may be composed of two.

SECOND ADHYA, *Ragabibaka,* the modes and their variations.

They say that singing was invented by *Mahadeo* and *Purbutty.* That the first had five mouths, from each of which issued a musical mode in the following order : 1, *Sree Raga ;* 2, *Bussunt ;* 3, *Beharowg ;* 4, *Puncham ;* 5, *Megh.*

To this they add *Natnarain,* which they attribute to *Purbutty.* These six modes they call Raga, and each has several variations ; but the six following are what are most common.

VARIATIONS OF SREE RAGA—1, *Malavee ;* 2, *Tirowenee ;* 3, *Gowree ;* 4, *Kadaree ;* 5, *Maddeemadwee ;* 6, *Beharee.*

VARIATIONS OF BUSSUNT—1, *Deysee ;* 2, *Deo-gurree ;* 3, *Byratty ;* 4, *Towree ;* 5, *Lellita ;* 6, *Hindowlee.*

VARIATIONS OF BOYROWUNG—1, *Boyrowo ;* 2, *Muddehmad ;* 3, *Bihrowee ;* 4, *Bungalee ;* 5, *Biratka ;* 6, *Sindavee ;* 7, *Poonargeya.*

VARIATIONS OF PUNCHAM—1, *Beybhass ;* 2, *Boopaiee ;* 3, *Kanra ;* 4, *Badhunsha ;* 5, *Malsree ;* 6, *Pathamunjeree.*

VARIATIONS OF MEGH—1, *Mullar* ; 2, *Sowrutty ;* 3, *Assavaree ;* 4, *Kowsekee ;* 5, *Gandhar ;* 6, *Harasingaree.*

VARIATIONS OF NATNARAIN—1, *Kammodee ;* 2, *Kulleyan ;* 3, *Aheeree ;* 4, *Soodhanuat ;* 5 *Saluk ;* 6, *Nutkummer.*

Some make only four variations of each Raga. Others in the place of *Bussunt, Punchem,* and *Megh,* use *Malkoosa, Hindowl,* and *Deepuc,* and make five variations of each. Others instead of *Bussunt, Behunga, Punchama* and *Megh,* use *Soodh Behungara, Hindowla, Dasker,* and *Soodhanut.*

There are two kinds of songs ; *Marug* being those invented by the *Dewlabs* and the *Rekehsir,* which are the same everywhere, and are universally held in the highest veneration.

In the *Dekhan* there are many who sing them in different ways, amongst which are the following: 1, *Soorejperkass ;* 2, *Penjtalisser ;* 3, *Sirbetoobehder ;* 4, *Chanderperkass ;* 5, *Ragkuddem* ; 6, *Shoomra ;* and 7, *Surtunnee.*

The other kind of songs are called *Deysee* (or local), each place having its peculiar ones, as *Dhoorpud* in Agra, Gwaliar, Bary, and that neighbourhood. In the reign of Rajah Man Singh at Gwaliar, three of his musicians named Naik Bukhshoo, Mujhoo, and Bhannoo, formed a collection of songs suited to the taste of every class of people. When Man Singh died, Bukhshoo and Mujhoo went into the service of Sultan Bahader Gujeratty, and being highly esteemed by that prince, introduced into his court this kind of songs.

The *Dhoorpud* consists of stanzas of three or four rhymical lines of any length. They are chiefly in praise of men who have been famous for their valour or their virtue. Th *Deysee* songs in the Telingee and Carnatic dialects, are called

Dherow; the subject is generally love. Those sung in Bengal, are called *Bungeela.* Those of Jownpoor, *Choolkutta.* Those of Dehly, *Kowl,* and *Teraneh.* These last were composed by Ameer Khosru of Dehly, with the assistance of Samut and Tetar; they are a delightful mixture of the Persian and Hindove style. Those of Mehtra, are called *Bishenpud,* consisting of stanzas of four or six lines, and are in praise of *Kishen.* Those of Sind, are called *Kamee,* and are on love and friendship. Those in the Terhut language, called *Lehcharee,* were composed by Bedyaput, and are on the violence of the passion of love. Those of Lahore are called *Chund.* Those of Gujerat *Juckee.* The warlike and heroic songs are called *Kirheh* and *Sadereh;* they are of different measures, and in various dialects. Besides those already mentioned, there are many others, amongst which are *Poorbee, Dehnosiree, Rumkully, Koryie, Soohoo, Deyskar,* and *Deysneck.*

THE THIRD ADHYA, *Purkeerenka,* treats of *Alap,* which is of two kinds. 1, *Ragalap,* the *Tan,* or symphony, which contains the subject of the air. 2, *Roopalap,* the air with the words.

THE FOURTH ADHYA, *Pirbendh,* is the art of composing *Geet* (or song), and consists of six things :—1, *Soor* ; 2, *Bered* (praise) ; 3, *Pud,* the person praised ; 4, *Tinna,* or Amen ; 5, *Tuntinna,* or Amen ; 6, *Neehrat,* Time,

Paut signifies the variations of the word *Tuntinna,* from three to twenty syllables. This therefore is an excess of time.

Taul, or measure. If the *Taul* contains six *Tuntinnas,* it is called *Meydenee;* if five, *Anundenee;* if four, *Debnee;* if three, *Bhawanee;* if two, *Terawely;* and it never consists of fewer.

The four *Adhyas* above described, are only divisions of *Soor*, or melody.

THE FIFTH ADHYA, *Taul*, treats of the nature and quantity of the measure.

THE SIXTH ADHYA, *Wadya*, of musical instruments, and which are of four kinds :—1, *Tut*, stringed instruments. 2, *Tit*, those made of skins, such as drums. 3, *Gheen*, any two things that produce sound by percussion. 4, *Sookhir*, wind instruments.

STRINGED INSTRUMENTS :—

The *Junter* has a neck of hollow wood an ell in length, at each end of which is fastened half of a gourd. On the neck are placed sixteen wooden frets, over which are strung six iron wires, fastened into both ends of the neck. The tone is varied, by means of the frets.

The *Bheen* resembles the *Junter*; but has only three strings.

The *Kinner* has a longer neck than the *Bheen*, and has the gourds with two strings.

The *Sirbheen* is like the *Bheen* excepting that it has not any frets.

The *Ambirtee*, the neck of this is smaller than that of the *Sirbheen*, and it has only one gourd, which is placed in the middle of the neck underneath, and one iron wire. The changes of the modes are played upon it.

The *Rebab*, in general, has six strings of gut; but some have twelve, and others, eighteen.

The *Sirmendel* resembles the *Canoon*. It has twenty-one strings, some of which are of iron, some of brass, and some of gut.

The *Saringee,* called also *Soorbotan,* is of the shape of a bow, with two hollow cups inverted at each end. It has one string of gut, resembling a bow-string. They hold under the string a small gourd, and play with a plectrum.

The *Adhowtee* is a gourd with two wires.

The *Kingerah* resembles the *Bheen,* but has only two strings of gut, and the gourds are smaller.

THE SECOND KIND OF INSTRUMENTS OR DRUMS :—

The *Pukuwej* is a hollow piece of wood in the shape of a citron, but flat at both ends, which are covered with parchment ; and it is held under one arm.

The *Awej* resembles two falconers drums fastened together. It is braced with strings of silk.

The *Dehl,* is another kind of drum well known.

The *Dheddeh,* is smaller than the *Dehl.*

The *Irdahwej,* is half the size of the *Awej.*

The *Duff,* is another kind of drum well known.

The *Khenjir,* is a little Duff hung round with small bells.

THE THIRD KIND OF INSTRUMENTS, THOSE OF PERCUSSION :—

The *Tal,* is a pair of brass cups, with broad mouths.

The *Kut-h Tal,* resemble small fish, and are made of wood or stone ; a set consists of four.

THE FOURTH KIND, OR WIND INSTRUMENTS :—

The *Shehna,* is the same as the Persian *Sirna,* or trumpet.

The *Mushk,* is composed of two reeds, perforated according to rule, and joined together in a leather bag. In the Persian language it is called *Nie Amban,* or the bagpipe.

The *Moorlee,* is a kind of flute.

The *Owpunk,* is a hollow tube, an ell long, with a hole in the centre, in which is placed a small reed

THE SEVENTH ADHYA, *Tirtya, or the Art of Dancing.*

The different kinds of singers.

Those who sing the ancient songs, which are the same everywhere, are called *Bykar ;* and those who teach them *Sehkar.*. The *Kerawunt* chiefly sing the *Dhoorpud.*

The *Dharhee* are those who sing the Penjaby songs, which they accompany with the *Dehdeh,* and *Kingerah.* Many of these sing in the field of battle the praises of heroes, to excite the troops to valiant actions. The *Kewall* are of this number, but sing chiefly the Dehly airs and Persian songs in the same style. The *Poorkeya,* the men accompany their voices with the *Awej,* and the women with the *Tal ;* formerly they sung the *Kirkeh,* but now the *Dhoorpud,* and such like. There are many beautiful women of this class. The *Duszun* are chiefly Penjaby women who play on the *Duff* and *Dehl,* and sing *Dhoorpud* and the *Sohlah,* or nuptial and birth-day songs. Formerly, they appeared only before women ; but now they will exhibit in public. The *Sezdehtaly,* the men of this class have large *Duffs,* and one of the women plays at once upon thirteen pair of *Tal,* placing them upon her wrists, backs of the hands, elbows, shoulders, back of the neck, and on the breast.

These are mostly natives of Gujerat and Mulwah. The *Nuthwah* dance with graceful motions, and sing and play upon the *Pukawej, Rebab,* and *Tal.*

The *Keertunnya* are *Brahmins* whose instruments are such as were in use amongst the ancient, *viz.,* the *Pukawej, Rebab,* and *Tal.* They are boys dressed like women, who sing the praise of Kishen. The *Bhugteyeh,* whose songs are the same as the last ; but they change their dresses, and are great mimics. They exhibit at night. The *Bhunweyeh* greatly resemble the last, but exhibit both in day and night. They dance in a surprizing manner in the compass of a brass dish, called in the Hindovee language *Talee.* They also sing: The *Bhena* play on the *Dhel* and *Tal,* and *sing:* They represent different animals: They draw up water through the nostrils: They run an iron spit down their throat into the stomach: They swallow a mixture of different kinds of grain, and then bring them up again separately, with other flights of hand. The *Kunjeree,* the men play on the *Pukawej, Rebab,* and *Tal,* and the women sing and dance: His Majesty calls them *Kunchenee.* The *Nut* play on the *Dhel* and *Tal,* dance upon the rope, and throw themselves into strange postures. The *Behroopee* exhibit in the day, and disguise themselves in such a manner, that old men seem to be youths, and youths old men, beyond detection.

The Jugglers are so dexterous, that they will seem to cut a man in pieces, and join him together again.

The AKAHREH, *or private Singing and Dancing.*

This is an entertainment given at night by great people to their own family. The performers are generally women of the house, who are instructed by proper people.

A set consists of four dancers, four singers, and four others who play the *Tal,* with two *Pukawej,* two *Owpunks,* one *Rebab,* one *Junter;* and two who stand by with torches. They are, for the most part, instructed by the *Nutwah,* who sometimes teach slaves of their own, and then sell them.

His Majesty is excessively fond of music, and has a perfect knowledge of its principles. This art, which the generality of people use as the means of obtaining sleep, serves to amuse him and keep him awake.

THE NAQQARAHKHANAH

AND

THE IMPERIAL MUSICIANS.

Translated from the original Persian.

BY

H. BLOCHMANN, Esq., M. A.

(From the "Ain-i-Akbari," Vol. I.)

AIN 19.

NAQQARAHKHANAH.

BY

H. BLOCHMANN, Esq., M. A.

Of musical instruments used in the *Naqqārahkhanah*, I may mention, 1, The *Kuwargah*, commonly called *Damāmah*; there are eighteen pairs of them more or less; and they give a deep sound. 2, The *Naqqārah*, twenty pairs, more or less. 3, The *Duhul*, of which four are used. 4, The *Karanā** is made of gold, silver, brass, and other metals: and they never blow fewer than four. 5, The *Surnā* of the Persian and Indian kinds; they blow nine together. 6, The *Nafir*, of the Persian, European and Indian kinds; they blow some of each kind. 7, The *Sing* is of brass, and made in the form of a cow's horn; they blow two together. 8, The *Sanj*, or cymbal, of which three pairs are used.

Formerly the band played four gharis before the commencement of the night, and likewise four gharis before daybreak; now they play first at midnight, when the sun commences his ascent, and the second time at dawn. One ghari before sun-rise, the musicians commence to blow the *Surná*, and wake up those that are asleep; and one ghari after sun-rise, they play a short prelude, when they beat the *Kuwargah* a little, whereupon they blow the *Karaná*, the *Nafir*, and the other instruments, without, however, making use of the *Naqqārah*; after a little pause the *Surnās* are blown again, the

* Or Karraná.

time of the music being indicated by the Nafirs. One hour later the *Naqqārahs* commence, when all musicians raise "the auspicious strain."* After this they go through the following seven performances :—1, The *Mursali*, which is the name of a tune played by the *Mursil;* and afterwards the *Bardāsht,* which consists likewise of certain tunes, played by the whole band. This is followed by a pianissimo, and a crescendo passing over into a diminuendo ; 2, The playing of the four tunes, called *Ikhlāti, Ibtidāi, Shírazi, Qalandári nígar quatrah,*† or *Nukhūd Qatrah,* which occupies an hour. 3, The playing of the old *Khwárizmite* tunes. Of these his Majesty has composed more than two hundred, which are the delight of young and old, especially the tunes *Jalálsháhí, Mahámir karkat (?)*, and the *Nauròzi.* 4, The swelling play of the cymbals. 5, The playing of *Ba miyān daur.* 6, The passing into the tunes *Azfar*, also called *Ráhi bálā*, after which comes a pianissimo. 7, The *Khwárizmite* tunes, played by the *Mursil,* after which he passes into the *Mursali* ; he then pauses, and commences the blessings on his Majesty, when the whole band strikes up a pianissimo. Then follows the reading of beautiful sentences and poems. This also lasts for an hour. Afterwards the *Surna*-players perform for another hour, when the whole comes to a proper conclusion.

His Majesty has such a knowledge of the science of Music as trained musicians do not possess ; and he is likewise an excellent hand in performing, especially on the *Naqqârah.*

* Probably blessings on his Majesty.

† Several of these names of melodies are unclear, and will in all probability, remain so. Perhaps the words *shírází qalandari*, "a hermit of Shiraz," belong to each other. *Nágar qatrah* means, behold the tear.

AIN 30.

THE IMPERIAL MUSICIANS.*

I CANNOT sufficiently describe the wonderful power of this talisman of knowledge (music). It sometimes causes the beautiful creatures of the harem of the heart to shine forth on the tongue, and sometimes appears in solemn strains by means of the hand and the chord. The melodies then enter through the window of the ear and return to their former seat, the heart, bringing with them thousands of presents. The hearers, according to their insight, are moved to sorrow or to joy. Music is thus of use to those who have renounced the world and to such as still cling to it.

His Majesty pays much attention to music, and is the patron of all who practise this enchanting art. There are numerous musicians at Court, Hindus, Irani, Turanis, Kashmiris, both men and women. The court musicians are arranged in seven divisions, one for each day in the week. When his Majesty gives the order, they let the wine of harmony flow, and thus increase intoxication in some, and sobriety in others.

* We have to distinguish *goyandah*, singers, from *khwanandahs*, chanters, and *sâzandahs*, players. The principal singers and musicians come from Gwaliar, Mashhad, Tabriz, and Kashmir. A few come from Transoxania. The schools in Kashmir had been founded by Irâni and Túrâni musicians, patronized by Zain ul-Abidin, king of Kashmir. The same of Gwaliar for its schools of music dates from the time of Rajah Mân Tunwar. During his reign lived the famous Naik Bakhshu, whose melodies are only second to those of Tansen. Bakhshu also lived at the court of Rajah Bikramajit, Man's son; but when his patron lost his throne, he went to Rajah Kirat of Kalinjar. Not long afterwards, he accepted a call to Gujrat, where he remained at the court of Sultan Bahadur (1526 to 1536, A. D.) Islem Shah also was a patron of music. His two great singers were Ram Doss and Mahapater. Both entered subsequently Akbar's service. Mahapater wa. once sent as ambassador to Mukund Deo of Orissa.

A detailed description of this class of people would be too difficult ; but I shall mention the principal musicians.

1. Miyan Tansen,* of Gwaliar. A singer like him has not been in India for the last thousand years.
2. Bábá Ramdas,† of Gwaliar, a singer.
3. Subhan Khan, of Gwaliar, a singer.
4. Srigyan Khan, of Gwaliar, a singer.
5. Miyan Chand, of Gwaliar, a singer.
6. Bichitr Khan, brother of Subhan Khan, a singer.
7. Muhammad Khan Dhari, sings.‡
8. Bir Mandal Khan, of Gwaliar, plays on the *Sarmandal*
9. Baz Bahadur, ruler of Malwah, a singer without rival.
10. Shihab Khan, of Gwaliar, performs on the *Bin*.
11. Daúd Dhari, sings.
12. Sarod Khan, of Gwaliar, sings.
13. Miyan Lal, of Gwaliar,|| sings.

* Regarding Tansen, or Tansain or Tansin, Ram Chand is said to have once given him one kror of tankahs as a present. Ibrahim Sur in vain persuaded Tansen to come to Agrah. Abulfazl mentions below his son Tantarang Khan ; and the Padishahnamah (11, 5—an interesting passage) mentions another son of the name of Bilas.

† Badaoni (11,42) says, Ram Dass came from Lakhnaw. He appears to have been with Bairam Khan during his rebellion, and he received once from him one lakh of tankahs, empty as Bairam's treasure chest was. He was first at the court of Islem Shah, and he is looked upon as second only to Tansen. His son Sur Das is mentioned below.

‡ Dhari means 'a singer,' a musician.

|| Jahángir says in the Tuzuk that Lál Kaláwant (or Kalanwat, *i. e.*, the singer) died in the 3rd year of his reign, "sixty or rather seventy years old. He had been from his youth in my father's service. One of his concubines, on his death, poisoned herself with opium. I have rarely seen such an attachment among Muhammadan women."

14. Tantarang Khan, son of Miyan Tansen, sings.
15. Mulla Is-haq Dharí, sings.
16. Usta Dost, of Mashhad, plays on the flute *(nai).*
17. Nának Jarjú, of Gwaliar, a singer.
18. Purbin Khán, his son, plays on the *Bín.*
19. Sur Das, son of Bábú Ram Das, a singer.
20. Cháud Khan, of Gwaliar, sings.
21. Rangsen, of Agrah, sings.
22. Shaikh Dáwan Dhari, performs on the *Karaná.*
23. Rahmatullah, brother of Mullá Is-háq, (No. 15), a singer.
24. Mir Sayyid Alí, of Mashhad, plays on the *Ghichak.*
25. Ustą Yúsuf, of Harát, plays on the *Tambúráh.*
26. Qásim, surnamed Koh—bar.* He has invented an instrument, intermediate between the *Qübüz* and the *Rabáb.*
27. Tásh Beg, of Qipcháq, plays on the *Qübüz.*
28. Sultán Hafiz Hussain, of Mashhad, chants.
29. Bahrám Qulí, of Harát, plays on the *Ghichak.*
30. Sultán Háshim, of Mashhad, plays on the *Tambúráh.*
31. Ustá Shah Muhammad, plays on the *Surná.*
32. Ustá Muhammad Amin, plays on the *Tambúráh.*
33. Hafiz Khwajah' Ali, of Mashhad, chants.
34. Mir' Abdullah, brother of Mir Abdul Hai, plays the *Qánún.*

* Koh-bar, as we know from the Pádishahnamah (1., 6, p. 335) is the name of a Chaghtai tribe. The *Nafais-ul-Maásir* mentions a poet the name of Muhammad Qasim Kohbar, whose *nom-de-plume* was Cabri. *Vide* Sprenger's catalogue, p. 50 (where we have to read *Koh-bar,* for *Guh-paz*).

35. Pirzádah,* nephew of Mir Dawám, of Khurásán, sings and chants.

36. Ustá Muhammad Hussain, plays the *Tambúrah*.†

* Pizzadah, according to Badaoni (111, 318) was from Sabzwar. He wrote poems under the *iakhalluc* of Liwai. He was killed in 995 at Lahor, by a wall falling on him.

† The Maásir i Rahimi mentions the following musicians in the service of the Khan Khanán—Aglic Muhammad Nai, son of Háji Ismáil, of Tabriz; Mauláná Acwáti, of Tabriz; Ustáb Mirzá, Ali Fathagi; Mauláná Sharaf of Nishápúr, a brother of the poet Naziri (p. 579), Muhammad Múmin, *alias* Háfizak, a Tambúrah-player; and Hafiz Nazr, from transoxania, a good singer. The Tuzuk and the Iqbálnámah mention the following singers of Jahángir's reign—Jahángírdad; Chatr Khan; Parwizdad; Khurramdad; Mak'hú; Hamzan. During Shahjahán's reign we find Jangát'h, who received from Shahjahán the title of *Kabrái;* Dírang Khan; and Lál Khan; who got the title of *Gunasamudra* (ocean of excellence). Lál Khan was son-in-law to Bilas, son of Tansen. Jagnath and Dirang Khan were both weighed in silver, and received each 4,500 Rupees.

Aurangzib abolished the singers and musicians, just as he abolished the court historians. Music is against the Muhammadan law. Khan Khan (11,213) tells a curious incident which took place after the order had been given. The court-musicians brought a bier in front of the Jharok'hah (the window where the emperors used to shew themselves daily to the people,) and wailed so loud as to attract Aurangzib's attention. He came to the window, and asked whom they had on the bier. They said, "Melody is dead, and we are going to the graveyard." "Very well," said the emperor, "make the grave deep, so that neither voice nor echo may issue from it." A short time after, the Jharok'hah also was abolished.

ORIENTAL MUSIC.

THE MUSIC OF HINDUSTAN OR INDIA.

BY

WILLIAM C. STAFFORD.

ORIENTAL MUSIC.

THE MUSIC OF HINDUSTAN OR INDIA.

BY

WILLIAM C. STAFFORD.

SIR WILLIAM JONES divides Asia into five great nations—the Indians, Arabians, Persians, Chinese, and Tartars ; all of whom, except the last, have their characteristic and national music. In Tartary he found few indications of musical knowledge ; though some of the branches of that vast mother of nations undoubtedly possessed great skill in the science.

India is one of those countries which lays claim to a very high antiquity, and to a very early proficiency in the arts and sciences. M. Bailly supposes the Indians cultivated Astronomy 3101 years before Christ. The computation, however, is irreconcilable with the commonly received opinion of the age of the world ; and we merely allude to it as a proof that the country which we now call Hindustan, was amongst the earliest settlements of the sons of Noah, and that a people renowed for learning and intelligence, dwelt there. "India," says Mr. Orme, "has been inhabited, from the earliest antiquity, by a people who have no resemblance, either in their figure or manners, with any of the nations contiguous to them ;" and, as Sir William Jones observes, however degenerate the Hindus may now appear, we cannot but suppose, "that in some early day, they were splendid in arts and arms, happy in government, wise in legislation, and eminent in knowledge." We shall not, however, pursue the inquiry into their antiquity, nor into their proficiency, in arts and sciences, except to give a sketch, as succinct as circumstances will allow, of their musical pretensions.

The Hindus believe, that music was invented by Brahma himself or by his active power, Sareswati, the goddess of speech ; and that their mythological son, Narad, invented the *vina*, the oldest musical instrument in use in Hindustan, —which was also called *Cach'hapi* or *Testudo*. Among inspired mortals, the first musician is believed to have been the sage Bharat, who was the inventor, they say, of *Natacs*, or dramas, represented with songs and dances, and the author of a musical system that bears his name. There appear to have been in the ancient Hindu music, four principal *matas*, or systems, and almost every kingdom and province had a peculiar style of melody, and very different names for the modes, as well as a different arrangement and enumeration of them.

In the sacred books of the Hindus, their ancient system of music is said still to be preserved. These, however, have never been translated ; and probably never will be : nor do we think they would repay the time and trouble which such a task would require. To the learned natives, however, the *theory* of the art appears to be known, though the *practice* is entirely lost.

The Hindus have thirty-six ancient melodies, of a very peculiar nature, called *raugs*, [or ragas] and *raugines*, [or ragines.] There are various popular traditions as to their origin ; and many miraculous powers are assigned to them. "Of the six raugs," says Sir William Ouseley,* "the first

* *Oriental Collec ions.*

five owe their origin to the god Mahadeo, who produced them from his five heads. Parbuttee, his wife, constructed the sixth; and the thirty *raugines* were composed by Brahma. Thus, of celestial invention, these melodies are of a peculiar genus; and of the three ancient genera of the Greeks most resemble the *enharmonic.* A considerable difficulty is found in setting to music the *raugs* and *raugines,* as our system does not supply notes, or signs, sufficiently expressive of the almost imperceptible elevations and depressions of the voice in these melodies; of which the time is broken and irregular, the modulations frequent, and very wild. Whatever magic was in the touch, when Orpheus swept his Lyre or Timotheus filled his softly-breathing flute, the effects said to have been produced by two of the six *raugs,* are even more extraordinary than any of those ascribed to the modes of the ancients. Mia Tousine, a wonderful musician in the time of the Emperor Akber, sung one of the night *raugs* at midday; the powers of his music were such, that it instantly became night; and the darkness extended in a circle round the palace, as far as the sound of his voice could be heard." Another of these *raugs*—the *raug Dheepuck*—possessed the singular property of occasioning the destruction by fire of whoever attempted to sing it. Akber is said to have commanded one of his musicians, named Naik Gopal, to sing it, and he, obliged to obey, repaired to the river Jumna in which he plunged himself up to the neck. As he warbled the wild and magical notes, flames burst from his body and consumed him to ashes; the effect of the third—the *Maig Mullar raug*—was to produce immediate rain, and tradition says, "a singing girl once, by exerting the powers of her voice, in this *raug,* drew down from the clouds timely and refreshing showers on the parched rice-crops of Bengal, and thereby averted the horrors of famine from the *paradise of region.*"* Of course no traveller now meets with singers possessed of these wonderful properties; but if he inquire for them in the west of India, he is told they are to be found in Bengal: in Bengal the inquirer is sent back to the west of India on the search.

The ancient musical instruments of India were of the lyre, the flute, and the drum kind, and it would appear that the violin was in use in some parts as far back as the early part of the seventeenth century.

"In a collection of Voyages and Travels, collected for the library of Lord Orford, there is one entitled, 'A true and almost incredible report of an Englishman, that, being cast-away in the good ship called the *Ascension,* in Cambaya, the farthest part of the East Indies, travelled by land through many unknown kingdoms,' &c., &c., by Captain Corvette, 1607-8, which contains many curious particulars of the people amongst whom he was thrown; and what is to our purpose here contains a passage, clearly describing the existence of the ancient violin. He arrives at Buckar 'standing on an island, in a gallant fresh river,' where dwelt a people called the Bullochies, '*men*-eators' and worshippers of the sun. The adjoining country of the Puttans was little better, for they met the travellers ***with fiddles in their hands,*** as if to welcome them, yet robbed and nearly murdered them."†

Francis Fowke Esq., in a letter to Sir William Jones, describes an Hindu instrument called the Been (or *vina* before mentioned) which is similar in construction to the Spanish Guitar. "The style of music," he says, "on this instrument

* Sir W. Ouseley's *Oriental Collections,* Vol. i., p. 74.

† *Quarterly Musical Review.*

is in general that of great execution ; I could hardly ever discover any rational air or subject. The music seems to consist of a number of detached passages, some very regular in their ascent and descent; and those that are played softly are both uncommon and pleasing. The open wires are struck from time to time in a manner that I think prepares the ear for a change in the modulation, to which the uncommonly full and fine tones of these notes greatly contribute; but the ear is always disappointed." He adds, "were there any other circumstances respecting the Indian music which led to the supposition, that it has at some period been much superior to the present practice, the style, scale, and antiquity of this instrument, would, I think, greatly confirm the supposition." There is an excavation at Mahabalipatam, described by Mr. Goldingham, in the Asiatic Researches,* which he imagines was originally intended as it is now used "as a shelter for travellers. A scene of sculpture fronts the entrance, said to represent Crishna attending the herds of Ananda. One of the group represents a man diverting an infant by playing on a flute, and holding the instrument as we do." In the same papers there is an account of the pagoda at Permuttum, on which there are several groups of sculptured figures; one of which represents two camels, "with a person on each, beating the naqua, or great drum."†

What we have hitherto said, must be considered as referring chiefly to the ancient music of Hindustan. Of the modern Hindu music and the sensations it excites, as Sir William Ouseley remarks, we can speak with greater accuracy. It is of the *diatonic* genera and "many of the

* *Asiatic Researches*, Vol. V.

† *Ibid.* p. 313.

Hindu melodies possess the plaintive simplicity of the Scotch and Irish, and others a wild originality, pleasing beyond description. Counterpoint seems not to have entered, at any time, into the system of Indian music. It is not alluded to in the M. S. treatises which I have hitherto persued; nor have I discovered that any of our ingenious Orientalists speak of it as being known in Hindustan."*

Sir William Jones says, "The Hindu system of music has, I believe, been formed on truer principles than our own; and all the skill of the native composers is directed to the great object of their art, *the natural expression of strong passions*, to which melody, indeed, is often sacrificed, though some of their tunes are pleasing even to an European ear."† If we do not admit Sir William's eulogy in the fullest sense, we must certainly allow, that many of the Hindu airs possess great merit. Dr. Crotch has inserted several of them in his "Specimens of Various Styles of Music;" some of which are original in their formation, and others are marked by a peculiar and pleasing tenderness. It would appear, that music is generally cultivated in India; and in central India, according to Sir John Malcolm, most of the villages have attached to them men and women of the Nutt or Bamallee tribes, who appear to be a kind of wandering gipsies, and have attached to them rude musicians and minstrels, whose music and songs form the chief entertainment of the peasantry. These musicians are divided into two classes, Chárims and Bháts; they boast of a celestial origin, and exercise an influence of a very powerful description over the people.

* *Oriental Collections.*

† Sir William Jones's *Second Anniversary Discourse before the Asiatic Society of Calcutta.* Works, Vol. III, p. 17.

In an account of Penang, given by Wilkinson in his "Sketches of China," it appears that the inhabitants cultivate a species of extempore song, rudely imitative of the art of improvisatrizing, so well known in Italy.

"Upon entering one of their boats, you immediately become a subject for their panegyric and eulogium ; and every part of your dress is severally described and sung in chorus by the sable songsters, in their savage polacca, which, although possessing more discord than harmony, has a kind of melancholic dissonancy, not altogether unpleasing to the ear."*

The Hindus have a Gamut "consisting of seven notes like our own, which, being repeated in their several *ast'haus*, or octaves, form a scale of twenty-one natural notes. The seven notes which form the Gamut are expressed *sa, ra, ga, ma, pa, da, na,* or *sa, ri, ga, ma, pa, dha, ni* ; and, when written at length, stand thus : *kauredge ; rekhub ; gundhaur ; muddhum ; punchum ; dhawoth ; neekhaudh.* Of these seven words, (the first excepted) the initial letters are used, in writing music, to express the notes. Instead of the initial of the first, or lowest *kauredge,* that of the word *sur* is used, which signifies, emphatically, the *note* being, as it were, the foundation of the others, and named *swara,* or the *sound,* from the important office which it bears in the scale."†

Sir William Jones says, "As to the notation, since every Indian consonant includes, by its nature, the short vowel *a,* five of the sounds are denoted by single consonants, and the two others have different short vowels, taken from their

* Letter on 'Oriental Music,' in the *Quarterly Musical Review and Magazine*, Vol. viii., p. 20.

† Sir William Ouseley's *Oriental Collections*, Vol. i., p. 76.

full names; by substituting long vowels, the *time* of each note is doubled, and other marks are used for a further elongation of them. The octaves above and below the mean scale, the connexion and acceleration of notes, the graces of execution, or manner of finger in the instrument, are expressed very clearly by small circles and ellipses, by little chains, by curves, by straight lines, horizontal or perpendicular, and by crescents, all in various positions. The close of a strain is distinguished by a lotus flower; but the time and measure are determined by the prosody of the verse, and by the comparative length of each syllable, with which every note, or assemblage of notes, respectively corresponds. If I understand the native musicians, they have not only the chromatic, but even the second, or new enharmonic genus."*

The regular Gamut of the Hindus applies very nearly to our major mode; *ut, ri, mi, fa sol, la si, ut.* When the same syllables are applied to notes, which compose our minor mode, they are distinguished by epithets expressing the change.

The Hindus reckon twenty-two *S'rati's,* or quarters and thirds of a tone, in their octave. Their modes are very numerous; in the days of *Crishna,* they say they amounted to sixteen thousand. One of their musical authors, SOMA, enumerates nine hundred and sixty possible variations of the musical scale, but he selects from them, as applicable to practice, only twenty-three primary modes. It should be observed, that the Hindu word *raga,* which is rendered mode, properly signifies a passion, or affection of the mind; each mode being intended, according to BHERAT'S definition of it, to move one or other of our simple or mixed affections.

* *On the Musical Modes of the Hindus.* Works Vol. iv., p. 157.

Mr. Paterson, in his notice of the "*Gamas, or Musical Scales of the Hindus,*" expresses an opinion, that the ancient Hindus were confined, in their music, to thirty-six melodies, *viz.*, "the six ragas, and thirty ragines," which were fixed respectively to particular seasons of the year, and times of the day and night, and probably were, in early times, applied to the service of different deities. Now the Hindus would consider a performer who sung a raga out of its appropriate season, as an ignorant pretender to the character of a musician.

The principal instruments in use in modern Hindustan, are the *tamboura* which has a body formed of a gourd, with a long neck, or finger-board, and three strings, two of which are turned in unison, and one an octave below. These strings are struck with a plectrum, shaped like a heart. The *sauringas*, or *syringas*, resemble an European violin. The strings are of gut; they are sometimes four, and sometimes five in number: and they are tuned in fourths, played with a bow, and stopped on the finger-board in the manner of a violin; the Cashmerian *sauringas* are larger, and are held and played in the manner of that instrument.

The Hindu *cithara* is furnished with wires, and is played with a bow. The common pulsatile instrument in use is a small *kettle-drum*. Two of these instruments are fastened to the sash which goes round the waist, and are beaten with the fingers, both hands being used.

In those parts of India which are under British dominion, the same style of music is cultivated which is current in the mother country; and Calcutta, in particular, has been visited by some distinguished artists, both vocal and instrumental.

The orchestra of the theatre in that city,—in 1824, consisted, besides the violins, of a double bass, two violon cellos, two bassoons, two flutes, two clarionets, two horns, two trumpets, and kettle-drums. It was under the direction of Mr. Delmer ; and the most distinguished amongst the singers were Dr. Wilson, Mr. and Mrs. Bianchi Lacy with Mesdames Cooke, Kelly and Miss Williams. Concerts were given, sometimes by foreigners, but generally by Englishmen, the price of admission being sixteen Rupees. The charge of the higher class of professors for lessons was from eight to sixteen Rupees.

MUSIC OF THE HINDUS.

BY

J. NATHAN.

(From "Musurgia Vocalis.")

MUSIC OF THE HINDUS.

BY

J. NATHAN.

THE Hindus considered music invented for the purpose of raising the mind by devotion to the felicity of the divine nature, and have airs faithfully handed down by their ancestors in *Sastras*, where the whole science of harmony is personified in six *Ragas*, or, as we may call them, major modes ; to each of which is attached six *Ragnis*, or minor modes of the same strain, representing so many princes with six wives to each. But as the Indian allegories speak much more expressively to the eye than to the ear, we learn from appropriate paintings to the several modes, that the performance of each undivided melody is exclusively restricted to some season of the year, or point of time in the twenty-four hours, at which only it is opportune or admissible.*

I here omit a full discussion of Hindu music, because the pages of the Asiatic Researches have been already devoted

* According to Hindu belief in the absurd account given in the Sanscrit language, the supreme God having created the world by the word of his mouth, formed a female deity named Bawaney, who, in an enthusiasm of joy and praise brought forth three eggs. From these were produced three male deities, named Brimah, Vishnou, Sheevah. Brimah was endowed with the power of creating the things of this world, Vishnou with that of cherishing them, and Sheevah with that of restraining and correcting them. Seraswaty, the wife of Brimah, presides over music, harmony and eloquence ; she is also said to be the inventress of the letters called *Devanagry*, by which the divine will was first promulgated among mankind. This goddess is supposed to have a number of inferior deities, called *Rags* or *Ragas*,

to the inquiry. Lieutenant-Colonel Tod, however, imagines the Hindus to have derived the notion of the seven notes from the seven planets, whence they obtained an octave with its semitones. It is also possible (he avers) that as they converted the ascending and descending notes into Grahas or planetary bodies, they may have added them to the harmonious numbers, and thus produced the No-Ragini or nine modes of music, so called from the nine passions excited by the powers of Harmony. He believes, that they had not only the diatonic, but the chromatic scale ; for, although the latter has been referred to Timotheus in the time of Alexander, it is more probable, that it was brought from the banks of the Indus.

acting in subordination to her ; they preside over each mode. The Ragas are accompanied each with five Raginies or Ragnis, female deities or nymphs of harmony ; they have each eight so is or genii, and a distinct season is appointed for the music of each *Rag*, during which only it can be sung or played, and this at distinct and stated hours of the day or night.

There once existed, say the Hindus, a musical mode belonging to *Deipec* or Cupid, the inflamer; but it is now lost, and a musician who attempted to restore it was consumed with fire from heaven.

T) Nared, the son of Brimah, is ascribed the invention of a fretted instrument named *Bene*.

SCIENTIFIC INTELLIGENCE.

(*From the "Journal of the Asiatic Society,"*
Vol. XXV., 1834.)

WILLARD'S TREATISE

ON THE

MUSIC OF HINDUSTAN.

WITH the exception of Sir William Jones' valuable and learned essay in the third volume of the Asiatic Researches, we have had little information on the music of the Hindus, beyond a notice of the adaptation of the rags to the different seasons and hours in Gilchrist's Hindustani Grammar, and occasional cursory (generally disparaging) mention of the existing practice of the art at nâches, in noisy processions, or on the Ghâts, by travellers ill capable of appreciating the peculiarities of the science of sweet sounds among the nations of the East. The instruments themselves are pretty well known; Solwyn's magnificent work contains accurate drawings of most of them, which have been copied into other more popular works.

The present volume, therefore, a child of long promise, and consequently of high expectation, was received with avidity, as the author was known to be a skilful performer himself on several instruments, and to have enjoyed local advantages of observation from his appointment at the native court of the Nawab of Banda: neither has his little volume disappointed us, being a familiar and pleasing account of his subject, intended for the general reader, and rendered more inviting by frequent allusion to the music of the West both ancient and modern. An author in the present day labours under evident disadvantages, in attempting to describe what the music of the Hindus was in the flourishing period of their literature and religion, when poets and priests were also musicians, modulating and singing their own compositions. To have persued the subject as an antiquary, would have required extensive knowledge of Sanskrit, and sufficient familiarity with the varied metre of its heroic, and erotic poetry, to do without aid from native professors; for the present cultivators of the science are for the chief part of the most ignorant and abandoned classes; so that the very art is held to be disreputable among the more respectable ranks, just as among us the noble drama is forsworn by many, from the abuses which have crept into our theatres. Still in these degenerate days there are exceptions, and the sacred *Vin* may occasionally be heard pouring forth a strain of rhapsody that carries the imagination back to the fabulous age of *Rishes* and *Gandharbas.*

Our author treats successively of the Gamut, of time, of oriental melody, rags and raginees (giving a long catalogue of compound rags) instruments, vocal compositions, and of the peculiarities of manners and customs exemplified in the songs of Hindustan. Then follows a brief account of the most celebrated musicians, a copious glossary of musical terms, and copper-plate tables of the varieties of time or metre with their native characters and values.

"The musicians of Hindustan never appear to have had any determined pitch by which their instruments were regulated, each person tuning his own to a certain height, adapted by guess, to the power of the instrument and quality of the strings, the capacity of the voice intended to be accompanied, and other adventitious circumstances. From this it may be observed that it is immaterial which note is designated by which letter." Sir William Jones makes the Kharaj, or key-note, on the *Vin*, to correspond with A, but the author thinks it would be more systematic to tune it to *ut* or C, the key-note of the natural scale of Europe. This depends upon whether it was the intention to speak of the diatonic intervals, or of the absolute pitch of the instrument. "The notes of an octave are divided into 22 minor sub-divisions instead of twelve semitones, as is done with us: these are called *Srúti*, and each of them has a distinct name assigned as follow :—

	Soor.	*Abbreviated for Solfaing.*	*Srutis comprised.*
C	*Kharaj*	*Sa*	Butra, Cumodutee, Mundrica, Chhundavuttee.
D	*Rikhab*	*Ri*	Duyavatee, Reictica, Runjunee.
E	*Gandhar*	*Ga*	Sivee, Crodhee
F	*Maddham*	*Ma*	Bugra, Prusarunee, Preetee, Marjunee.
G	*Panchum*	*Pa*	Kshuttee, Recta, Sidpunee, Ulapunee.
A	*Dhyvat*	*Dha*	Mundutee, Rohinee, Rummya.
B	*Nikhad*	*Ni*	Oogra, Joobhanka.

The intervals between the first and second, fourth and fifth, and fifth and sixth notes are divided into four parts; those between the second and third, and sixth and seventh, each into three parts; and those between the third and fourth, and seventh and eighth, which with us are reckoned semitones, each into two parts." Captain Willard asserts under the division 'time,' notwithstanding the authority of Tartini and Dr. Burney, that no musician can execute measures of five notes in a bar—"There is *beautiful melody* in Hindustan comprising *seven* and other unequal number of notes in a measure, and that they *have* musicians in abundance that are able to execute it. We should much doubt this fact.

Indian Harmony is mostly confined to a monotonous repetion of the key-note during the flights cf their vocal or instrumental melody ; for it is melody which has ever constituted the soul of the national music in India as among the Greeks and Egyptains. Our author has the following general observations on this subject.

1. Hindustani melodies are short, lengthened by repetition and variations.

2. They all partake of the nature of what is denominated by us Rondo, the piece being invariably concluded with the first strain, and sometimes with the first bar, or at least with the first note of that bar.

3. A bar, or measure, or a certain number of measures, is frequently repeated with slight variation, almost *ad lib.*

4. There is as much liberty allowed with respect to pauses, which may be lengthened at pleasure, provided the time be not disturbed. The author corrects Sir William Jones' rendering of *Rág* by the expression, 'mode,' or key, for which the Hindus have the distinct word *t'hat* :—*rág* signifies rather '*tune*' or '*air*.'

The personification of *rágs* and *ráginees*, and the series of pictures called ragmalahs, are too well known to require any remark ; it would have increased the interest of the work to European readers had the descriptions of these been accompanied by engravings of a selected series of drawings, but we are aware that this could not have been easily done in India. The sixteen melodies set to music (always excepting the impossible 7-quaver airs) form, however, an interesting part of the author's labour ; the effect of metre is strikingly marked in some of these airs.

We cannot resist pointing out the close resemblance of the 9th (a Persian ghazal) to the hexameter verse; by transposing the first and second section in each line and adding one long foot the metre becomes perfect:

Ashvagari dil burda za man (to) jalva numái,
Kajkulahi zar rin kamari (ham) tanga qubái,
Man bavasalash ky rasam in (ast) bas ki barahash,
Khaka shavam rozi (ta) bosam (man) kafi pai.

which may be anglicized in the metre of the original:—

(Dilburda za man-ashvagari—jalva numá, &c.)

Oh thief of my heart, eye me not so—shining so brightly
With head dress awry—girdle of gold—boddice bound tightly
When, when shall we meet! Ah not in life—not till my ashes
Lie strew'd in thy path—kissing thy feet—treading so lightly.

CATALOGUE OF INDIAN MUSICAL INSTRUMENTS.

BY

COL. P. T. FRENCH.

(From the Proceedings of the Royal Irish Academy, Vol. IX., Part I.)

CATALOGUE OF INDIAN MUSICAL INSTRUMENTS,

PRESENTED BY

COLONEL P. T. FRENCH.

CAPTAIN MEADOWS TAYLOR read the following :—

Having been called upon to describe the valuable Collection of Musical Instruments of India, presented by Colonel P. T. French to the Academy, I will now proceed to do so, in the order in which they have been numbered. I have to regret that I have not been able to tune any of them : had this been possible, their uses and effects would have been much more readily understood than they can be by mere description ; but the greater number of these instruments require steel wire strings of a quality made especially for them by wire-drawers in India, which is not obtainable in this city. I have therefore to depend upon descriptive detail alone, with notices of the uses to which they are put by native musicians of India, according to my own experience.

NOS. 1, 2, 3, in CATALOGUE. NATIVE NAME झं (Jhang).

METAL CYMBALS OF VARIOUS KINDS.

These are used as accompaniments to all native music ; but in the north more frequently in connexion with that of a religious character than in the south, where in all shapes they are universal. The larger kinds, whether of silver or of bell metal, when clashed together, have an effect similar to those in use in our own military bands, and form fitting unison with the hoarse bray of trumpets, the shrill pipes and flageolets, the drums, and large choruses of male voices, by which the temple music, chaunts hymns, and the like, is generally executed. Cymbals differ in form and sound: some have the effect of large gongs; others of a softer and more tinkling character, are used with softer music. In all, however, the effect for the most part is to assist in marking the time, which is done very skilfully and evenly by the performers.

In the south of India another kind of cymbal is used, which is in the form of two cups, of bell metal, and of which there is no specimen here. Of these one is held in the left palm, secured by a cord passed round the hand, and is struck by the other, which is held loosely in the right. Players on these cymbals are extremely dexterous, and produce a not unpleasing accompaniment to the voice, or to instrumental music, by striking the cups together in such a manner, outside, inside, and upon their edges, as to form notes in accordance with the voice, or the other instruments by which it may be accompanied. This cymbal accompaniment is played with more execution than may be conceived possible from the nature of the instrument. I have heard *professors* even play solos upon it, which, if not very intelligible as to tune, were at least curious in execution and diversity of *time*, as suited to the various styles of music. Cymbals are used both by Hindu and Mahomedan musicians.

4. थाला (*Thalla*).—GONG.

This needs no particular description. It is beaten in temple music, or as calls to sacrifice or ceremony at different hours of the day, and is used by many of the professional religious mendicants of the country, more especially those who are accompanied by bulls or goats which perform tricks. The thalla or gong, is not used as an accompaniment to vocal music, nor to any but the loud, crashing and generally dissonant music of temple ceremonies. It is not used by Mahomedans except when struck as a clock, noting the hours of the day as shown by the water-clock or hour-glass, and in this respect indeed it is common both to Hindus and Mahomedans.

5. गंटे (*Gunte*).—Bell.

As a musical instrument, the bell is used somewhat in the same manner as the cymbals before mentioned, but more rarely. No ceremony of sacrifice or oblation, however, is ever performed without preliminary tinkling of the bell, which is repeated at certain intervals according to the ritual. No set of sacrificial utensils is complete without one. To describe the use of the hand bell at particular periods of ceremonial observance, would lead me into digressions which have no reference to the subject in hand ; but there can be no doubt that the practice of using it is as ancient as Hinduism itself, and the rituals, liturgies, and works on ceremonial observances, define the use to be made of it. By Mahomedans, the use of the bell in any form that I am aware of is unknown.

6. घुंघरू (*Goongooroo*).—Ankle Bells.

These strings of small bells are used by all dancers, male or female, Hindu or Mahomedan. They are tied round the leg, above the ankle, and produce a faint clashing sound as the feet move in steps, which mingles not unmusically, with the dance music, or songs which accompany the dance ; and they not only serve to mark the time, but to keep the dancer or singer in perfect time and accord with the musicians. These bells are the symbols of their profession with all dancers and singers, and to some extent are held sacred. No dancer ties them on his or her ankles before performance, without touching his or her forehead and eyes with them, and saying a short prayer or invocation to a patron saint or divinity, Hindu or Mahomedan. Nor is it possible, after a female singer or dancer has once been invested with them—a ceremony which is very solemnly performed, and attended with much cost—to abandon the professional life so adopted. He or she "has tied on the bells," is even a proverb, to signify that the person alluded to has devoted himself or herself to a purpose from which it is impossible to recede. Strings of these small bells are also used for horses, and tied round the fetlocks of prancing chargers with gay tinsel ribbons or pieces of cloth, also round the necks of lap-dogs, and some of a large size round those of a favourite plough or cart bullock. The latter are identical with sleigh bells. No post runner in India travels without a string of them tied on the end of his pole on which is slung the leather bag he carries ; and on a still night their clashing sound, besides being heard at a great distance serves to scare away wild beasts and to cheer the runner on his lonely path.

7. सिंग (*Seeng*).—Horn.

Used universally through India for signals, watch setting, processions, and the like, both by Mahomedans and Hindus, though the performers. for the most part, are Hindus of low caste. In every village of Central or Southern India, it is the business of one or more of the watchmen to blow the horn at sunset, and again at certain hours during the night, or when the watchmen go their stated rounds. In large cities every *mahulla* or ward has a horn-blower attached to its night watchmen or police; and there is seldom a guard or detachment of native irregular troops without one. In all processions, temple services, and especially at marriages and other festive occasions, this horn is indispensable; and wailing blasts for the dead are played upon it at the funerals of Hindus of the lower classes and castes, or equally so at the cremations of Hindu princes.

No native authority traverses the country without one, frequently several, in his train; and as towns or villages are approached, the great man's advent is heralded by flourishes of the instrument, blown by the performer, who struts at the head of the cavalcade. These blasts are answered by others from the town or village gate, whence the local authorities come out to meet the visitor and present their offerings of welcome. On these occasions, the horn-blowers on both sides vie with each other in producing their grandest effects, and the discordance is generally indescribable.

Itinerant mendicants of many classes use this instrument, both Hindu and Mahomedan; and by the men in charge of droves of cattle carrying grain or merchandize, such as Brinjarees, Comptees, and others, it is sounded at intervals along the road to cheer up their bullocks and keep them from straggling, as well as at their departure from or arrival at one of their stages.

In tone a good Seeng, or horn, is not unlike a common bugle, but has much more power, and in the hands of a good player much more compass. In playing the high notes in many of the calls, shrill quivering cadences are produced, which have a startling and peculiarly wild effect as heard from the walls of some ancient fortress, or from village towers and gates as night falls, and more especially in the otherwise unbroken stillness of night.

I have never heard tunes played or attempted by native horn-blowers, though the modulations of the tones of the instruments are frequently sweet and pleasing; nor are they used in concert with other music, but always independently, as I have already explained. There can be no doubt, I think, that this kind of horn is of very ancient origin and use; and I observe in the Museum of the Academy one ancient Irish or Celtic instrument, if not indeed others, identical with the Indian Seeng, and which, like it, were most probably used in battle, or for the purposes already detailed. In shape, in the peculiar adaptation of their joints, and in the form of the mouth-piece, they are identical.

8. तुतुरि (*Tootoore*).—Small Trumpet.

Used chiefly in religious music at temples, and in other religious ceremonies. It always accompanies the next in order, and may be called the tenor trumpet, the other being the bass. No calls or modulations are blown upon it, but it is sounded at intervals, several being employed, with a wild shrill effect, in concert with the pipes on which the tunes are played.

9. कर्ना (*Kurna*).—Large Trumpet.

Like the preceding, this is used chiefly in religious processions, or in festivals in honour of local divinities. It has a few hoarse bass notes, which contrast with the shrill tenor of the Tootoore, and appear incapable of other modulation.

These instruments are almost invariably played by Brahmins or priests attached to Hindu temples, and by persons attached to the retinues of the Gooroos, Swamies, or spiritual princes of the country, who possess large ecclesiastical jurisdiction, and are provided with them, as a mark of high rank, which is not allowable to others. Occasionally, also, they are met with in the Nobuts, or musical establishments attached by royal permission to nobles of high rank, Mahomedan as well as Hindu; and they are sounded at the five stated periods of the regular daily performance; but they do not exist in all cases, for there are distinctions in the classes of instruments, according to the rank of persons privileged to play the Nobut, which involve the presence or otherwise of the *kurna*, those of the highest rank only being able to use it. The Nobut, as a peculiar institution of native music, will be explained hereafter. The *kurna*, or large trumpet, is esteemed by all Brahmins to be the most ancient instrument of music in existence, and the sound of it to be especially pleasing to the gods, in various particular ceremonies, and at solemn parts of sacrifice. I need not, however, occupy the time of the Academy with such legends.

It is perhaps worthy of remark, however, that in the procession on the Arch of Titus at Rome, one of these trumpets, precisely similar in shape to that of this collection, is being carried with the sacred candle-stick with seven branches, and other trophies from the Temple at Jerusalem; and thus it may be inferred that it was used in the ancient Jewish ceremonies.

10. होलार चा सुनाडे (*Holar cha Soonai*).—11, 12, *Do.*

Tenor or Second.—Reed Pipes.

These instruments, which all belong to the same class, are of universal use in all parts of India. What bagpipes are to Scotland or Ireland, these pipes are to India. Although flageolets in appearance, their sound is precisely similar to that of the bagpipes, only perhaps more powerful, and in the hands of good players more melodious. They have seven and eight holes, respectively, and thus would appear to have no great compass; but in execution, whether from the effect of the lips and tongue upon the reed mouth-piece, or the manner of fingering upon the holes, combinations are formed which include semitones and quarter notes, and thus the expression of chromatic passages *ad libitum*, of which native prayers are very fond, is given, which, in reality, are very effective. From their great power of sound, these pipes are unpleasant if the performers be near; but at a distance in the open air, and specially among mountains, the effect is much subdued, and often attains much wild beauty and softness. As I have already stated, their use is almost universal. They are, in fact, the only regular out-door instruments of Indian music, and are employed on all occasions, whether in domestic or public religious ceremonials, processions in festivals, temple music, and the like; and the music played upon them varies with the occasion on which they are used. Marches, and military music exceedingly like pibrochs in character—pieces for marriages, for rejoicings, for funerals, welcomings, departures—familiar ballad airs, and the stated music of the Nobut, have all separate modes and effects. In the Mahratta country, in which I know them best, the simple melodies of the people, joyous or plaintive, are performed with a style of execution which is often surprising; and combinations of musical effect are introduced which are equally curious and interesting.

In the Nobut or honorary band of musicians attached to noblemen, temples, or shrines of saints, Mahomedan or

Hindu, the best performers obtainable are generally employed; and the performance is accompanied by drums, tenor and bass, and large kettle-drums, which are tuned with the pipes, and form useful aids to the general effect. The music played is generally traditional, as no written music is ever played from; but skilful players not unfrequently invent new airs, which are founded upon the several modes of recognised divisions of music, and these are taught to pupils, thus perpetuating continual changes, whether for different hours of the day or night, or for extraordinary occasions. Not unfrequently, very sweet-sounding flageolets are used by Mahratta musicians in company with these pipes, which have the effect of mollifying their shrillness; but I do not find any specimens of them in this collection.

In the Mahratta country the players of these pipes are called *gursee*, and the office of piper is hereditary in every village or town, accompanied by portions of land, and certain proportions of the crops of the village at harvest, and other hereditary dues and privileges, in common with other members of the hereditary twelve villages councilmen. The office of "*gursee*" involves sweeping the village temples, lighting the lamps, and officiating at certain ceremonies; and on all occasions of marriages, festivals, funerals, and the like, the *gursee* is entitled to certain perquisites, the rights to which are strictly preserved and universally admitted.

14. होलार चा सुर. 15. *(Holar cha Soor)*.—Tenor and Bass Drones.

The pipes are invariable accompanied by drones, tenor and bass, or first and second bass, of which Nos. 14 and 15 are specimens. The instruments have but one note each, which is played without intermission by different persons. They have the exact effect of the drones of bagpipes, and can be tuned to any key which the leading instruments require, by altering the position of the mouth-piece or reed, and the pipes are tuned to different keys in the same manner.

16. पुंगि (*Poongi*).—SNAKE-CHARMER'S PIPE.

These instruments have six notes, and three semitones. Simple. plaintive airs, generally in minor keys, can be played upon them; but they are not used with other musical instruments, and belong exclusively to the snake-charmers and various tribes of jugglers, acrobats, and the like. By the snake-charmers, a few notes only are played, which seem to have the effect of rousing the snakes to be exhibited, usually cobra de capellos, to action; and as the reptiles raise themselves on their tails, expand their hoods, and wave themselves to and fro, the players become more excited, while the motion of the snakes is accelerated by the rapidity of their execution. So also in feats of jugglery, or sleight of hand, the *poongi*, accompanied by a small hand drum, seems to assist the performer, especially when throwing knives or balls into the air, catching them in succession, and throwing them up again.

I think there is no doubt that the tones of this instrument have an effect upon all snakes, especially cobras, though this is denied by many. As an instance of this, I may mention that one very large cobra, which frequented my garden at Ellichpoor, and of which every one was in dread, was caught by some professional snake-charmers in my own presence by means of the *poongi*. It was played at first very softly before the aloe bush, underneath which the snake lived in a hole ; gradually the performer increased the tone and time of his playing, and as the snake showed its head, he retreated gently till it was fairly outside, and erected itself in a defiant manner. At that moment another man stepped dexterously behind, and, while the snake's attention was absorbed by the player before, threw a heavy blanket upon it, seizing it by the head under the jaws. The head was then pinned down by a forked stick, and the fangs and teeth extracted by strong pincers. The snake was then turned loose, apparently completely cowed and exhausted, and finally transferred to a basket for education as a performer. There was no mistake as to the identity of the reptile ; for a portion of its tail had been shot off in an attempt to destroy it. The same men afterwards drew snakes from the thatch of my house, all of which seemed to obey the fascination of the pipe.

17. सुरसोटा *(Soor Sotta)*.• 18. तांबुरा *(Tumboora)*.

19. Do. 20. Do.—Four Stringed Lutes, large and small.

The four instruments, 17 to 20, are called *soor sotta*, o. *tumboora*, and are only variations of the *tumboora*. They consist of a large grourd as a body, and a stringboard without frets, with pegs at the end, along which the wires, one brass and three steel, are stretched over a bridge, below which each string is fitted with a glass bead, which improves the tone and assists in tunning. No performance of varied character is made on these instruments. They are tuned to one chord, in whatever key is required—generally of C—and the finger passed rapidly across the strings : or the notes are played separately, but quickly, so as to form the chord in vibration.

Almost all Hindu and Mahomedan singers use these instruments in preference to any other. They are, in fact, only helps to the voice, and afford a simple accompaniment which marks the time, while it does not interfere with the singer's execution. So much ornament is employed by professional native singers, that they prefer to rely upon their vocal powers alone for success; and it is esteemed a mark of inferiority to use any other adventitious aid than the simple chord of the *tumboora*. In most instance the singer plays himself, though I have occasionally seen two or three instruments, of different sizes and tones, employed where the singer was sure of correctness of time, and accord. The *tumboora*, therefore, is confined to the use of singers, male or female, or to accompaniments in recitations, the chanting of sacred works and hymns, and of scales and exercises in singing. It is never used in company with pipes or flageolets, or indeed with any other instruments; but, as I have described it, the effect is simple, and often very charming when a good instrument is used which has a mellow tone.

21. सितार (*Sitar*).—Guitar, or Lute, for Performance.

The *sitar* is another instrument expressly intended for the performance of species of music, though I have heard it used occasionally by Rajpoot minstrels as an accompaniment to the voice. It has five wire strings, three steel for treble, and two brass for bass, and eighteen frets, or, with the nut, nineteen; and it will be seen by a glance, and its capability for execution is considerable, though the metallic strings always produce a jangling effect, which is unpleasant. The *sitar* can be altered to any key by moving the frets up or down, and a skilful musician knows how to do this exactly. The execution with which it is frequently played is wonderful, and the performer can execute chromatic passages at will, extending to fourths of origiual notes.

22. सुर श्रृङ्गा (*Soorsringa*). 23. कछवा (*Kuchwa.*)

Numbers 22 and 23 are instruments of the same character as 21, for performance only. 23 differs from 21, not only in respect to its size and power, but in having two strings only to play upon, tuned in thirds, from strings in the centre, which are tuned to the chord of the key or primary note; and two smaller strings at the side, which represent a high octave, and can be struck as necessary. In playing, the chord in the centre is not always struck, but only occasionally for effect. This instrument, which is difficult of execution, is not often met with. 22 has only sixteen frets, but eight strings, six from the top and two at the sides, which lie under those played upon, and are used in combination with them for peculiar resonant effects. This variation of No. 21 is, however, uncommon, and confined perhaps to the Guzerat country.

24, 24A, 25. ताउसि (*Taoosee*).

This is another variation of the *sitar*, No. 21. No. 24 has seventeen frets, with six playing strings; but below them are eleven strings of very fine steel wire, which are tuned to eleven separate notes in the direct scale, and are not played upon. Their use is to effect modulations by vibration of sound, which imparts softness to the melodies executed by the hand. No. 25 is an instrument of the same character, but with twelve lower strings, which are tuned as in the preceding, and with the same object.

The *Vina*.—The best instrument, however, and the most powerful and melodious of this character, is the *vina*, which is wanting to this collection. In form it does not differ much from the preceding, but it has much more power and sweetness, though the peculiar effect of notes sounded upon brass and steel strings is never absent. The finger board of the *vina* with nineteen frets is 2½ octaves, and the frets themselves represent the following notes in English music:—

D, D♯, E, F, F♯ G, G♯, A, B♯, C, C♯, D, D♯, C, F, F♯, G♯, A, D. To hear, so as to understand, any really classical Hindu music, it should be played upon this instrument; and I have occasionally met with some very learned and accomplished performers, principally from Mysore and the South of India. One of these men, after playing many Hindu airs and variations upon them, changed the key of the instrument, and began a piece which was familiar to me, though from *him* unaccountable; it was, in fact, a great portion of Beethoven's Sonata in A; and he explained that, having once taught an English lady a good deal of his own music, which she played upon the piano, she had in turn taught him this Sonata, which he preferred, he said, above all other "English Music," and his version of it, considering the defects of his instrument, was really very beautiful. The fact of nineteen frets expressing the notes I have enumerated, and their extension according to the Hindu system of fingering, affords satisfactory proof of the capabilties of the *vina*, which is honourably mentioned by Sir William Jones in his Essay on Hindu Music, as the standard instrument of India.

26. सारंगि (*Sarungi.*) 27. सरीदा (*Sarrooda*).
28. चिकारा (*Chikara*).

These are the ordinary violins or fiddles of India, and are played in the same manner, though differing from them in some respects, as the instruments in use with us. Of the three, No. 26 is the most commonly employed. 87, *Sarrooda*, may be called the tenor or second fiddle, and accompanies 26 in chords, played by the bow, or by hand as a guitar. 28 is an inferior fiddle, which is mostly to be seen in the hands of strolling players, or mendicants, reciters of short plays or poems, and ballad singers. The *Sarungi* has four strings of cat-gut ; it is played with a bow ; and the execution upon it by accomplished performers is frequently striking and pleasing, while the tones are nearer perhaps in quality to the human voice than those of any other instrument with which I am acquainted. Considering its small size and rude shape, the tone is much more sweet and powerful than would be conceived from its appearance, and this may be accounted for in two ways. First, that the sounding board is of parchment, stretched over the wooden frame ; and, secondly, that below the gut-strings which are played upon, there are eleven others of fine steel wire, tuned exactly with the scale, and thus the effect of the notes played is perhaps increased by vibration upon the wire notes beneath.

The *Sarungi* is used by Mahomedan musicians more than by Hindu ; and I imagine it may have been introduced into India by the Mahomedans, possibly from Persia. It forms an excellent accompaniment to the voice ; and an old friend of mine, an excellent musician and violin player, the late Captain Giberne, Bombay Army, used to prefer one of these instruments to his own violin for concerted pieces in which the violin took a sophrano part. The capability of the *Sarungi* for the execution of chromatic passages and harmonies is, to some extent, equal to our own violin ; but it would be quite possible to improve the native instrument without altering its character, and in such case it might prove a useful addition to our own orchestral effects.

From its size, the *Sarrooda* is more powerful, but more difficult of execution ; and it combines the effect of a guitar, as it is sometimes played in accompaniment, and the violin.

29. सारमंदल (*Sar Mundal.*)

This may be styled the Indian dulcimer. It is by no means common, and therefore good execution upon it is not often met with, nor indeed at any time is it very pleasing, owing to the continual jangle of the wire strings.

30. बीन (*Been*).

Wire-strung guitar, which is chiefly used by mendicants and religious devotees in recitations, hymns, and other sacred singing. In some degree it resembles the *vina* but has not its power or sweetness, nor indeed capability of execution. This instrument has twenty-three frets, and there are five strings to be played upon, with two others at the side for occasional effects.

31. तुंतुंनि (*Toontoonee*).

An instrument with one wire string, and of a rude character. It is invariably used by mendicants and common ballad singers in the Dekan, and the wire is struck rapidly by the finger, or a quill, as an accompaniment to the voice. The string can be tuned to any key required.

32. डफडे (*Duffde*). 33. (*Duffde*). 34. हलक्या (*Hulkya*).
35. डायरा (*Dayra*). 36. डफ (*Duff.*)

These five instruments belong to one class, the common tambourine drum of India, which is played, partly by sticks, partly by the hand. The performer holds two long thin pieces of wood or twig in his left hand, which he rests upon the frame of the instrument, which is strung over his shoulder, while with the right he beats it with a short thick drumstick. The measure and tone can be changed and varied by the manner in which the notes are played by the sticks in the left hand, and in this respect the drummers are very expert. These instruments form the ordinary accompaniments to the horn, No. 7. Every village, or watch on town bastions, fort walls, and the like, has one ; and in native armies the *duff* is beaten furiously on occasions of attack. In all sorts of processions, festivals, and the like, they are employed ; but they do not aspire to the refinement of other drums of a more scientific character, which will be described in turn.

37. ढोल (*Dhôl*). 38. 39. ढोलकि (*Dholkeé*).—
ORDINARY DRUM AND LITTLE DRUM.

Both played by hand as accompaniment to the voice, or struck with a stick when in concert with pipes or loud instruments. Both these instruments are of universal use, but are seldom employed by professional musicians.

40 पखवाज (*Pukhwaj*).—TENOR AND BASS DRUM.

Which is used exclusively as accompaniment to the voice, and in all concerted music. Some musicians prefer the *tubla*, which will be described hereafter; and perhaps the *pukhwaj* is employed more than the other by Hindu professionals. On this instrument-players are exceedingly expert; and by the manner in which both sides, tenor and bass, are played by the hand, the points of the fingers, and occasionally the palms, the notes which are produced assist the voice; while the time, however complicated, is kept with the greatest exactness. This drum is tuned by the side cords, and by a composition laid on the centre, which assists the sound; and a piece of dough is usually put upon the bass side, which tempers the skin, and keeps it in tune. Among instrumental performers this drum, or the *tubla* is considered the standard instrument, and all others, whatever they may be, are tuned to it.

41. हुडुक *(Hoodook)*. 42. डाक *(Dák)*.

These drums are used by ballad singers, mendicants and the like, and need no particular description. The latter use them in concert with begging petitions in the name of some divinity, which are often sung to wild or melancholy cadences.

43. वाह्या *(Bahya)*. 44. जिल्ला *(Jilla)*.—COMMON COPPER KETTLE DRUMS.

Which need no particular explanation; both are played with sticks. They are often found with small parties of village musicians, and in concert with pipes.

45. सबांल *(Sumball)*.—TENOR AND BASS DRUM.

Of the same character as No. 40, *Pukhwáj*; but not so melodious in tone, nor so much used.

46. तबला (*Tubla.*)

These drums, tenor and bass, rank with the *Pukhwaj*, and are preferred by many players. They are tied in a cloth round the waist, when played, and the hands are exclusively used, with extraordinary execution. The tone is mellow and delicate, and, harmonized with the violins, forms an excellent accompaniment to the voice. The *tubla* drums are made of copper, and, while equally sweet, have perhaps more resonance than the *pukhwaj*, which is of wood.

Drum-playing on these instruments is quite an art among Indian performers. They mark the time, which is of a very complicated nature, and differs in many respects from ours, to suit the varied modes of the music. On this account, and from the very florid passages required, years of study and practice are required by the perfomers.

47. नल (*Nul*).—Kettle-Drums.

Generally used on horseback, much like our own, and beaten by sticks. In native cavalry, and in our own irregular cavalry regiments, they are carried in front on the march, and by their sonorous notes the line of progress is indicated to prevent straggling.

48. डुगडुगा (*Doogdooga*):—Small Hand Drum.

Used chiefly by mendicants and ballad singers.

49. नोबत (*Nobut.*)

This instrument, which is the largest kettle-drum used in India, gives the name to the "*Nobut*," or honorary music before alluded to. It has a deep, mellow sound, and is played and used much like our own bass drum. With it are usually associated the smaller kettle-drums, 43 and 44 ; and a performance upon the drums alone forms part of every period of playing throughout the day, though they accompany the pipes and trumpets in all other music executed.

50. शङ्क (*Shunk*).—Conch Shell.

Is not used as a musical instrument, but is sounded during religious ceremonials, in processions of Hindu worship, and before idols. No tune, so to speak, can be played upon it ; but the tone is capable of much modulation by the lips, and its clear, mellow, humming notes, heard at early morning and eventime from Hindu temples and the groves about them, have a peculiar though melancholy effect, not without charm.

The above concludes the catalogue of these instruments, and as the foregoing details may be esteemed incomplete without some notice of Hindu music as a science, the following remarks upon it, brief as they must necessarily be, may serve in some respects to supply the deficiency. I do not put them forward as original ; for it would be impossible for me, without a greater acquaintance with Hindu music than I possess, to write anything more complete than Sir William Jone's essay, which gives details to a greater extent than those with which I can presume now to occupy the time of the Academy.

First, then, as to notation—we find the Hindu gamut to be in essentials similar to our own. There are eight notes in their scale, which form the foundation of the primary modes, or "Swaras," and which are named as follows :—

Sharja.	Punchama.
Rishaba.	Dhaivata.
Gandhara.	Nishada.
Madhyama.	

of which the initial letters form the gamut :—*Sa, Ri, Ga, Ma, Pa, Dha, Ni, Sa,* corresponding with our *Ut, Ri, Mi, Fa, Sol, La, Si, Ut,* and the Hindu scale may be thus written :—

A B C D E F G A

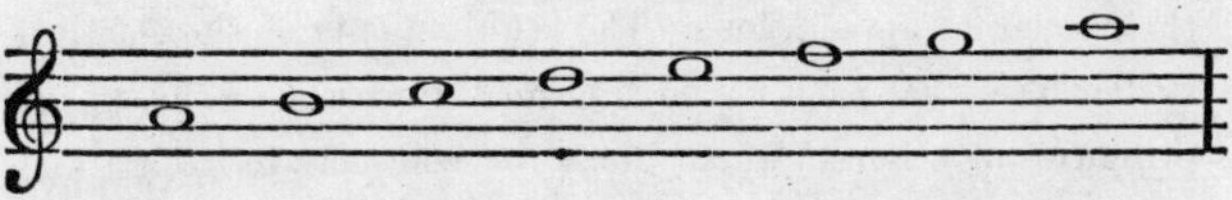

SA, RI, GA, MA, PA, DHA, NI, SA.

But the Hindus have adopted no especial symbols, like ours, to express sound or time ; and in writing music, according to the ancient system, the air and time of the melody are expressed by lengthening or shortening the vowels attached to each initial consonant, and repeating the notes as they may fall together in the air.* This in itself, it will be admitted, is rude and unsatisfactory ; but by certian signs, such as dots, curves, and other marks, the written notation becomes intelligible to performers ; and as taught at present, the scales, and vocal and instrumental exercises of learners, some of which are extremely complicated and difficult, consist of repetitions of the primary notes of the gamut, in the time and tune intended.

Each note is divided into halves, thirds, and fourths, which are defined by signs and marks attached to the notes of the

* In like manner our own music might be written and read from the notes themselves.

gamut, and can be expressed by the voice; or, taking the vina as the standard instrument, on and between the frets, by a manner of fingering known to performers and teachers; and the *Sarungi* or violin, can be used with similar effect.

Again, taking each fundamental sound separately, the classical definition or doctrine of sounds admits and defines seven variations to each, which become the leaders of a series of other modes. Thus we find 7×12=84 modes: seven primary, and seventy-seven secondary, which are known under their separate appellations. The requirements of the classical system are, that each melody formed upon any of the above primaries or other adjuncts should be complete in itself; and no deviation from this rule is recognised or permitted. The modes are distributed over the hours of the day and night; and no professor of Hindu music, or educated performer, would be held excusable by a critical audience, if he transgressed propriety so much as to introduce at a wrong period songs, or instrumental performances, which belonged to another.

In illustration of this rule, Sir William Jones observes:— "A melody, or phrase, commencing with

D. E. F♯. G♯. A. B. C♯. D.

where the first semitone appears between the fourth and fifth notes, and the second between the seventh and eighth, as in the natural scale; and the G♯ and C♯, or ga and ni, of the Indian authors, form our major mode of D;—such a melody must end with the fifth note from the tonic, and it would be a gross violation of musical decorum to sing it at any time except the close of day."

Another mode of division, which is perhaps more modern, is the division of the six primary notes into fifty-four modes, by an allegory. Bhairava, Malava, Sriraga, Hindola, Dipaca, and Megha, are six nymphs, each of whom is married to a Ragini, and each has eight children. Thus we have six nymphs, as primary notes ; six semitones, as husbands ; and forty-eight children, as minor modes or divisions ; making fifty-four in all.

A third system divides of rags or modes into six primary, and thirty secondary. Each of these is known by the note which begins it or ends it. As an example, the Sriraga corresponds with our major scale ; Sa, or A, is its principal notes, with Pa, or E, diminished by one "*sruti*," or part of a note. Thus, we find that this mode represents the ordinary scale, ut, re, mi, sol, fa, la, si, ut, with a minor tone, or three *srutis*, between the fifth and sixth notes.

I have mentioned in my descriptions of the instruments, that chromatic and enharmonic passages of great intricacy can be executed upon several of them — the *vina*, the *sarungi*, &c. This will be accounted for by the fact of the system of music prescribing twenty-two *srutis* or divisions of notes, to each whole octave ; or furnishing each note, or those which according to the requirements of the particular mode may need it or the particular melody in the mode, with semitones, thirds, and quarters of notes, as may be necessary. It would seem, however, as if more than "twenty-two *srutis*" to an octave were inadmissible ; and the notes to which any number of *srutis* is admissible is determined by the key note, or primary.

"Semitones," says Sir William Jones, "are placed as in our own diatonic scales, the intervals between the fourth and fifth, and first and second are major tones ; but that between fifth and sixth, which is minor in our scale, is major in theirs.

The two scales are made to coincide by taking a '*sruti*' from Pa, or E, and adding it to Dha, or F; or, in Indian terms, by raising Savaretna to the class of "Santa," and her sisters. Every *sruti* is a little nymph; and these nymphs, or *srutis*, or quarter-tones of the fifth note, Pa, or E, are called malini, Chapala, Sola, and Savaretna."

In like manner, every note has its fairy attendants attached to it; and these being furnished with names, the separate portions of each are known at once, in their proper order, and without confusion, to scientific Hindu musicians.

There are many Sanscrit, as well as Teloogoo, Canarese, and Tamul works on music, still in existence. Indeed, in the south of India music appears to have been maintained and cultivated as a science, long after it had ceased as such in the north. Mahomedan historians of the period relate, that when the Dekhan was invaded by Alla-oo-deen Togluk, in A. D. 1294, and the conquest of the South of India completed by the Mogul general, Mullik Kafoor, several years afterwards, the profession of music was found to be in a condition so far advanced of the north, that singers, male and female, musicians, and their Brahmin instructors, were taken with the royal armies and settled in the north. The works that remain on the subject have been examined by competent oriental scholars, who have discovered that music as a science held a high place among ancient Hindus, and became the subject of learned, though pedantic, treatises on doctrines of sound, variations of scales accord of musical instruments, divisions of modes, singing, and instrumentation; but nowhere does it appear that the laws of harmony had ever been discovered or invented; and, as a consequence, all Indian music is wanting in this most essential particular.

This, and the pedantic divisions into modes, so jealously guarded from infringement, have prevented Hindu music and its science from that improvement and extension which have been attained elsewhere. In this respect music is, like all other sciences of the Hindus, and their philosophy, unprogressive and effete. In performance upon the *vina* or *sarungi*, the performer's ear, and the capabilities of the instrument, lead players into thirds, fifths, and octaves, with the laws of which they are unacquainted ; but all singing and playing are in unison, and whether trebles, tenors, or basses, which are often joined, and in all instrumental music, the execution is of the same character. It is needless to say that this inevitably produces monotony, and causes Indian music to be generally uninteresting, if not repellant, to European ears.

I am bound to state, however, that very little of the really good or classical music of the Hindus is ever heard by European ears. What is ordinarily played to them is the commonest ballads and love songs, with modern Persian and Hindustani ditties, sung by ill-instructed screaming dancing women, at crowded native durbars, marriages, and other ceremonials. The late Nawab Shumsh-ool Oomrah, of Hydrabad, for instance, used to cause from ten to twenty sets of dancers and singers to stand up together, each set consisting of several women as singers, and a proportion of instrumental performers. All sang and played together whatever they pleased, and the clamour of different tunes, with all their varied accompaniments, was quite indescribable. It is no wonder, therefore, that the English guests stopped their ears, and declared native music to be abominable. Need I say, that, were all the best singers and bands of Dublin to play the most beautiful music at their command at the same moment, the effect might even be more painfully hideous !

But music of much intrinsic beauty, nevertheless, exists ; and the ancient rágs or modes, with their simple melodies, and the marvellously difficult, and often charming scales, *droopuds* and *laonees*, and other exercises of vocal and instrumental performance, and the plaintive and beautiful ballads of the Rajpoots and Mahrattas, would, I think, amply repay collection by one competent to make it. It would be a grateful gift to the musical world at large, were the Government of India to undertake a complete collection and exposition of the best Hindu and Mahomedan music, as it exists in the north of India, in Rajpootana, and Guzerat, in the Southern Provinces, and midway in Maharashtra and Bundelkund. The music of all these provinces differs as much in character as national music in Europe, and there is a great deal of it that is very interesting. How many of the old rágs or modes are illustrated by love songs ! and how many of the chivalrous events of ancient and mediæval times are subjects of ballads much like our own, descriptive, picturesque, and most original both in subject and music ! In the Mahratta country, I can state of my own experience that ballads and love songs are innumerable, whether of the old Mahomedan period, the Mahratta risings against them, and the more recent English and Mahratta wars, and are full of local adventure and spirited description ; while in all the grades of love songs, under their several local denominations, there are scores, nay, hundreds, in every province of India, worthy of being rescued from their present obscurity, and of being preserved among the musical records of the world.

In his Essay, and to illustrate the manner of notation of the ancient Hindu system, Sir William Jones has quoted a very simple air of Soma's, who was one of the most ancient Hindu writers on music, and composers. This, with a few airs contributed by Colonel Tod, in his work on the Rajpoots, form nearly all the Hindu music now on record ; and these, with some common tunes picked up from ordinary singing men and women at nautches, are the only specimens of Indian music now available for reference or comparison. There is much to be regretted, I think, in this, not only because national music is always valuable in an ethnological point of view, but because it would afford most interesting comparisons with the ancient national music of Europe, which it so much resembles. I venture to offer a very simple contribution,—a plaintive Hindu air of the most ancient class, to which I have adapted English words in partial paraphrase of the original Hindee, and to which one of my daughters has added enough accompaniment to admit of its being sung by a soprano voice to the pianoforte.

I cannot close this paper without adverting to the value and importance of this collection of musical instruments, which I consider to be unique. I have never seen so large a one in the possession of any native connoisseur, and my impression is that there is nothing so complete in any European museum. A few, and very few, instruments are wanting to make it perfect, and these might be easily supplied. On these grounds, therefore, I consider that this Academy is under peculiar obligations to Colonel French for his valuable donation,—valuable alike from its original cost and expense of transport, and as an illustration of the musical tastes and acquirements of India ; and I have no doubt that suitable acknowledgment will be made to him.

INDIAN AIR.

Kurna na päee bāt.

Words by M. T., from Hindu Ballad, Accompaniment by A. M. T.

Andanti.

I had treasured up to — tell My stream - - ing eyes were
dim, with weary tears, which then, a-las! un - headed
fell Rude blows the bitter wind, Cold

is the dri - ving rain ; Nor place I
find to dwell. Ah ! me; from them un -
kind no pitying word, no shelter - ing love I find.

Ah ! now I vainly cry
Dear lord, dear heart so fondly loved,
Thou would'st not see me lie
So desolate, nor fail that love so truly proved.
Rest ! rest, oh, breaking heart ;
Peace cometh now to thee, that nought had ever mov'd,
Ah ! why delay thy dart
Kind death—take me to him, that never more we part.

ORIGINAL HINDEE WORDS.

Kurna na päẹe bát
Ab myn. Peea soo jeea ke bat
Oodowjee ! tahreean, myn bulaeen leongi ho !
Mohe le'chulo oonhen ke pas.

MUSIC

BY

LIEUT.-COL. JAMES TOD.

(From Annals and Antiquities of Rajast'han.)

MUSIC.

BY

LIEUT.-COL. JAMES TOD.

(From Annals and Antiquities of Rajast'han, Vol. I, page 538 *to* 540.*)*

As Muralidhara, or the "flute-holder," Kaniya is the god of music; and in giving him the shepherd's reed instead of the *vina* or *lyre,* we may conjecture the simple bamboo *(bhans)* which formed the first flute *(bhansli)* was in use before the *Chatara,** the Grepcian *Cithara,*† the first invented lyre of Apollo. Thus from the six-wired instrument of the Hindus we have the Greek *Cithara,* the English *Cithern,* and the Spanish *guitar* of modern days. The Greeks, following the Egyptians, had but six notes, with their lettered sym-

* From *cha,* 'six' and *tar,* 'a string or wire.'

† Strabo says, the Greeks consider music as originating from Thrace and Asia, of which countries were Orpheus, Musæus, &c.; and that others "who regard *all Asia, as far as India,* as a country sacred to *Dionysius* (Bacchus,) attribute to that "country the invention of nearly all the science of music. We perceive them sometimes describing the *cithara* of the Asiatic, and sometimes applying to flutes the epithet of Phrygian. The names of certain instruments, such as the *nabla,* and others likewise, are taken from barbarous tongues." This *nabla* of Strabo is possibly the *tabla,* the small tabor of India. If Strabo took his orthography from the Persian or Arabic, a single point would constitute the difference between the *N* (ن) and the *T* (ت).

bols ; and it was reserved for the Italians to add a seventh. Guido Aretine, a monk in the thirteenth century, has the credit of this. I, however, believe the Hindus numbered their's from the heavenly bodies—the Sun, Moon, Mercury, Venus, Mars, Jupiter, Saturn,—hence they had the regular octave, with its semitones : and as, in the pruriency of their fancy, they converted the ascending and descending notes into *grahas*, or planetary bodies, so they may have added them to the harmonious numbers, and produced the *no-ragini*, their *nine* modes of music.* Could we affirm that the hymns composed and set to music by Jydeva, nearly three thousand years ago, and still chaunted in honor of the Apollo of Vrij, had been handed down with the sentiments of these mystic compositions (and Sir W. Jones sanctions the idea,) we should say, from their simplicity, that the musicians of that age had only the diatonic scale ; but we have every reason to believe, from the very elaborate character of their written music, which is painful and discordant to the ear from its minuteness of sub-division, that they had also the chromatic scale, said to have been invented by Timotheus in the time of Alexander, who might have carried it from

* An account of the state of musical science amongst the Hindus of early ages, and a comparison between it and that of Europe, is yet a desideratum in Oriental literature. From what we already know of the science, it appears to have attained a theoretical precision yet unknown to Europe, and that, at a period when even Greece was little removed from barbarism. The inspirations of the bards of the first ages were all set to music ; and the children of the most powerful potentates sang the episodes of the great epics of Valmika and Vyasa. There is a distinguished member of the Royal Asiatic Society, and perhaps the only one, who could fill up this *hiatus* ; and we may hope that the leisure and inclination of the Right Hon'ble Sir G. Ousely will tempt him to enlighten us on this most interesting point.

the banks of the Indus· In the mystic dance, the *Ras-mandala,* yet imitated on the annual festival sacred to the sun—god Heri, he is represented with a radiant crown in a dancing attitude, playing on the flute to the nymphs encircling him, each holding a musical instrument :—

> "In song and dance about the sacred hill ;
> "Mystical dance, which yonder starry sphere
> "Of planets, and of fixed, in all her wheels
> "Resembles nearest, mazes intricate,
> "Eccentrick, intervolved, yet regular
> "Then most, when most irregular they seem ;
> "And in their motions harmony divine
> "So smooths her charming tones, the God's own ear
> "Listens delighed."
>
> *Milton, Book V.*, 155.

These nymphs are also called the *no-ragini,* from *raga,* a mode of song over which each presides, and *no-rasa,* or 'nine passions,' excited by the powers of harmony. May we not in this trace the origin of Apollo and the sacred nine ? In the manner described above, the *ras-mandal* is typical of the zodiacal phenomena ; and in each sign a musical nymph is sculptured in *alto-relievo,* in the vaulted temple dedicated to the god,* or in secular-edifices by way of ornament, as in the triumphal column of Cheetore.

From Annals and Atiquities of Rajast'han, Vol I, page 543 *to* 544.

This mystic dance, the *ras-mandal,* appears analogous to the Pyhrric dance, or the *fire*-dance of the Egyptians. The

* I have often been struck with a characteristic analogy in the sculptures of the most ancient Saxon Cathedrals in England and on the Continent, to Kanya and the *Gopis.* Both may be intended to represent divine harmony. Did the Asi and Jits of Scandinavia, the ancestors of the Saxons, bring them from Asia ?

movements of those who personate the deity and his fair companions are full of grace, and the dialogue is replete with harmony.* The Chobis† of Mat'hura and Vindravana have considerable reputation as vocalists; and the effect of the modulated and deep tones of the adult blending with the clear treble of the juvenile performers, while the time is marked by the cymbal or the soothing monotony of the tabor, accompanied occasionally by the *múrali* or flute, is very pleasing.

From Annals and Antiquities of Rajast'han, Vol. I, page 648 *to* 649.

Every chief has his band, vocal and instrumental; but Sindia, some years since, carried away the most celebrated vocalists of Oodipoor. The Rajpoots are all partial to music. The tuppa is the favourite measure. Its chief character is plaintive simplicity; and it is analogous to the Scotch, or perhaps still more to the Norman.‡

* The anniversary of the birth of Kaniya is celebrated with splendour at Sindia's Court, where the author frequently witnessed it, during a ten years' residence.

† The priests of Kaniya, probably so called from the chob or club with which, on the annual festival, they assault the castle of Kansa, the tyrant usurper of Crishna's birthnight, who, like Herod, ordered the slaughter of all the youths of Vrij, that Chrisna might not escape. These Chobis are most likely the Sobu of Alexander, who occupied the chief towns of the Punjaub. and who, according to Arrian, worshipped Hercules (*Heri-cúl-es* chief of the race of Heri), and were armed with clubs. The mimic assault of Kansa's castle by some hundreds of these robust church militants with their long clubs covered with iron rings, is well worth seeing.

‡ The *tuppa* belongs to the very extremity of India, being indigenous as far as the Indus and the countries watered by its arms; and though the peculiar measure is common in Rajast'han, the prefix of *Punjabi* shows its origin. I have listened at Caen to the viola or hurdy-gurdy, till I could have fancied myself in Méwar.

The Rana, who is a great patron of the art, has a small band of musicians, whose only instrument is the *shehna*, or hautboy. They played their national tuppas with great taste and feeling ; and these strains, wafted from the lofty terrace of the palace in the silence of the night, produced a sensation of delight not unmixed with pain, which its peculiarly melancholy character excites. The Rana has also a few flutes or flageolet players, who discourse most eloquent music. Indeed, we may enumerate this among the principal amusements of the Rajpoots ; and although it would be deemed indecorous to be a performer, the science forms a part of education.*

Who that has marched in the stillness of night through the mountainous regions of Central India, and heard the wander sound the *tooraye* from his turreted abode, perched like an eyrie on the mountain-top, can ever forget its graduated intensity of sound, or the emphatic *hem ! hem !* 'all's well,' which follows the lengthened blast of the cornet reverberating in every recess.†

* Chund remarks of his hero, the Chohan, that he was "master of the art," both vocal and instrumental. Whether profane music was ever common may be doubted ; but sacred music was a part of early education with the sons of kings. Rama and his brothers were celebrated for the harmonious execution of episodes from the grand epic, the *Ramayuna*. The sacred canticles of Jydeva were set to music, and apparently by himself, and are yet sung by the Chobis. The inhabitants of the various monastic establishments chaunt their addresses to the deity ; and I have listened with delight to the modulated cadences of the hermits, singing the praises of Pataliswara from their pinnacled abode of Aboo. It would be injustice to touch incidentally on the merits of the minstrel Dholi, who sings the warlike compositions of the sacred Bardai of Rajast'han.

† The *tooraye* is the sole instrument of the many of the trumpet kind which is not dissonant. The Kotah prince has the largest band, perhaps, in these countries ; instruments of all kinds—stringed, wind, and percussion. But as it is formed by rule, in which the sacred and shrill conch-shell takes precedence, it must be allowed that it is any thing but harmonious.

A species of bagpipe, so common to all the Celtic races of Europe, is not unknown to the Rajpoots. It is called the *mêshek*, but is only the rudiment of that instrument whose peculiar influence on the physical, through the moral agency of man, is described by our own master-bard. They have likewise the double flageolet ; but in the same ratio of perfection to that of Europe as the *mêshek* to the heart-stirring pipe of the north. As to their lutes, guitars, and all the varieties of tintibulants (as Dr. Johnson would call them), it would fatigue without interesting the reader to enumerate them.

NOTES ON THE MUSICAL INSTRUMENTS

OF THE

NEPALESE.

BY

A. CAMPBELL, Esq., M.D.,

(From "Journal of the Asiatic Society of Bengal" Vol. VI, Part II.)

NOTES ON THE MUSICAL INSTRUMENTS

OF THE

NEPALESE.*

BY

A. CAMPBELL, Esq., M.D.

It is almost unnecessary to allude here to the two chief classes of men forming the population of the valley of *Nepal;* but to save repetition, it may not be amiss to mention, that the instruments underneath enumerated are common to the Newars and the Parbuttiahs, both designations being understood in the widest sense. This difference, however, exists, in the classes of each tribe using them; among Parbuttiahs none but the lowest castes furnish professional musicians, and there are no amateurs of this science among the rude highlanders, who now rule *Nepal.* The Newars, on the contrary, are as a people, extremely fond of music, and many of the higher and middle castes practise it professionally, and indulge in it as amateurs. Their labors in the field are generally accompanied, and their weary return from it at certain seasons enlivened, by the plaintive strains of the rural flute (*bansuli*) as the sharper tones of the *Mohalli* (flageolet), and at marriages, births, feasts, fairs, and religious processions, a preceding band of music, is an

* The figures refer to models presented by Dr. Campbell and deposited in the Museum.—Ed.

indispensable portion of the smallest ceremony; nor is it uncommon, on the festival day (of which the Newars have nearly 100 annually) to see a joyous jolly fellow, with his flageolet, or cymbals, as the case may be, trudging along towards the scene of rejoicing, piping a national air on the former, for his own amusement and that of all passengers, or drumming with the latter, in unison to his thoughtless but cheering whistle.

As a general rule, however, professional musicians, among the Newars, as with the Parbuttiahs, are from among the lowest castes, *Kúllás* and *Kúsúlliahs*, from the majority from the former, *Damais* and *Sarkis* from the latter.

The instruments used by the people are as follows: I exclude the imitations by the Goorkhas, of British ones, with which their military bands are furnished, the chief of which are the *bagpipe*, made and played on the *Sarkis*. The flute, either English, or imitation of the flageolet, and a variety of horns, trumpets and bugles.

No. 1.—*Phúnga (Newari)*, is a trumpet-shaped instrument made of copper, about three-and-half feet long, two inches in diameter at its large extremity, and tapering gradually to the mouth-piece, where its bore is diminished to the diameter of $\frac{1}{8}$th of an inch, it is formed of three pieces, the one fitting into the other is of very rude workmanship, and costs cnly about two Nepalese Rupees.* The length of this instrument, and its slender make, require some support, when being used; it is consequently furnished with three pieces of stick, which, when fitted into one another, form a rod of four feet in length to which the *Phúnga* is attached, by a bit of ribbon, at its expanded end, the rod crossing the

* A Nepalese Rupee worth about 12 or 12½ annas of Company's currency.

instrument at right angles. The player holding the opposite end of the rod in his right hand elevates the instrument at pleasure, bringing it to the perpendicular when used in a crowd, but carrying it horizontally under other circumstances. The *Phúnga* belongs exclusively to the Newars, is called by them, "the musical instrument of the Gods," and is played on at every religious ceremony and at every temple, within the valley, when the setting sun gives the signal for the performance of the evening sacrifice.

No. 2.—The *Mohalli* (*Newari*), or Nepalese flageolet. Is rudely executed, and from the most ordinary materials. Its mouth-piece is nothing more than a bit of palm leaf folded, and cut into a convenient shape ! the body of the instrument is made of two pieces of sál wood, bound together by slips of bambú, and hollowed out longitudinally, apertures or stops, (8 in number) being made for the fingers to play on ; its trumpet or dilated extremity, is made of copper, gradually increasing in calibre, from the diameter of an inch to that of four inches at its open termination. The complete instrument costs about two-and-a-half Nepalese Rupees. The *Mohalli* belongs exclusively to the Newars, and many persons of this tribe use it, who are not professional musicians. Its tones are sharper than those of the *bansuli* or common Indian flute, and the national tunes adapted to it are lively and pleasing, even to a British ear. To the Newars it seems to sound magically, for it has the power of inducing the poorest and most fatigued laborers, to join in the dance, and it is the constant accompaniment to their songs of merriment at feasts and weddings.

No. 3.—The *Singha* or *Narsingha*, the Nepalese horn. It is made entirely of copper, is, when put together, in the shape of a cow's horn, and about four feet long, is composed of four pieces, and tapers gradually from its wider extremity, where its calibre is four inches in diameter, to the mouth-piece, where the bore is not more than a quarter of an inch across. The *Singha* is used exclusively by the lowest castes among the Parbuttiahs, and is in considerable demand among the lower castes of the plains of India. Its blast is loud, deep, but not musical, and its professors seem unable to mould its tones into anything like harmony. It is rudely manufactured, and costs about three-and-a-half Nepalese Rupees.

No. 4.—The *Nag-phêni* or *Turi*, a Parbuttiah instrument exclusively. It is only different from the last in being of a smaller size and having three vertical turns in its shaft, like a French-horn. Its noise, for music it scarce produces, is anything but harmonious. It is made of sheet copper, tinned over, and costs one Rupee eight annas.

No. 5.—The *Bansuli*, " or rural flute" of Sir W. Jones. It is much more like the common English fife in its tones, and is identical with it in form ; is used by the Newars and Parbuttiahs.

No. 6.—The *Saringi*. This is the same as the instrument of that name used in India, and represents our European violin, in so far as it is stringed and scraped upon, with a horse-hair bow, but it is at best a miserable instrument. In *Nepal* it is only played on by the lowest caste Parbuttiahs, and by begger boys, from among whom I have not seen or heard of any Pagamnis. The dancing girls, imported from *Benares* annually for the amusement of the durbar, have their accompanying fiddlers ; but these being foreigners, are not alluded to here.

No. 7.—The *Sitar*, or three-stringed guitar of India, is used by a very few persons in *Nepal*, whose proficiency is most wretched. Professors of this instrument from the plains of India find some encouragement from the Goorkhas,—at least an occasional performer of tolerable skill may be heard at their court.

No. 8.—Cymbals of various size, from that of a tea-cup, to the dimensions of a wash-hand basin, are used by the Newars and Parbuttiahs, to the same extent as in Hindustan ; all religious ceremonies requiring music, all jattras, or processions of the Gods, as well as of marrying, and feasting mortals, are accompanied by the discordant noise of these untuned instruments. They are made of mixed metals, the chief of which is denominated *Phulia*, and is composed of zinc, copper and tin, in various proportions, according to the tone intended for the cymbal.

No. 9.—*Múrúlli* of the Parbuttiahs, *Beaugh* of the Newars, is a small clarionet, about nine inches long, with eight stops, made of a single piece of bambu, the mouth-piece being formed by blocking up one end of the canal with a bit of wood, except a small slip through which the air is breathed. The tone of this instrument is sweet, and the airs played on it pleasing and plaintive. It costs about eight annas.

No. 10.—*Dhol* (Drum). The same as the Hindustani one, except in the greater length of barrel, in one of the varieties.

No. 11.—*Dholuck*, differs from the *Dhol* in having one end only covered with leather, and played on, is used by the Parbuttiahs but not commonly ; a nearly similar drum is used by the Newars, and called by them *dishi*.

No. 12.—*Beh (Newari)*, commonly called *Krishna-beh*, is the pastoral flute of that God (KRISHNA) so celebrated in history, and so famous in his loves,—is a common reed, with a spoon-shaped shield at the mouth-stop ; has seven stops along its shaft.

Specimens of these instruments were deposited in the Museum of the Asiatic Society of Bengal in January last. I do not feel at present competent to give any correct account of the state of the science of music among the Nepalese. In general it may be stated that the Newars are capable of forming bands, containing performers on all the instruments above enumerated, whose music is far from discordant altogether of the simplest construction. The orchestra attendant on a Hindu play enacted here last year was upwards of 50 strong, and in some of the melo-dramatic portions of the performance, the tunes were not only enlivening and harmonious, but of a highly inspiriting caste. The Nepalese have no written music, so far as I have been able to ascertain. Among the numerous volumes of Sanscrit literature, collected by Mr. HODGSON in *Nepal*, he informs me there is a very large one of the scenic and musical acts, which he infers must have flourished very considerably in union with each other, previous to the Goorkha conquest of the valley. In these works the musical science is deemed of sacred origin. The Nepalese music is most probably identical with that of the plains, the Hindu portion of which is traced to the same fountain.

MUSIC OF CEYLON.

BY

JOHN DAVY, M.D., F.R.S.

(From "An Account of the Interior of Ceylon and of its Inhabitants.")

MUSIC OF CEYLON.

BY

JOHN DAVY, M. D., F. R. S.

Almost every Singalese is, more or less, a poet; or, at least, can compose what they call poetry. Love is not their great inspiring theme, but interest;—a young Kandyan does not indite a ditty to his mistress's eye-brows; the bearded chief is the favourite of his muse, to whom he sings his petition in verse, whether it be to ask a favour, or beg an indulgence. All their poetry is sung or recited: they have seven tunes by which they are modulated. Their most admired tune is called "the Horse-trot;" from the resemblance which it bears to the sound of the trotting of a horse.

Of their music, which is extremely simple, they are very fond, and prefer it greatly to ours, which, they say, they do not understand. The whole amount of their tunes does not, I believe, exceed the number already mentioned.

Their most common instruments are those of which figures are given:—

No. 1.—The Berrigodea, a kind of long drum, is made of jack-wood, covered with deer's skin; and beat with the hands.

No. 2.—The Doula, made like the former, is beat at one end with a stick, and at the other with the hand.

No. 3.—The Tam-a-tom, is beat with two sticks, the extremities of which are bent to form circles, and kept in a state of tension.

No. 4.—The Udakea, is beat with the fingers.

No. 5.—The Tallea, made of brass, is beat with a stick.

No. 6.—The Horanawa; its mouth-piece is of talipot-leaf, its middle-piece of wood, and the other parts are of brass. The fusiform piece of wood attached, is to separate the bits of leaf forming the mouth-piece, and enlarge the orifice.

No. 7.—The Venah, or Venavah, has two strings of different kinds, one made of a species of flax, and the other of horse-hair, which is the material also of the string of the bow, which with bells attached to it, is used as a fiddle-stick. The hollow part of the instrument is half a cocoa-nut shell, polished, covered with the dried skin of a lizard, and perforated below.

All these instruments, with the exception of the Venavah and Udakea, are very noisy, and are seldom used, excepting in temples and in processions. Each kind of drum has a different sound. The Horanawa, the Kandyan pipe, is extremely shrill, and its notes are not unlike the Highland bagpipe. The Venavah is rarely seen, excepting in the hand of some strolling lame or blind son of Apollo, who wanders about the country from house to house, amusing the villagers, and supporting himself by his simple instrument. The Udakea is the favourite domestic instrument. It is usually beat during the recital of a poem, and is the general accompaniment of the song. At night it is often to be heard in the houses of the Singalese, particularly of the better sort; many of whom spend hours together listening to it, and are in the habit of being lulled to sleep by it; for "nothing (they say) is so tranquilising as sweet poetry, and the gentle Udakea."

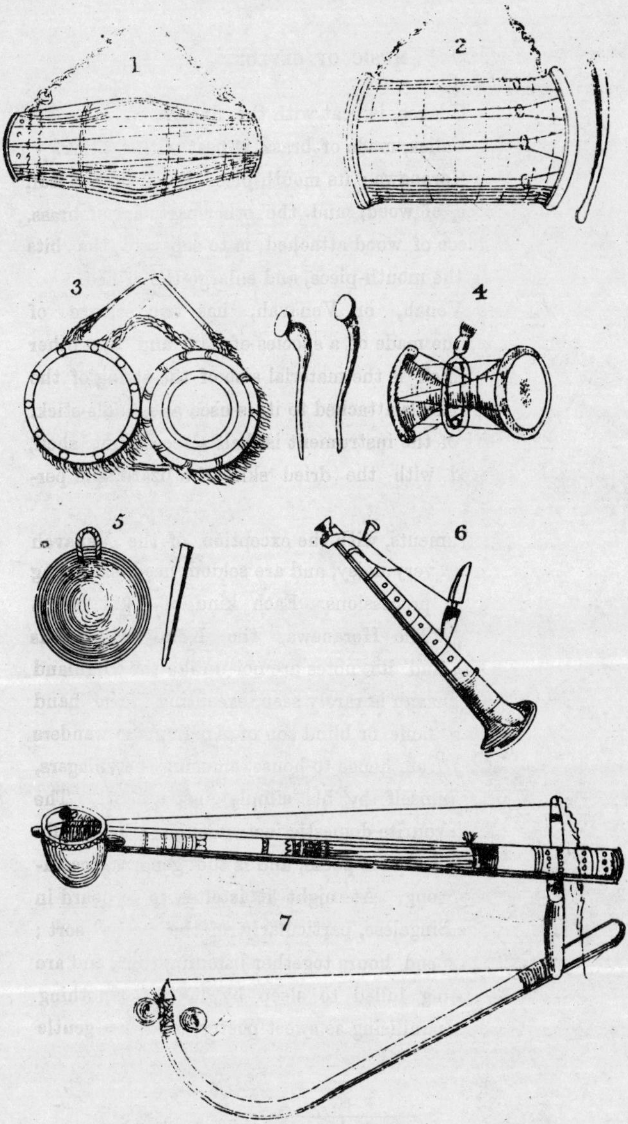
1
2
3
4
5
6
7

MUSIC AND DANCING.

BY

CRAWFURD, Esq.

(From the "History of the Indian Archipelago," Vol. I.)

MUSIC AND DANCING.

(JAVANESE.)

BY

CRAWFURD, Esq.

MUSIC.

After this account of the state of the *medical art* among the Indian islanders, I shall proceed to describe their *music.* Each tribe has its distinct national airs, but it is among the Javanese alone that music assumes the semblance of an art. These people have, indeed, carried it to a state of improvement, not only beyond their own progress in other arts, but much beyond, I think, that of all other people in so rude a state of society. This is most remarkably displayed in the construction and composition of their musical instruments and bands. These instruments are either *wind* instruments, *stringed* instruments, or instruments of *percussion.* The two first are remarkably rude, and it is only in the last that the perfection of Javanese music is to be discovered. I shall offer the reader a short description of all these in succession, and afterwards proceed to give a description of their musical system.

In doing this, I am happy to say, that my own deficiencies are supplied by the skill and learning of Dr. Crotch, the well-known auther of the "Specimens of the various Styles of Music." I supplied this gentleman with a variety of Javanese airs, taken down by my friend Mr. Scott of Java, and he had the advantage of inspecting the fine collection of musical instruments belonging to Sir Stamford Raffles at the Duke of Somerset's. On the subject of Javanese music he addressed a letter to me, the words of which I shall quote without alteration on every material point.

Of the wind instruments the rudest and earliest is the *Angklung.* This instrument is confined to the mountaineers of Java, particularly those of the western end of the island. It consists of a number of tubes of bamboo cane, cut at the end like the barrels of an organ, and of graduated lengths so as to form a gamut or series of notes. The tubes are loosely placed in frames, so as to move when the frame is shaken; and the whole of its rude notes consists in nothing more than the vibration produced by this motion. A troop of forty or fifty mountaineers will be seen dancing in wild and grotesque attitudes, each individual playing upon an *Angklung,* himself and his instrument decked with feathers. Among the musical instruments of the neighbouring island of Bali is a large wind instrument, in appearance like a German flute, but in sound and the manner in which it is blown more resembling a clarionet. It is about four feet in length, and five or six of them usually play in a band. The *suling* and *serdum* are sorts of flutes or fifes in use among the Malay tribes, played alone, and never in a band.

These, I think, are the only native wind instruments known to the Indian islander at present. The fife or flute they acquired from the Hindus, as its Sanskrit name *bangsi* points out. Trumpets they acquired from the Persians and Europeans, as we learn from their names, *nasiri* and *salompret.* The *sruni* is a kind of native hautboys or trumpet, which we read of in native romance, without ever seeing.

Of stringed instruments they have three, the *chălempung*, the *trawangsa*, and the *rabab*. The *chălempung* has from ten fifteen wire strings, and is played in the manner of a harp. The *trawangsa* is an instrument resembling a guitar, which is occasionally found among the Sandas or mountaineers of Java. This is the same sort of lute which we hear of among the Malays under the name of *Káchapi*. The *rabab*, an instrument borrowed from the Persians, is a small violin of two strings played with a bow, and producing perfect intonation. This is played by the leader of the band in a Javanese Orchestra, but is wanting in the music of those tribes who have had little intercourse with the western nations of Asia. It is a handsome little instrument, made of ivory, with a front of parchment.

The instruments of percussion are numerous. The drum is a native instrument, and recognised by many different names, according to the dialects of the people. Besides the native varieties, they are indebted to the Arabs and Europeans for others. The native drum struck with the hand is a rude instrument, and Dr. Crotch pronounces, upon a very good one in the collection of Sir Stamford Raffles, that, " the sound is feeble and unmusical."

Next to the drum may be mentioned the well-known instruments called *gongs*. The word, which is correctly written *gung*, is common to all the dialects of the Archipelago, and its source may be considered to be the vernacular language of Java; if, indeed, it was not originally borrowed from the Chinese. The *gong* is a composition of copper, zinc and tin, in proportions which have not been determined, some of them are of enormous size, being occasionally from three to four feet in diameter. They have a nob in the centre, which is struck with a mallet covered at top with cloth or elastic gum. They are usually suspended from a rich frame, and the tone which they produce is the deepest and richest that can be imagined. Dr. Crotch says of those he inspected, "A pair of gongs was suspended from the centre of a most superb wooden stand richly carved, painted and gilt. The tone of these instruments exceeded in depth and quality any thing I had ever heard."

The next instrument of percussion to be mentioned may be described as a variety of small gongs, of which one is laid in a wooden frame upon strings to support it. These, according to their varieties, are called by the names of *Ketuk* and *Kampul.*

A series of similar vessels or gongs, arranged in a double row upon a wooden frame, go under the name of *Kromo* and *Bonang.* "The tone of this singular instrument," says Dr. Crotch, "is at once powerful and sweet, and its intonation clear and perfect."

The last class of instruments of percussion are the *Staccados,* in the Javanese language called *Gāmbang.* These are of greater variety than any of the rest. The first I shall mention is the wooden Staccado, or *Gambang Kayu.* This consists of a certain number of bars of a hard sonorous wood of graduated lengths, placed over a wooden trought or boat, and struck with a little hammer. This instrument is common throughout every part of the Archipelago, particularly among the Malay tribes, and is often played alone. The second kind of Staccado resembles this, differing from it only in having the bars made of metal instead of wood.

They each assume different names in the copious language of Java, according to the number of bars, or notes, or other modifications of their construction. The tone of the wooden Staccado is sweet, but not powerful; that of the metallic one stronger. A modification of the latter is known by the name of *Gănder.* This consists of thin plates, instead of bars of metal, supported by tightened cords, instead of resting on the sides of the wooden boat or trought; below each bar, there is a bamboo tube to improve the sound. On the fabrication of all those instruments, Dr. Crotch observes, after viewing those at the Duke of Somerset's, that he "was astonished and delighted with their ingenious fabrication, splendour, beauty and accurate intonation."

The instruments now described, according to their arrangement, the omission of some instruments, or the insertion of others, are divided into bands or Orchestras, pitched on the same scale in perfect unison, and each appropriated to some particular description of music, or some particular occasion. The word *Gamălan,* which we so often hear in the mouths of the Javanese, expresses these bands or sets. There are no less than seven of them. The first is called *Manggang,* and is the simplest and most ancient. Some of the principal instruments mentioned in the description I have given are omitted in it; it is played at public processions. The name of *Gamalan Kodok Ngorek,* or the band resembling "the croaking of frogs," a name which it sometimes bears, was probably given to it from its want of harmony, after the Javanese became acquainted with the more improved and perfect ones.

The next band is the *Sălendro,* the most perfect of all, whether for the number of instruments of which it consists, or the number of notes in each of this. The *Pelag* is like the *Sălendro ;* but some of the instruments have fewer notes, and all are larger and louder. The *Miring,* as its name implies, partakes of the nature of the *Sălendro* and *Pelag.* These three bands are more particularly employed as accompaniments in the different kinds of dramatic exhibitions.

The *Gamălan Choro Bali,* or band according to the fashion of Bali, omits the *răbab* or violin, an instrument borrowed from the Mahomedans ; for which, I presume, are substituted in the native country of it, the flutes or clarionets which I have described. In other respects it resembles the *Sălendro,* and has the instruments as large and loud as those of the *Pelang.*

The *Săkaten* is only distinguished from the *Pelag* by the still greater size and louder sound of the instruments. This is played only before the monarch, and on very solemn occasions, such as the great religious festivals.

The *Srunen* is the martial music of the country. In this band, as its name implies, trumpets are introduced, or some wind instruments similar to them--a complete band of either kind will cost from two hundred to five hundred pounds Sterling.

On the style and character of Javanese music, the following are Dr. Crotch's very interesting observations: "The instruments," he observes, "are all in the same kind of scale as that produced by the black keys of the piano-forte ; in which scale so many of the Scots and Irish, all the Chinese, and some of the East Indian and North American airs of the greatest antiquity were composed. The result of my examination is a pretty strong conviction that all the real native music of Java, notwithstanding some difficulties which it is unnecessary to particularize,* is composed in a common enharmonic scale. The tunes which I have selected are all in simple common time. Some of the cadences remind us of Scots music for the bagpipe; others in the minor key, have the flat seventh instead of the leading note or sharp seventh—one of the indications of antiquity. In many of the airs the recurrence of the same passages is artful and ingenious. The irregularity of the rhythm or measure, and the reiteration of the same sound, are characteristic of oriental music. The melodies are in general wild, plaintive and interesting." It is almost unnecessary to add, that the Indian islanders are unacquainted with the art of writing music; the tunes, of which there are a great variety, are handed down from memory.

In the plates accompanying this work will be found the scales or gamuts of the principal instruments of percussion, with five Javanese tunes, and one Malay air, selected by Dr. Crotch, to which are added, by himself, the b es and chords.

DANCING.

The love of *dancing,* in a variety of shapes, is a favourite passion of the Indian islanders. It is somewhat more, indeed, than an amusement, often mingling itself with the more serious business of life. Dancing, as practised by them, is neither the art, as it exists among the savages of America, nor among the Hindus and Mahomedans of Western India.

* The difficulties here alluded to are, in our present state of information, believed to be the consequence of some errors which had found their way into the original manuscript furnished to Dr. Cr tch.

Like the latter, they have professed dancing women, who exhibit for hire ; but like the former, they occasionally dance themselves, and in public processions, and even more serious occasions, dancing forms a portion of the solemnities.

Whatever be the occasion in which dancing is exhibited, it is always grave, stately and slow, never gay nor animated. As in all Asiatic dancing, it is not the legs but the body, and especially the arms, down to the very fingers, that are employed. Dexterity, agility or liveliness, are never attempted. To the gravity and solemnity which belong to the inhabitants of a warm climate, any display of agility would appear as indecorous, as their stately and sluggish minuet dancing appears insupportably tiresome to our more volatile and lively tempers.

The dancing of the Indian islanders may be considered as of three kinds,—their serious dances on public occasions, the private dances of individuals at festivities, and the exhibitions of professed dancers.

Of the first kind are the war dances of the people of Celebes. If a warrior throws out a defiance to his enemy, it is done in a dance in which he brandishes his spear and kris, pronouncing an emphatic challenge. If a native of the same country runs a muck, ten to one but he braves death in a dancing posture. When they swear eternal hatred to their enemies, or fidelity to their friends, the solemnity is accompanied by a dance. There is a good deal more vivacity on these occasions than I ever saw exhibited on any other of the same kind.

All orders executed in the presence of a Javanese monarch, on public occasions, are accompanied by a dance. When a message is to be conveyed to the royal ear, the messenger advances with a solemn dance, and retreats in the same way. The ambassadors from one native prince in Java to another follow the same course when coming into and retiring from the presence of the sovereign to whom they are deputed. When the persons whose business it is to let the tiger loose from his cage into the hollow square of spearmen, as above mentioned, have performed their duty, and received the royal nod to retire, an occasion, one would think, when dancing might be spared, they do so in a slow dance and solemn strut, with some risk of being devoured by the tiger in the midst of their performance.

Previous to the introduction of the Mahomedan religion, it appears to have been the custom of all the oriental islanders, for the men of rank, at their public festivities, when heated with wine, to dance. Upon such occasions, the exhibition appears to have been a kind of war dance. The dancer drew his kris, and went through all the evolutions of a mock fight. At present the practice is most common among the Javanese, with every chief of whom dancing, far from being considered scandalous, as among the people of Western India, is held to be a necessary accomplishment.* Respectable women never

* In Dampier's time, and I suppose to the present day, the people of Mindanao followed the same practice. "It was not long before the general caused his dancing women to enter the room, and divert the company with that pastime. I had forgot to tell you, that they have none but vocal music here by what I could learn, except only a row of a kind of bells without clappers, sixteen in number, and their weight increasing gradually from about three to ten pound weight. These were set in a row, on a table in the general's house, where, for seven or eight days together, before the circumcision day, they were struck, each with a little stick, for the biggest part of the day making a great noise, and they ceased that morning. So these dancing women sung themselves, and danced to their own music. After

join in it, and with that sex, dancing is confined to those whose profession it is. In the most crowded circle of strangers, a Javanese chief will exhibit in the mazes of the dance with an ordinary dancing girl, or, in other words, with a common prostitute. I have often seen the sultan of Madura, a most amiable and respectable prince, in this situation. The dance at such time is nothing more than the slow and solemn pacing exhibited on other occasions.

The professed dancers differ little but in inferiority of skill, from the common dancing girls of Hindustan. Those who have been often disgusted with the latter, will find still less to interest them in the former. The music to which the dancing is performed is, indeed, generally incomparably better than that of Western India, although the vocal part of it is equally harsh and dissonant. Now and then a single voice of great tenderness and melody may be found, but whenever an effort is made at raising it for the accommodation of an audience, it becomes harsh and unmusical. The songs sung on such occasions are often nothing more than unpremeditated effusions, but among the Javanese, to whom I am now more particularly alluding, there are some national ballads, that might bear a comparison with the boasted odes of the Persian minstrels.

this the general's women, and the sultan's sons, and his nieces, danced. Two of the sultan's nieces were about 18 or 19 years old the other two were three or four years younger. These young ladies were very richly dressed, with loose garments of silk, and small coronets on their heads. They were much fairer than any women I did ever see there, and very well featured; and their noses, though but small, yet higher than the other women, and very well proportioned"—*Dampier's Voyages*, Vol. I, p. 342.

The singular fact of the sovereign having, among the Javanese, the most beautiful and admired of his concubines instructed to dance, and their exhibiting their performance in public, accords with what I have stated respecting the condition of women among the Indian islanders.*

* Commodore Beaulieu's account of a dance exhibited before the King of Achin is somewhat peculiar, but very characteristic:—"Then came fifteen or twenty women, who ranged themselves by the wall side, and each of them having little drums in their hands, sung their king's conquests, making their voices answer the drums. After that there came in, at a little door, two little girls, very oddly dressed, but very handsome, and whiter than any I ever saw in so hot a country. Upon their head they had a sort of hat, made of spangles of gold, which glittered mightily, together with a plume about a foot and a half high, made of the same spangles. This hat hung down upon one ear. They had large ear-pendants of spangles of gold, hanging down to their shoulders. Their neck was covered with necklaces of gold, and upon their shoulders was a sort of jacket of gold, curiously engraven, under which was a shift, or waistcoat of cloth of gold, with red silk, covering their breast, and a very broad girdle, made of gold spangles. Their girdle was tied above the haunches, from which there hung a cloth of gold, with straight breeches underneath, which were likewise made of cloth of gold, and did not pass the knees, where several bells of gold hung upon them.

"Their arms and legs were naked, but, from the wrist to the elbow were adorned with bracelets of gold and jewels, as well as from the ancle to the calf of their leg. At their girdle each of them had a sword, the hilts and scabbards of which were covered with jewels; and in their hands a large fan of gold, with several little bells about it. They advanced upon the carpet with a profound gravity, and, falling upon their knees before the king, saluted him, by joining their hands, and lifting them up to their head; then they began to dance, with one knee upon the ground, making several motions with their body and arms; after that they danced upright, with a great deal of agility and cadence, sometimes putting their hands to their swords, another time making as if they shot a bow, and sometimes as if they had a shield and hanger in their hands. This lasted about half an hour, after which they kneeled before the king, and, in my opinion, were pretty well tired, for each of them had above forty pounds weight of gold upon her. However, they danced with a very good grace, and if our French dancing-masters had seen them, they would have owned their performance not to have been what we account barbarous."—*Harris's Collection of Voyages*, Vol. I, p. 732.

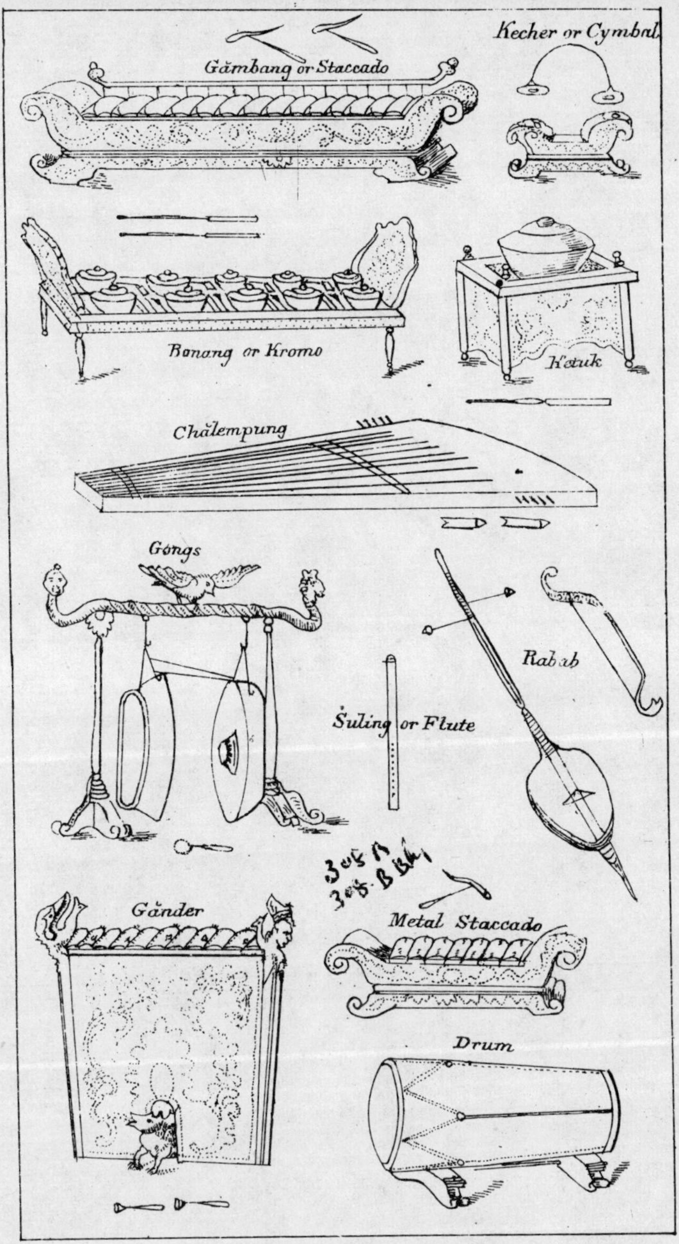

JAVANESE MUSICAL INSTRUMEN.

Scale of the Gambang Kayu or wooden Staccado.

Gambang gangsa or metal Staccado.

The Bonang or Kromo. Note of the Gong. Note of the Cymbal.

Bandi Lori.

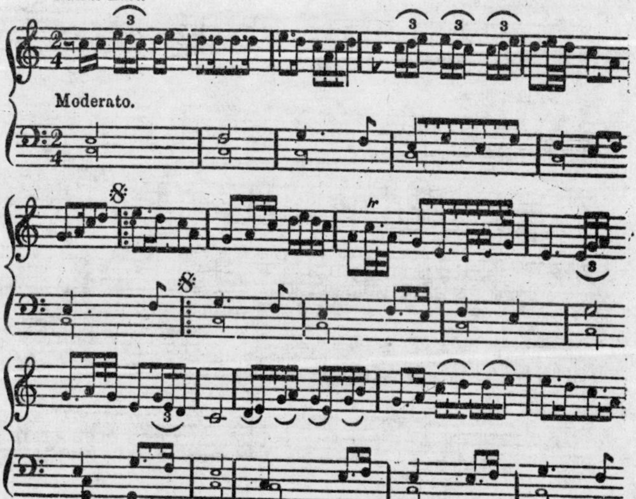

Lompong Keli

Sumadang

Galati Mungup

Raja Santul

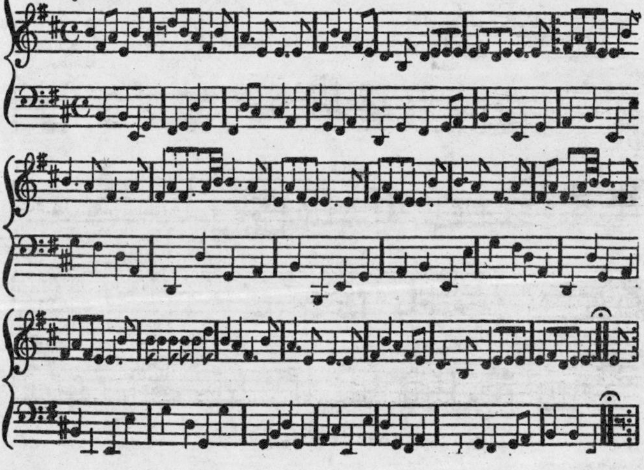

END OF VOL. I.

PART II.

FROM

THE INDUSTRIAL ARTS OF INDIA.

BY

GEORGE C. M. BIRDWOOD, C.S.I., M.D., EDIN,

1880.

MUSICAL INSTRUMENTS.

Indian Musical Instruments are remarkable for the beauty and variety of their forms, which the ancient sculptures and paintings at Ajanta shew have remained unchanged for the last two thousand years. The harp, *chang,* is identical in shape with the Assyrian harp represented on the Nineveh sculptures, and the *Vina* is of equal antiquity. The Hindus claim to have invented the fiddle bow. At Kalka, in the Ambala District of the Panjab, the "Jew's harp" *Mu-chang* ["mouth-harp"], is made at certain seasons of festivity and sold by hundreds. Musical Instruments are made in most of the large towns and cities, and those of Srinagar [Cashmere] and Delhi in the Panjab, of Murshedabad in Bengal, and of Tamkur in Mysore, are specially prized. They are also made of marked excellence at Parashram and Malwan, both in the Ratnagiri Collectorate of the Bombay Presidency. Delhi, Bareilly and Channapatna in Mysore are noted for the manufacture of wire for musical instruments. The Conch shell used in India as a wind instrument is often beautifully mounted in silver and gold. It is the Turbinella rapa of naturalists, and all that is required to make it sonorous is to drill a hole through its base. When blown into, the wind passing through the different whorls, produces a loud, sharp, and piercing sound, which is heard far and wide, and hence its great esteen as a war trumpet. It is used in religious services to call the attention of the gods to their worshippers; and also at the conclusion of certain ceremonies. The Conch shell used for pouring water on the gods is a smaller one, the Mazza rapa of naturalists. Both these species, and a third, the Voluta gravis, are used in the manufacture of the bracelets of Dacca.

ON

THE HINDU DIVISION OF THE OCTAVE, WITH SOME ADDITIONS TO THE THEORY OF SYSTEMS OF THE HIGHER ORDERS.

BY

R. H. M. BOSANQUET.

(*Proceedings of the Royal Society of London. From March* 1, 1877 *to December* 20, 1877.)

"On the Hindu division of the Octave, with some additions to the theory of systems of the higher orders."* By R. H. M. Bosanquet, Fellow of St. John's College, Oxford. Communicated by Prof. Henry J. S. Smith, F. R. S., Savilian Professor of Geometry in the University of Oxford. Received January 5th, 1877. Read 8th February.†

My attention has been recently drawn to some publications which appear to afford trustworthy information concerning the musical intervals in use among the Hindus.‡ In particular it appears that the foundation of their system is a division of the Octave into 22 intervals, which are called S'rutis. I propose to discuss this system in the light of the theory formerly communicated to the Royal Society; and as it is one of what I have called the higher systems, and the theory of such systems has not been sufficiently developed, I take the opportunity of adding what is necessary for the classification, discussion and practical treatment of the principal systems of this character.

Some light may be thrown on the object of the paper by the following quotation from the work of Fetis before referred to. After an exhaustive treatment of the various accessible scales, tunes, &c., from the artistic point of view, he sums up in the following words:—

"Dailleurs, pour établir d'une maniére certaine l'état véritable de la musique indienne de nos jours, il faudrait

* Sometime after the paper was read, the author's attention was called to M. Fetis's work, a reference to which is embodied in the paper.

† See Proc. Roy. Soc., Vol. XXV, p. 540.

‡ "Hindu music, from various authors," Part I, S. M. Tagore, President, Bengal Music School, &c , Fetis, Histoire Générale de la Musiqueval.

qu'elle eût été étudiée sur les lieux par un musician possidant une connaissance compléte del'art et de la science, ce qui n'a pas eu lieu Jusqu'an Jaurd' hui. Cette étude exigerait, pour être bien faite, non seulementle savoir technique, mais un esprit observateur dégagé de tout systéme préconcu. Dans ces conditions seulement, on parviendrait á déterminer avec exactitude la nature de la tonalité des chants de l' Inde moderne, ce que n'ont fait ni Fowke, ni W. Ouseley, ni Willard, ni même W. Jones; car leurs appréciation â ce sujet n'ont pas la rigoureuse précision qué est indispensable dans les recherches de ce genre."

The point of the present paper, so far as it relates to Hindu music, is, that until we have a general means of producing and controlling such systems as are likely to be met with on instruments with fixed tones (*e. g.*, the harmonium) and of thus comparing such systems with actual facts, we can have no certainty as to the results, at least in the present state of musical education.

Fetis employs the principle of the comparison of intervals with equal temperament semitones, which is the basis of the writer's methods ; but he uses it only for the purpose of speculating on the connexion between the Hindu system of 22, and a division of the Octave into 24, or of each semitone into two equal parts, a comparison by which nothing appears to be gained.* The use of method for instituting comparisons with perfect consonances has escaped him. And yet it appears (Fetis, Vol. II, p. 278) that the Vina (the historic instrument of Indian music) is tuned by concords, forming a complete major chord on the open strings. This

* Proc. Roy. Soc., 1875, Vol. XXIII, p. 390 ; and "An Elementary Treatise on Musical Intervals and Temperament" (Macmillan, 1876.)

is enough of itself to suggest the necessity of an inquiry into the relations between the system of 22 and perfect concords.

The Hindu scale has several forms ; that which is described by most of the writers, and seems accepted as fundamental, is represented commonly as follows, S'rutis being such that 22 of them make an Octave :—

S'rutis.	*Hindu names.*	*European names.*
4	Sa	C
	Ri	D
3	Ga	F
2	Ma	F
	Pa	G
4	Dha	A
3	Ni	B
2	Sa	C

The above scale is called the Shadja Gráma.

Another form called Madhyama Gráma is precisely similar to the above, except that the intervals *Pa Dha* and *Dha Ni* are inverted ; so that we have

3	Pa	G
	Dha	A
4	Ni	B

There is a third principal form, the constitution of which appears uncertain, but the two above given are suggestive, and are enough to make clear to us the general nature of the arrangement.

In fact, if we suppose for a moment that the fifths and thirds of this scale are perfect, which is not exactly true, we see that the first form, *Shadja Gráma*, is the form we should give to the scale in just intonation, when we wish to retain the ordinary second of the key, and raise the sixth of the key, so as to form a good fifth with the second (*e. g.*, in the key of C we should raise *a* to *a* so as to get the good fifth, *d-a.*) The other form, *Madhyama Grāma,* corresponds to the diatonic scale as ordinarily given.

Are the S'rutis all equal in value ? The native writers say nothing about this, but the European ones for the most part suggest that they are not. For instance, an English reviewer recently wrote, "A S'ruti is a quarter tone or a third of a tone according to its position in the scale." This appears to be a misapprehension arising from the modern idea that each interval of a tone in the scale is necessarily the same. But the language in which the different forms of the scale is described distinctly indicates that a note rises or falls when it gains or loses a S'ruti ; consequently we may infer that the S'rutis are intended to be equal in a general sort of way, probably without any very great precision.

We shall now show that the fifths and thirds, produced by a division of the Octave into 22 equal intervals, do not deviate very widely from the exact intervals, which are the foundation of the diatonic scale.

For this purpose we shall only need to recall the values of the perfect fifth and third in terms of equal temperament semitones of 12 to the Octave. A simple calculation will give us the values of the corresponding intervals of the system.

The perfect fifth is 7·01955 semitones,

or $7\frac{1}{51}$ nearly.

The perfect third is 4—·13686 semitones,

or $4-\frac{1}{7\cdot3}$ nearly.

To find the interval in semitones made by x units of the system of 22, we have

$\frac{12}{22}x$ or $\frac{6}{11}x$

Hence we obtain the following values :—

SYSTEM OF 22.

Intervals.	No. of units.	Interval in semitones.	Exact interval in semitones.
Major third ...	7	3·8182	3·8631
Fifth	13	7·0909	7·0195

Hence the fifth of the system of 22 is sharp by about ·07, or $\frac{1}{3}$ of a comma very nearly.

The major third is flat by ·045, or $\frac{1}{5}$ of a comma nearly.

(Comma of $\frac{81}{80}$=·21506.)

The system of 22 possesses, then, remarkable properties; it has both fifths and thirds considerably better than any other cyclical system having so low a number of notes. The only objection, as far as the concords go, to its practical employment for our own purposes lies in the fifths; these lie just beyond the limit of what is tolerable in the case of instruments with continuous tones. (The mean tone system is regarded as the extreme limit; this has fifths $\frac{1}{4}$ of a comma flat.) For the purposes of the Hindus, where no stress is laid on the harmony, the system is already so perfect that improvement could hardly be expected.

It is thus wrong to suppose that the system of 22 would need much tempering to bring its concords into tune. These are probably quite as accurate as rough and poorly toned instruments admit of.

But although the consonance error of fifth and third is small, it is far otherwise with the deviations of the other intervals of the scale from the values to which Europeans are accustomed.

SYSTEM OF 22.

Interval.	*Difference of.*	*Units.*	*Interval.*	*Exact Interval.*
Fourth	.. Fifth and Octave	2	4·9091	4·9805
Major tone	.. Fourth and fifth	4	2·1818	2.0391
Minor tone	.. Third and major tone	3	1·6363	1·8240
Major semitone	.. Third and fourth	2	1·0909	1·1174
Minor third	.. Fifth and third	6	3·2727	3·1564
Minor semitone	.. Major third and minor third.	1	·5454	·7067

In regarding these numbers we must remember that, as far as European musicians are concerned, the deviation from equal temperament is the most important thing in a melodic point of view; and this is expressed in every case by the notation adopted for the intervals. Intervals which deviate widely from equal temperament sound out of tune to the European ear; and, as harmony is not employed, the justification which derivation from perfect concords is felt to give in harmony has no opportunity of asserting itself.

The only method by which it will be possible to make reliable investigations on the intervals practically used in India will be to provide some instruments suitable for manipulating the system of 22 divisions in the Octave, and then to compare its intervals with those given by the Indian musicians. It will thus be possible to find out what is the extent of the tempering, if any, which they employ. The education of the European ear is as yet so imperfect that no reliance can be placed on estimations of intervals, other than integral numbers of equal temperament semitones, if made by ear only, even with skilled musicians. The habit of estimating fractions of intervals numerically by ear is completely uncultivated among us; and the value to be set on the dicta of casual European observers is in consequence little or nothing.

I shall presently indicate the mode in which the principles of the generalized key-board permit us to construct an instrument that will deal practically with this system of 22, and exhibit in a graphical manner the singular laws of harmony to which its notes are subject.

Theory of the Higher Systems.

Let us recall what is meant by the order of a system.

(The letters E. T., are used as an abbreviation for "equal temperament.")

The E. T., fifth is 7 semitones; the Octave is 12 semitones.

$\therefore$ 12 E. T., fifths = 7 octaves = 84 semitones.

The perfect fifth, on the other hand, is (very nearly) $7\frac{1}{51}$; so that 12 perfect fifths $= 84\frac{12}{51}$.

And in other systems there is always a small difference between 12 fifths and 7 Octaves. Now the simplest way in which this can be treated is to make this small difference the unit of the system. When this is done the system is said to be of the first order.

But sometimes this small difference is more than one unit: if it is divided into two units, we say that the system is of the second order; if into three, of the third, and so on.

The forms of arrangement into scales and laws connecting the harmony of fifths and thirds depend primarily upon the orders of systems.

Referring back for the details of the investigation to my previous communication already cited, I recall only that the systems of each order proceed by differences of 12, and that for the first three orders they are as follows :—

Order				
1.	17	29	41	53
2.	22	34	..	118
3.	15	27	39	..

The accompanying illustration (Diagram I.) will make clear what is meant by saying that the system of 22 is a system of the second order. The numbers are the characteristic numbers of the system; they are arranged in order of fifths, *i. e.*, they proceed by differences of 13, 22, being always cast out. The departure of the sharp fifths from E. T. is represented by displacement in a vertical direction.

Then the circle of 12 fifths has its terminal points 2 units apart.

Similarly in systems of the rth order, the circle of 12-fifths has its terminal points r units apart.

In the illustration we see how the notes may be introduced which form the intervals intermediate between the terminal points, thus the note 1 is introduced midway between 0 and 2.

Diagram I.

Characteristic numbers of system of 22 in order of fifths.

c	g	d	a	e	b	f♯	c♯	g♯	e♭	b♭	f	c
2 1 0	13	4	17	8	21	12	3	16	7	20	11	2 1 0

Formation of Thirds.

Thirds may be formed either by the notes of the circle of fifths with which we start, or by the notes of another circle any number of unites above or more generally below the first.

In the system of 22 we have seen that the third is 7 units. Looking at the circle of fifths, the third by 4 fifths up is 8 units. We may form the third to any note therefore by ascending through 4 fifths of the series and then descending one unit; *i. e.*, the third is formed in the circle of fifths, one unit below that which contains the fundamental.

This mode of formation has not been previously considered. It leads to the following observation, which is important in the practical employment of the system :—

Modulation through a third, in systems of this character, cannot be generally treated as equivalent to modulation through any number of fifths.

We proceed to a further classification of the higher systems, based on this property.

By definition, the interval between the two ends of the circle of fifths is r units. Let r circles of fifths be placed in juxta-position, so that corresponding pairs of notes are all one unit apart, and consider the third formed with the starting point of the uppermost series.

Then we shall define a system as being of class x, when the third lies in the *xth* series below the upper one.

In the system of 22, the third (7) to c (0) lies one series below that in which c is, so that we may define the properties of the system of 22 by saying that it is of order 2 and class 1.

The simplest systems of higher orders are those which form their thirds either by 4 fifths up or 8 fifths down in the same series; those may be spoken of as of order r class o, and order r class r respectively. Both have been considered in my paper already referred to.

I proceed to indicate shortly the general expressions by means of which systems can be discussed.

The departure of the third formed by 4 fifths up is

$$4\frac{r}{n}.$$

In a system of class x, the third is x units lower, and its departure is

$$4\frac{r}{n}-x.\frac{12}{n}=-4\ \frac{3x-r}{n}\ \ldots\ldots\ldots\ldots\ldots\ldots\ (i)$$

And this has to be compared with the departure of the perfect third,

$$=-{\cdot}13686$$

$$=-\frac{1}{7{\cdot}3}\text{ nearly.}$$

So that for a determination of the class of any system n of the *rth* order, we have the approximate condition.

$$3x-r=\frac{n}{29{\cdot}2}\text{ nearly}\ \ldots\ldots\ldots\ldots\ldots\ (ii)$$

DIAGRAM II.

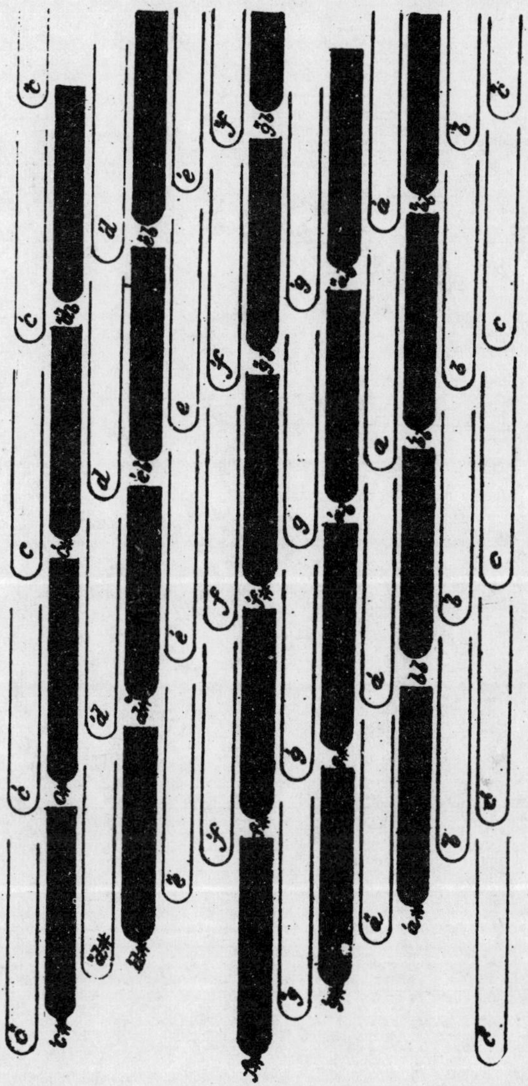

The formulæ (*i*) and (*ii*) are sufficient for any required discussion; they present no difficulty, and I confine myself to a statement of a few of the principal results.

The departure of the third of all systems of order 2, class 1 is represented by

$$-\frac{4}{n}.$$

The system of 34, of order 2, class 1, presents both fifths and thirds of exceptional excellence. This system may be of interest for modern purposes.

Systems of the third order and first class have equal-temperament thirds; for (*i*) vanishes when $x=\frac{r}{3}$: or, more generally, a system has E. T., thirds when the number of the class is $\frac{1}{3}$ that of the order.

System of order r class x which make 3x—r, negative need not be considered, as their thirds are sharper than E. T. thirds

In the third order, class 2, there is a good system of 87.

In the fourth order, class 2, there is a good system of 56.

Neither of these are likely to be of practical interest.

Practical Applications.

In the light of the foregoing investigation we see that the generalized key-board, as hitherto constructed, is of limited application; it is capable of controlling only systems which form their thirds by either 4-fifths or 8-fifths down.

The systems included by these conditions are all those of the first order, positive and negative, and all systems of any order of class o or class r. These embrace all that are likely to be interesting with reference to European harmonious music, with the possible exception of the system of 34 above alluded to.

The principles of the position on which the key-board is founded are, however, applicable to all higher systems; and I shall presently investigate its transformations. The key-board of the second order thus obtained will afford a means of controlling, in a convenient manner, systems of the first class in that order, and dealing with facility with either the Hindu system of 22, or the system of 34 above mentioned.

But before proceeding to discuss these arrangements, it is desirable to provide the extension of our notation, which is necessary for dealing with systems of the rth order and classes other than r and o.

Generalized Notation.

The notation which I have hitherto employed has always assumed that the deviation, or departure, due to a circle of 12-fifths is identical with one unit of the system employed.

Thus C—1C represented both the departure of 12-fifths and the smallest interval, or unit, of the system.

In non-cyclical systems, and in systems of the first order, this representation is consistent and satisfactory; but in systems of higher orders these two conceptions diverge. The departure of 12 fifths and the unit of the system can no longer be represented by the same symbol.

The choice we will make is, that the symbol of elevation or depression shall represent primarily one unit of the system. Thus c—/c will always represent the unit, but will only represent the departure of 12 fifths in systems of the first order.

C—/ /c will be the departure of twelve-fifths in systems of the second order; *c—/ / /c* in systems of the third order, and so on.

It follows that, in a continuous series of fifths, at the point where two consecutive series of the notation join, the difference of the marks, on the two notes which constitute the joining fifth, wiil be *r*.

Thus the following are fifths which join the unmarked series to that next above it :—

In the 1st order, *b*—/*f*♯,
2nd „ *b*—//*f*♯,
3rd „ *b*—///*f*♯

and so on.

We now require only to find the thirds. Introducing the conditions that the system be of class x, we find the third as follows :—Pass up four steps in the series of fifths, and then *x* units down.

Example.—Order 2, Class 1.

Third to C :

4 Steps up give *e*,

1 Unit down *e*, which is the required third.

Third to C :

4 Steps up give / /*d*♯,

1 Unit down /*d*♯, which is the third.

Whence, in order 2, class 1, *b*, *e*, *a*, *d* (letters of the memoria—technica word) form thirds by one mark up, and all remaining notes by one mark down.

Similarly, in a system of order *r* clsss *x*, *b*, *e*, *a*, *d* form thirds with *r*—*x* marks up, and all the remaining notes with *x* marks down.

Transformations of the generalized Key-board.

It is only necessary to require, in the construction of the generalized key-board, that all the keys shall equally fit all the bearings, to render it possible to produce any required position system with a sufficient number of the ordinary keys. This requirement has always been attended to in the plans for the sake of simplification ; though the important results which flow from it were not originally foreseen. But it is found that unless the attention of the maker is specially directed to the point, the nature of the finishing processes does not secure the result in question ; there is, however, no difficulty in securing it when it is desired.

The distance of the end of the key on the plan (projection on a horizontal plane) from a line of reference drawn from right to left determines the form of the key completely.

There are 12 such fundamental positions ; so that we may describe the pattern of any key completely as a function of a series of numbers running from 1 to 12. After 12 the same patterns recur, with reference to a new standard line, such that the old 12 has the same position as the new *o*.

The ordinary arrangement of a series of 12 fifths may be simply exhibited by writing under each note of the series the number of which its pattern is a function.

Direct Key-board.

c	*g*	*d*	*a*	*e*	*b*	/*f*♯	/*c*♯	/*g*♯	/*d*♯	/*a*♯	/*f*	/*c*
1	2	3	4	5	6	7	8	9	10	11	12	1

Increase of the numbers denotes increased height as well as increased distance from the front ; so that according to this, the original arrangement, rise on the key-board corresponds to rise in the series of fifths.

Inversion.

Before the key-board was originally constructed, it became matter for investigation how far it would be advantageous to make rise in the series of fifths correspond to fall on the key-board and *vice versâ*.

It is a question of manipulation; the advantages are in some cases rather evenly balanced, and it is very desirable to examine this arrangement practically.

The example of transformation will bear upon this problem:—

It is possible to convert a generalized key-board of the "direct arrangement" above described into an "inverted one" by re-arranging the keys.

Inverted Key-board.

c	*g*	*d*	*a*	*e*	*b*	/ *f*♯	/ *c*♯	/ *g*♯	/ *d*♯	/ *a*♯	/ *f*	/ *c*
12	11	10	9	8	7	6	5	4	3	2	1	12

To complete this transformation in an extremely practical manner, we have only to determine the condition that white and black notes shall remain the same.

Looking at the key-board of an ordinary piano, which presents the same order of white and black, we see that, as far as colour is concerned, it is symmetrical about two points, *d* and *a*♭. Portions of a key-board, therefore, which terminate in these points, or in points equi-distant on opposite sides from either, present when inverted from right to left, the same sequence of black and white as before.

The most convenient arrangement for this purpose consists of a compass of keys from *c* to *e*, any number of octaves included.

When inverted, *i. e.*, when the note on the extreme right is placed in the same row on the extreme left and so on, such an arrangement presents the same sequence of black and white as before.

The *e* becomes *a c* and the sequence of patterns is that of an inverted series.

General transformation of the rth order.

Systems of the *rth* order were defined as those in which the ends of the circle of 12 fifths include *r* units of the system. Similarly the key-board of the *rth* order may be defined as that which has *r* unit intervals ($r-1$ notes) in the vertical line between the ends of a circle of 12-fifths.

It is easy to obtain the condition of arrangement in the general case. The difference of level of the ends of the series of 12-fifths, must amount to 12 steps by course of fifths, and to *r* steps by course of units. Consequently the whole difference of level of the ends of the series of fifths must be made up of 12 *r* primary steps, or steps made by the patterns; each step in course of fifths must be made up of *r* primary steps, and each step in course of units must be made up of 12 primary steps.* In this manner, with a sufficient supply of notes of the 12 given patterns, a generalized key-board of any order can be at once arranged.

Although system of any order can always be constructed in this manner, it will not generally be the case that they can be played upon with facility—simply because the large space covered by related notes cannot be, in the general case, brought within reach of the hand. By any system can be demonstrated in this manner.

KEY-BOARD OF THE SECOND ORDER.

The key-board of the second order furnishes results of some interest. It can be easily arranged according to the foregoing rules. The peculiarity in the result is, that performance on a complete system of the second order and first class, by means of it, is nearly as easy as performance on system of the first order by means of the key-board formerly constructed. The problem of representation and performance is thus solved both of the Hindu system of 22, and for the system of 34, the interest of which has been already indicated.

Diagram II. (p. 382) represents a portion of the key-board of the second order.

C—/*e*—*g* is a major triad, whence the major thirds are better situated for the finger than on the first order key-board with positive systems ; but the presence of continuous rows of keys in all twelve divisions is somewhat less advantageous than in that arrangement.

C—/*e**—*g* is the minor triad.

In the general transformation of the *rth* order, transformation with regard to colour (white or black) is not generally practicable. For the most general purpose it would be necessary to have a sufficient supply of keys of both colours for every pattern ; for any particular case the requirements are more limited.

* Any common factor of r and 12 may be divided out, since it is only necessary that the two classes of steps should be to each other as $12 : r$.

HINDU MUSIC.

BY

SOURINDRO MOHUN TAGORE.

Reprinted from the "Hindoo Patriot,"

7th September 1874.

HINDU MUSIC.

THE *Hindoo Patriot* of the 15th September last contained a criticism on Mr. C. B. Clarke's report on Hindu Music, embodied in a letter, dated the 17th May 1873, and addressed to the Director of Public Instruction. After an interval of about eight months Mr. Clarke thought fit to answer that criticism in an essay in the *Calcutta Review,* and it gave rise to a learned and interesting controversy, in the columns of the *Indian Observer,* between Mr. Aldis, Principal of the *Martinere,* an accomplished critic, and Mr. Clarke. The controversy has closed only lately. Other papers have also had their say on the subject. We watched with interest the current of criticism on Mr. Clarke's essay, and now that all parties have apparently exhausted themselves on the subject, we may, we think, with propriety, say a few words in reply to the author of the report, who has provoked this war of words. We are sorry to perceive that he still persists in his original misconception of the real character of Hindu Music; that he supports his errors by committing fresh errors; and that the more he proceeds, the more he involves himself in a maze of hopeless delusions. His mathematicism has proved a snare for himself in his attempt to unweave the web of Hindu Music. We believe he is a searcher after truth, and if he will, in a kindly spirit, accept the light which we, in all humility, offer to him, he may yet find out that priceless treasure. We will now proceed to an examination of Mr. Clarke's critical dissertation.

At first sight it would seem as if Mr. Clarke's chief object in writing the essay was to mystify the subject by enveloping it in a cloud of mathematicism. But no one is better aware than himself that mathematics is no more indispensable for one to be a musician than it is indispensable for him to be a painter or statuary. In learning music the student requires, above all things, an educated ear capable of detecting and feeling the sense of all tonal combinations. The susceptibility of an art being examined by mathematical tests is some thing different from mathematics being indispensable to its comprehension or acquisition. Principles of music, embodied into scientific theories, may be based on mathematics, but it does not necessarily follow that one must know mathematics in order to understand those principles. We may say without fear of contradiction that those principles which go to form the science of Acoustics enter fully into Hindu Music. But that science in its improved form is still incomplete and imperfect. "The state of our knowledge of Acoustics," justly observes Professor Graham, "one of the most subtle and difficult of sciences, is still too incomplete to permit of the formation of a perfect theory of music." There is nothing to make us regret that the principles of Acoustics, as they exhibit themselves in our music, differ in form from the European system. We shall have occasion to shew as we proceed that the science of Acoustics, as it exists among the Hindus, is quite sufficient for all purposes as regards the application of its principles to music. Mr. Clarke, we hope, will permit us to produce the testimony of eminent European professors of music to prove that mathematics, instead of contributing to the exposition and development of music, does much to mystify and obscure it. Dr. Weber says, "I must vindicate myself on the allegation, that, according to the foregoing division, harmonial acoustics, and in particular the mathematical doctrine of intervals, is not mentioned as a part, much less as the basis, of the doctrine of musical composition. For, most teachers of musical composition imagine that the theory of musical composition must necessarily be founded on harmonic acoustics, and, on this account commence their books of instruction with arithmetical and algebraic problems and formulas. But this seems to me, calling it by its proper name, nothing else than a mass of empty vagaries and an unseasonable retailing of erudition,—pedantry. For, one may be the profoundest musical composer, the greatest contrapuntist; one may be a Mozart or a Haydn, a Bach or a Palestrina, without knowing that a tone is to its fifth as 2 to 3; and it is, in my honest conviction, a mistake of teachers of musical composition, betraying a decided want of understanding of the subject, to mix, as they do, with the doctrine of musical composition, such demonstrations by fractions, powers, roots and equations, and other mathematical formulas, from which to proceed in teaching the theory of musical composition. To me it appears just as it would be for one to commence a course of instruction in painting, with the theory of light and colors, of straight and curved lines; musical instruction, with the study of harmony; and instruction in language, with the philosophy of speech; or, to demonstrate the principles of grammar to a child, in order to teach him to say—papa and mamma." Dr. Marx's observation of mathematics in relation to music are more pointed. He says, "our object, however, is not to calculate, but freely to invent; and this requires no mathematical calculations but a higher faculty which enables us to detect and feel the sense of the different tonal combinations; and, therefore, might be called artistic consciousness." The great Aristoxinas takes the same view, forcibly enforces the same doctrine and will not allow either reason or mathematics to have any share in the arrangement of the intervals. He thought sense the only judge. He therefore determined the 4th, 5th, and 8th by the ear, and the difference of the 4th and the 5th found out the interval of the tone.

Professor Graham, in his essay on the theory and practice of musical composition, while dwelling upon the injurious effect of mathematics on music, says,—"In Italy we may hear persons who cannot read music, singing very agreeably in two, or three, or four parts, in harmony. Do such persons know any thing of the harmonic ratios of the sounds they combine together in this way? They have no more idea that even an octave is in the ratio of 1:2, than they have of the distance between the earth and the moon. Similar false applications of mathematics have tended greatly to produce that mysterious obscurity which has hitherto been artificially thrown over the beautiful and inviting regions of musical melody and harmony."

But it is not necessary to go so far as Italy. The truth contained in the above extract is of universal application, and may be perceived in all countries in the fact that the greatest musicians and the most tasteful composers did not pretend to a knowledge of mathematics. Who amongst the students of oriental music is ignorant of the names of MIRJA BULL-BULL of Persia, AKHWAL-U-SOBBHA and NICOMACHUS of Arabia, HERMES TRISMEGISTUS of Egypt, the great CONFUCIUS and CHAONG of China, OSMAN EFIENDI of Turkey, ASAPH of the Hebrews, THAN SEN, AMEER KHUSRU, NAYAKA GOPAL, HURIDAS SWAMI, and RAJA MAN, HAHA, HUHU, SARANGADEVA, NARADA, BHARAT, and NARAYANADEVA of India? And yet who will venture to say that any one of them was a mathematician? The extracts we have given, we hope, will prove sufficiently the futility of Mr. Clarke's infallible test of mathematics.

We admire Mr. Clarke's boldness in venturing upon a discussion on the merits of Hindu Music with, as it appears, scarcely any knowledge of its elementary principles. He has no knowledge of Sanskrit, and is but very imperfectly acquainted with Bengali. He had recourse to a native guide, who seems to be equally ignorant of the Sanskrit language as of the musical literature of his country. And the result is that the critic is made to betray his ignorance of the simplest things in our musical system, such as the term Rága and the number of Rágas in use, of the construction of the Sitara and its capacity, though it is the simplest and the most popular of Hindu musical instruments. He attacks the Srooties which he does not evidently understand, though they form the very base-work of the musical system of the Hindus. That we are not wrong in our estimate of the critic's knowledge of the subject of his criticism will be perceived as we examine his theories one by one.

First as regards his views of Rága in Hindu Music. In saying "there are 36 modes in use amongst the Hindus," he evidently supposes that Rága and Mode are synonymous. Let us see how Danneley defines the term "mode." "A mode," he says, "or a scale is called major, when its third diatonic note is composed of four chromatic degrees; or is the fifth diatonic—chromatic note of the scale, called also the major third; as, C—natural, E—natural, C—sharp, E—sharp &c. A mode or scale is said to be minor when the third note, called the minor third, is composed of but three chromatic degrees; as C E—flat D F—natural; in opposition to major, the third note of which is composed of four chromatic degrees." Let us again see what view Captain Willard takes of Rága in Hindu Music:—

"Mode in the language of the musicians of this country (India) is, in my opinion, termed *Thát* and not Rága or Ráginee." "The word mode," he continues, "may be taken in two different significations—the one implying manner of style, and the other of key; and, strictly speaking, this latter is the sense in which it is usually understood in music." Neither is tune Rága as has been apparently construed by our critic in the following:—

"It is true that a European melody written in the fundamental mode can introduce and sometimes will introduce all the twelve notes in the octave, whereas the Hindu tunes cannot."

We will again quote Willard. "It is true," he says, "that a Ráginee (or Rága) is not to be considered exactly in the same situation as a tune is amongst us. It is not strictly a tune according to the acceptation of the word."

Tune and Rága are thus so distinct from each other that one cannot be used for the other without a confusion of ideas. Rága is not joined by regular and symmetrical forms, and may not terminate in the same key as the tune. Moreover, one Rága may be multiplied into innumerable tunes when its *angas*, namely *bibádí*, *anubádí*, *sambádí*, *graha*, *nyasa*, &c., are so arranged as to follow each other in regular succession. Again, Rága is not divided by a *bivájiká-rekhá* or bars, as the tune is. The truth is the English language has not a corresponding term for the Rága. To express it by the term mode would be nearly as accurate as to express the idea of quinine by the word *chiretta* in Bengali. How could *chiretta* be translated into English or quinine into Bengali when there is no term for *chiretta* in English and no term for quinine in Bengali? In the same way there is no equivalent term for Rága in English, nor one for mode in Bengali. The idea which the word Rága conveys has not its counterpart in English.

To enable Mr. Clarke to form a correct idea of the term Rága, and to prevent his confounding it with mode, we beg to recommend for his perusal such learned treatises as *Rágá-Bibodha, Rága-Sarvaswa Sára, Rágáranava, &c.*

As we have observed above our critic has not only no idea of Rága, but he is also ignorant of the number of its varieties. In one part of his essay he says, "Hindu Music, which employs 36 modes, &c." If he attempts to give a *swaragráma* of all the 36 modes he refers to, he will perceive the distinction between mode and Rága. He would have, however, avoided the mistake into which he has fallen, if his researches on the subject had extended a little beyond hearsay. The following stanza will occur to the most superficial enquirer who has but a rudimentary knowledge of the literature of Hindu Music :

सङ्गीतमारभत् कृष्णो मुरलीनादमोहितः ।
गोपीभिर्गीतमारब्धमेकैकं कृष्णसन्निधौ ॥
तेन जातानि रागाणां सहस्राणि च षोड़श ।

नारद संवाद ।

"KRISHNA, enchanted by the music of his flute, began singing, and the GOPIKÁS (sixteen thousands in number) followed him one by one, and thus are produced sixteen thousand Rágas."

Nárada Sambáda I, Chapter.

Again, our critic says, "It (Bengali Music) employs also seven notes only of the octave in simple tune and nine in more elaborate ones, &c."

The confidence with which the above lines are written is in keeping with his general knowledge of Hindu Music. To whom is he indebted for that invaluable morsel of truth that Bengali music employs nine notes in elaborate tunes? We would take the liberty to commend him to the following lines which occur in all respectable Sanskrit works on music:

ओड़वः पञ्चभिः प्रोक्तः स्वरैः षड्भिश्च षाड़वः ।
सम्पूर्णः सप्तभिश्चैय एवं रागास्त्रिधा मताः ॥

सङ्गीत दर्पण।

"There are three classes of Rāgas (in Hindu Music): that class which is produced by a *grāma* consisting of five tones is called *odava*, and that produced by a *gráma* of six tones is called *shādava*, while the third one produced by a *grāma* of seven tones is called *sampúrna*."

Sangita Darpana.

It may be observed here in passing that the diatonic scale which Mr. Clarke has used for our षड्ज gráma is a wrong one. The diatonic scale somewhat resembles the *saptaka* but not quite.

After giving a very short and meagre description of the Sitara, the simplest and the most popular musical instrument in use amongst the natives of this country, he says:

"But the frets (of the Sitara) are then inconveniently close together." It would be difficult to obviate objections in a case which depends upon practice. What may appear inconvenient to any other person may be one of the easiest musical feats to a practised player. We, for our part, shall be very happy to demonstrate this practically if our critic wants a practical demonstration. We do not know on what authority he ventures to make the statement that "the Sitara cannot play D flat." Any body can do it. We find no difficulty in playing it with *Múrchchhaná* and can practically shew it without displacing the frets. Here, again, is another illustration of the mischief of hearsay knowledge. There would have been no chance of mistake if statements had been made on the authority of an expert or of one who possessed some practical knowledge. Mr. Clarke, in another place, says, "Hindu Music employs melody only without harmony." This is a very unqualified assertion. It is true that Hindu Music abounds in melody, but it is not void of harmony. The following quotation from NÁRADA's work will best explain our meaning :—

गानस्य दशविध गुणवृत्तिस्तद्यथा, रक्तं पूर्णमलङ्कृतं
प्रसन्नं व्यक्तं विकृष्टं श्लक्ष्णं समं सुकुमारं मधुर-
मिति गुणाः । तत्र रक्तं नाम वेणुवीणादि-स्वराणा-
मेकोवे रक्तमित्युच्यते ।

There are ten kinds of properties of a song. These are :

रक्तं पूर्णमलङ्कृतं प्रसन्नं व्यक्तं विकृष्टं श्लक्ष्णं समं
सुकुमारं मधुरम् ।

but all of them are not to our present purpose ; रक्तं (*Raktang*) only serves our purpose well, and its definition is as follows : रक्तं (*Raktang*) is that which is produced by a combination of the sounds of all stringed-instruments, wind-instruments, and those of other kinds.

This is harmony. *Vide* सङ्गीत दर्पण and अद्भुत रामायण ।

The disadvantage of writing with an imperfect knowledge of his subject has betrayed the critic into absurd blunders at almost every step. We have another instance in the following extract :

"The Sitara thus stands in the mode, and can be made to stand in any one of the thirty.six modes employed in Hindu Music. This connection between the Sitara and the modes in use renders it certain that either the modes are derived from the Sitara or that the Sitara has been invented to play those particular modes. This latter seems to me highly improbable."

It is impossible to have two opinions on a point which does not admit of a doubt. To say that the Rágas were derived from the Sitara would be as much as to say that the goose was produced from the quill. The Sitara is an instrument of yesterday's invention. It was, according to Captain Willard, invented by AMEER KHUSROO in the beginning of the 12th century. Even the Víná, the most ancient of the Hindu instruments of music, of which the modern Sitara is a clumsy imitation, was invented by the great NÁRADA long after the Rágas had been practised on the throat. That this most ancient instrument, whose invention is almost coeval with the origin of Hindu Music, did not precede but follow the Ragas will appear from the following extracts familiar to every student of Sanskrit music :

रागाः कण्ठगताः स्मृताः

"The Rágas are known to be located in the throat."

Ergo they are not derived from the Sitara or any other instrument.

दारवी गात्रवीणा च द्वे वीणे गानजातिषु ।
सामगी गात्रवीणा तु तस्याः शृणुत लक्षणं ॥
गात्रवीणातु सा प्रोक्ता यस्यां गायन्ति सामगाः ।
स्वरव्यञ्जनसंयुक्ता तस्या दारुविनिर्म्मिता ॥

There are two kinds of Víná in music, namely, दारवी (Dáravi) or that which is made of wood and गात्रवीणा (Gátravíná) or that which is to be found in the human body. Now गात्रवीणा (Gátravíná) is called Sámagí because the *Sáma-Veda* singers wholly depended upon this Víná in singing hymns from the *Sáma-Veda*. It is capable of producing both tones and articulate sounds. Dáravivíná, which is made of wood, is an imitation of the Gátravíná.

निविश्य दृष्टिं हस्ताग्रे शास्त्रार्थमनुचिन्तयन् ।
सममुच्चारयेद्वाक्यं हस्तेन च मुखेन च ॥
यथैवोच्चारयेद् वर्णांस्तथैवैनान् समापयेत् ।

नारदीयशिक्षा ।

"Looking at the fingers and following the directions of the *Sástras* the words should at once be sounded both by the mouth and by the hand."

Again :—

नृत्यं वाद्यानुगं प्रोक्तं वाद्यं गीतानुवर्त्ति च ।
अतो गीतं प्रधानत्वादत्रादावभिधीयते ॥

सङ्गीत नारायण ।

"Dancing follows instrumental music, and music follows singing, hence singing being of prime importance it should here be first explained."

It is thus clear that the Rágas were neither derived from the Sitara nor from the Víná.

Mr. Clarke in a kind of condescending style reproves us for our obstinacy in maintaining that C sharp is the same as D flat. His words are :—

"Probably my Bengali friends will be surprised to hear that C sharp is never the same as D flat that in the instruments like violin that can be stopped anywhere, &c." We forbear urging any thing in defence of our position. If we have erred we have erred with the safest authorities on the subject. What Dr. Adolph Bernnard Marx, Professor of Music at the University of Berlin, says on this point, will, we suppose, be accepted as a conclusive settler of the dispute. "The attentive student," he states, "will, however, soon observe that two keys have each two different names and that *c flat* is the same as *b*, and *f flat* is the same as *e*. Such sounds which only differ in name but are indeed the same (as regards pitch) are termed enharmonic sounds. Thus *b* and *c flat*, *e* and *f flat*, *b sharp* and *c*, *c* sharp and *d flat*, *a flat* and *g sharp* are enharmonic sounds or notes. It may at first appear strange that each sound should thus have two different names; and the student may be inclined to ask why not call the black keys always *c sharp*, *d sharp*, &c., &c., or *d flat*, *e flat* &c., &c.. Why is *e* to be called sometimes *f flat*, and *f* sometimes *e sharp*. For this apparent superfluity of names there are very good reasons; they are indispensable for the sake of clearness and precision in musical notation, but their necessity will more fully appear in the study of the theory and practice of musical composition."

Again, the critic asks, "if there is no difference between G sharp and A flat, why have European musicians permitted in using two for one and the same thing?" The reply is a simple one, and a reference to Mr. John Hullah's work would have saved him the trouble of this enquiry. The words of Mr. Hullah are that they "are used for transposition, modulation, minor scale and chromatic scales." In Sanskrit they are used to mark the ascending and descending of a scale.

We are free to confess that we made the assertion, which is disputed, not on the authority of Sanskrit works, but from what we observed in English music. As Dr. Weber states:—

"When must a tone be written as the elevation of a lower one, and when as the elevation of a higher one? This is a point to which we have not yet attended. For the present it is sufficient to know that sometimes the one takes place and sometimes the other, just according to the different relations under which the tone occurs."

Again:

"It may, however, be further observed in respect to this matter that such a tone should not properly sound so high in the first case as in the second, *e. g.*, the key between C and D, when it occurs as C sharp it is not quite so high as when it appears as D flat, F sharp is not quite so high as G flat, E flat is not so low as D sharp, E sharp is not quite so high as F, F flat is not quite so low as E, C double sharp is not quite so high as D or E double flat, &c; This difference between C sharp and D flat, F sharp and G flat, and the like, is called an *enharmonic difference*; (which we call the difference of Srooties). These differences, however, are extremely small and thus imperceptible to our ear, and we may with entire propriety and convenience have but one and the same key for all tones differing only enharmonically; they may also be called *enharmonically parellel tones.* Thus only one and the same key C sharp and D flat, for A sharp and B flat, for C double sharp and D and E double flat, &c.

"Whatever be the bearing of this circumstance in other respects, in one certainly it is very convenient; for if, instead of the mere twelve keys which we now have within the compass of one octave, we should have a distinct key exclusively for C sharp and another for D flat, &c., one for E and another for F flat, and still another perhaps for D double sharp, &c., our pianofortes must be overloaded with an endless multitude of keys."

Thus we have been spared the trouble of entering into a vindication of our position, though Dr. Weber's explanations do not appear to us to be quite satisfactory. We hold that there must be difference between G sharp and A flat according to the division by *Srooties.* Mr. Clarke, should he admit this theory, must confess to a conversion to our doctrine; but should he deny the *Srooties* (quarter tones) he will only contradict himself. Any how his statements and his apparently professed creed are at variance with each other. All that we say is that he is right only when he admits the *Srooties.*

With regard to our critic's complaints as expressed in the following extracts, we sympathize with him on his want of knowledge of the Sanskrit language in which the theories of the art of music are clearly expounded:

"My Bengali critics assert that I do not understand what Srooties (or very sharp, very flat) are in Bengali music. How can I if the Srooties are not defined."

Again:

"But my Bengali critics while they go on piling heaps of hard terms about Srooti, &c., also omit altogether to define that of which they say I fail to discover the accurate meaning."

We are really sorry for our critic. We tried to make the idea of Srooti clear to him by a periphrasis in which the use of hard terms was unavoidable. And any definition that we may attempt will always fall short of his comprehension because of his ignorance of Sanskrit. But we will make another effort. The definitions in Sanskrit as given in *Sangita Ratnávali* are the following :

स्वल्पमात्रश्रवणान्नादानुरणनात्मिका ।
श्रुतिरित्युच्यते भेदास्तस्या द्वाविंशतिर्मताः ॥
षड्जादिकपरिज्ञानं श्रुतीनां फलमेव तत् ॥
ध्वनिमञ्जरी ।

A Srooti is formed by the smallest intervals of the sound and is to be perceivable by the ear. It is of twenty-two kinds.

श्रवणात् श्रुतिः

"Every distinct audible sound is a Srooti."

Again :

———————स्वराः श्रुतिसमुद्भवाः ।
श्रुतयः स्थानसम्भूताः स्थानानि त्रीणि तत्र हि ।
हृत्कण्ठः शिर इत्यासां द्विगुणादुत्तरोत्तरं ।
प्रत्येकं स्थानमेतच्च द्वाविंशतिविधं भवेत् ।
हृन्मूर्द्धनाभिकालग्ना नाड्यो द्वाविंशतिः शुभाः ।

"It is a Srooti because it is to be heard by the ear. Tones are produced by Srooties, and the places from which Srooties arise are three in number, *viz.*, heart, throat, and head."

तास्व वक्रास्तयोर्द्धस्था ध्वनिता मरुताहताः ।

"To every one of these three places there are twenty-two strings attached, and from them when struck by the wind the Srooties are produced, and these Srooties in every place rise successively higher and higher, *i. e.*, those of the throat are of higher tone than those of the heart, and so on."

The critic's failure to understand the term Srooti has led him to a curious blunder in his attempt to give a division of the Srooties in the Hindu Swaragráma ; this will appear from the following passage :

"The tone from G to A is divided into three Srooties and the tone from A to B into two Srooties."

The truth is, within the interval from G to A which corresponds to our प to ध we have four Srooties, and in that from A to B which corresponds to ध to नि three Srooties, as the following couplet from *Sangita Nárâyana* which is borne out by similar authorities in other Sanskrit books, will prove :

चतस्रः पञ्चमे षड्जे मध्यमे श्रुतयो मताः ।
ऋषभे धैवते तिस्रो द्वे गान्धारे निषादके ॥

"There are four Srooties in पञ्चम, षड्ज and मध्यम or G, C, and F, three in ऋषभ and धैवत or D, and A, and two in गान्धार and निषाद or E, and B."

We also find the following passages on the point in Carl Engel : "Smaller intervals than semi-tones are in use with some Asiatic nations, and were employed by the Hindus long before our Christian era."

Further,

"The seven intervals of the Hindu scale which nearly correspond with our diatonic major scale, are subdivided into twenty-two Srooties corresponding to quarter-tones."

Mr. Clarke finds fault with us for using the term quarter-tone for Srooti. We owe him some explanation. We used the word in the absence of a better one, though we are fully aware that a quarter-tone is not a Srooti. The term is used in all English works where it is intended to convey the idea of a Srooti, and we thought that Mr. Clarke would have no difficulty in understanding it if similarly used by us. In English there are no corresponding terms for Srooti, Rága, Murchchhaná, Tála and several other words commonly used in Hindu Music, and in employing any one of them in an English composition on music the choice of words conveying an approximate meaning is unavoidable, and in such a case the writer cannot be said to misuse words except by the hypercritical.

Then Mr. Clarke puts the following query; "I therefore ask what is a Srooti, is it a quarter-tone as my opponents usually denominate it: or is it sometimes a quarter-tone—sometimes third of a tone?" We reply that a Srooti is sometimes a quarter-tone and sometimes the third of a tone. There are four Srooties between षड्ज and ऋषभ and therefore each Srooti between these two tones is a quarter-tone. Similarly there are three Srooties between ऋषभ and गान्धार and here each Srooti is the third of a tone. To prevent misconception it is necessary to add that except in the definite places pointed out there cannot be a quarter-tone and third of a tone in any and every place. As to our critic's dogmatical conclusion that "if the latter alternative (the third of a tone) is selected I think it may be demonstrated that music on such a scale is impossible." We have just proved that when a Srooti is the third of a tone between ऋ and ग it is quite in place and the tone is perfectly musical—nobody has yet questioned that the tone between ऋ and ग is an unmusical one.

To come now to his other queries. He asks, "How many Srooties are there between C and G in *Tārā*, the upper octave, and how many between A and B in *Mudárá,* the lower octave? And in answering this question it must be recollected that the distance from C and D or from A to B is the same in every octave." There lies couched in these queries an unconscious mistake, but for which there would have been no occasion for them. Between C and D in the upper octave there are four Srooties, and between A and B in the lower octave, three. We shall only remark that there is no difference in number between the three *saptakas*—the only difference that exists consists in the difference of value. The numbers do not increase in quantity but in quality. We have again recourse to *Sangita Ratnávalí* which says :—

एते तु ध्वनिभेदाः स्युः श्रवणात् श्रुतिसंज्ञिताः ।
उच्चैश्चभावमापन्नाः द्विगुणादुत्तरोत्तरं ।

"These are the different kinds of tones. Then these are called Srooties because they are heard and rise higher and highest up in tone (as they pass through the different quarters)."

The warning given in the last sentence of the extract from the critique is uncalled-for. The distance from C to D (or from A to B) is not the same in every octave, for there are four Srooties in the interval between C and D, while there are three only between A and B, and our critic does not, we hope, wish us to say that four is equal to three. We repeat that the different spaces are the same in the three octaves,—they differ from each other only in quality.

Again, he asks—"If between G and A the difference is divided into three Srooties, does any one of the Srooti intervals coincide with the semi-tones, or do the three Srooties divide the interval from G to A into three equal tones?" The question itself is wrong. Between G and A there are not three but four Srooties divided into four equal intervals. This is the truth which all Hindu Musical works teach and which reason approves.

The assurance implied in the following passage is not a little surprising. "It is impossible to challenge any Bengali performer to exhibit the Srooties on a Sitara, for there are no frets on the Sitara at the Srooti intervals so that the Srooti can only be performed by flicking the string, *i. e.,* altogether uncertainly."

This is going a little too far, to say the least of it. What will the writer do if he has to tune a Rága ? Will he flick the string merely or do something else ? Will it not be necessary to remove the frets as often and whenever necessary, and tune the Srooti so that Rága may come out ? His replies to these questions will serve for the explanations he seeks.

Our critic not content with his extravagant and dogmatic opinions makes the following challenge :—

"Can any Bengali singer be produced who can sing the quarter tones between C and D and afterwards the third note between G and A ? I will not say produced before me as I am about to pledge myself to a total disbelief in the whole thing, but any competent Professor of music such as Mr. Frye."

Security, it is said, is man's chiefest enemy, and this is noteably the case with Mr. Clarke. The feat he alludes to, is neither impracticable nor difficult. One who knows to sing can sing both the quarter-tone and the third note without difficulty. It is done every day by practised singers and has been in use amongst us from remote antiquity. Very distinct allusion is made to the feat in ancient Sanskrit works on music such as *Ratnāvalī, Rága Bibodha,* and the like, from which we make the following extract :

क्रमादुच्चोच्चतायुक्ता वीणाकण्ठे तु लक्षिताः ।
ताः स्वरमण्डलयन्त्रादौ दर्शयन्ति सुशिक्षिताः ॥

"Srooties or enharmonic tones rise higher and highest up in succession perceivable both in Víná or in the stringed instruments and in the throat."

It is thus clear that the Srooties are both tuned and sung. We shall be very happy to satisfy Mr. Clarke not only before Professor Frye, but any number of European musicians of the truth of our statement. The difficulty will lie with the challenger himself, who, we may be permitted to say, evidently seems to be incapable of appreciating the Srooties. His disbelief in them, however, does not disprove their existence any more than the disbelief of a blind man in the existence of colors disprove the colors themselves. Neither can it affect the truth that the Srooties or enharmonic tones have been used and recognised from time immemorial not only in this country but in Greece, Arabia, China, Persia and several other Asiatic countries. Nathan truly observes that the Srooties are extremely musical, and they are so called from their superior excellence as a species of music, the modulation whereof, according to Brossard, proceeds by intervals less than quarter-tones. This species was in great vogue among the Greeks by whom it was considered much easier of execution, but it is now lost. It is evidently of much of ancient date as Aristoxinus ascribes the invention to Olympus. Dr. Burney says that Dr. Russel procured him from Aleppo the Arabian scale of music, the octave of which consisted of twenty-four quarter-tones, all of which admitted of the same demonstration as the Srooties. The following extract from Dr. Graham is very much to the point. He says, "as to the Hindu, Persian and Chinese scales and the use of the quarter-tones and other minute intervals, we refer the reader to what we published on that subject in No. IV., of the new *Edinburgh Review* for April 1822, pp. 521-528. We have examined a number of Chinese wind and stringed instruments brought home in June 1837 and have found semi-tones in all of them. Professional musicians who followed Napolean to Egypt remarked the frequent and dexterous use of very small intervals by some singers." Can we help inferring that the tones in the instruments referred to were Srooties ?

Again Stafford, the musical historian, says :—" A late traveller assures us that the modern Egyptian performers make use of very minute intervals in singing passages of embellishment with a rapidity and volubility, the imitation of which would be difficult, if not impracticable, to most European singers." That they are in use among many uncivilized nations will be found in various works of note, from one of which we transcribe the following passage :—

" Even some uncivilized nations possess according to the accounts of the travellers such a discernment of intervals as to surpass our own—Councillor Telinius* informs us that the natives of Nukahiva, the principal island of the Marguisus Archipelago distinctly intone demi-semi-tones (quarter tones) in their vocal performances. The New Zealanders appear from Davis' account to be gifted with a remarkably fine ear for distinguishing quarter tones."

The Persians appear to have employed at an early period smaller intervals than semi-tones.† In France too a number of experiments were made with Viottis' performance, and it was ascertained that he employed a vast number of very

* Musical curiosities by E. Jones.

† Specimens of Popular Poetry in Persian as found in the adventures and in the songs of the people inhabiting the shores of the Caspian Sea by Chodgoho.

minute intervals in order to play perfectly tunes in all keys. The Swiss still retain the quarter tones in use.*

As for the assertion that the *Sangita Sára* does not contain anything like the theory of music, we will take the liberty to point out that in the book alluded to and in all Sanskrit works on the subject, the theoretical part of music is as fully dwelt upon as in any European treatise, only it is not mystified by obscuring mathematicism. As we have said elsewhere we hold that it is quite possible to build a rational theory of music without the aid of numbers. We will again trouble the critic with an extract from a Sanskrit work bearing on the point in question :

आकाशाग्निमरुज्जातो नाभेरूर्द्ध्वं समुच्चरन्।
मुखेऽभिव्यक्तिमायाति यः स नादः प्रकीर्त्तितः ॥
आद्यः कायभवो वीणासम्भवस्तु द्वितीयकः।
तृतीयश्चापि वंश्यादिसम्भवः स त्रिधा मतः ॥

सङ्गीतनारायणः।

"Sound, which is first produced by vibration and air within the human body, comes through the mouth and is called नाद (náda).

"Thus the sound arises first from within the body, secondly it is expressed in the form of words through the mouth, and thirdly by means of instruments. From this नाद (náda) or sound the whole system of music is evolved."

तत्र प्रथमोद्दिष्टस्य गीतस्य वच्यमाणत्वान्नादं
विना तदनुपपत्तेः प्रथमं तमेवाह तदुक्तं।
न नादेन विना गीतं न नादेन विना स्वरः।
न नादेन विना रागस्तस्मान्नादात्मकं जगदिति।

सङ्गीतनारायणः।

---

* C. S. P. 54.

"And singing is to be explained first, but without नाद (náda) singing is impossible and therefore sound is the root of all. Without sound singing is impossible, without sound tone is impossible, without sound Rága is impossible, and therefore नाद (náda) is the all pervading soul of the world."

The origin and nature of this नाद (náda) is as follows :—

आत्मा विवक्षमाणोऽयं मनः प्रेरयते मनः ।
देहस्थं वह्निमाहन्ति स प्रेरयति मारुतं ॥
नकारः प्राणवायुः स्यात् दकारो हव्यवाहनः ।
ताभ्यामुत्पाद्यते यस्मात्तस्मान्नादोऽयमुच्यते ॥

सङ्गीतनारायणः ।

नादाभ्यां जातत्वान्नाद इत्यर्थ ; or (न) vital air or power and (द) heat or vibration produced by heat originates náda (नाद) or sound.

Again :

नादाच्च श्रुतयो जातास्ताभ्यः षड्जादयः स्वराः ।
तेभ्यो रागः समुत्पन्नो गीतं तस्माच्च जायते ॥
अतो नादात्मकं गीतं वाद्यं गीतानुवर्त्ति च ॥

"From náda arises srooti, from srooti comes *swara* or tone, and from *swara* comes Rága, and from Rága comes Gíta, and therefore the soul of Gíta is sound. The instrumental music follows Gíta."

Hence it is, we contend, that our scale is natural and is well represented by M. Momigny's doctrine which holds that a true scale is derived from nature and requires no mathematical calculations.

Our critic observes with some emphasis that the Hindu boatmen whom he heard "employ occasional sharps and flats that could not be played on the Sitara." Apart from the question of the accuracy of the statement about the boatmen's songs we will simply dwell on the principle involved in the criticism, and say that there is not a single Indian melody with occasional sharps and flats which cannot be played on the Sitara. Let our critic name any melody and we will demonstrate our position.

In extolling the boatmen's songs as the best and the most approved specimens of Hindu music our critic makes the following remarks:—

"I think most Europeans who take the trouble to compare this (boatmen's song) with the best specimens in *Sangita Sára* &c., will readily credit my statement in my letter of 17th May 1873 (which appears to have much angered my Bengali critics) *viz.*, that 'while all Hindu musicians speak with contempt and almost abhorrence of the boatmen's songs, I have heard many Europeans declare that the boatmen's chants are the only music in Bengal that can properly be called music'."

There is such a refined appreciation of musical lore in the above that we know not what to say. But it requires no comment. We grieve to find that our critic drags other Europeans along with him to countenance his own idiosyncrasies. May we ask how many Europeans understand the language of the boat-man's song or its so-called musical cadence? All native boatmen do not sing in the same strain and in the same language. In the Eastern districts there are classes of boatmen who may be marked out by broad distinguishing characteristics. Their habits and manners are distinct and their songs are different in strain and language. The boatmen of Noakhally are not like the boatmen of Dacca, and the boatmen of Chittagong are quite unlike the boatmen of Dacca and Noakhally. Again, by far the greater portion of these boatmen are Mahomedans, who sing songs in Mahomedanized Bengali if we may so express ourselves. Can Mr. Clarke distinguish a native boatman as to his nativity by his song and its language ? Besides the three large classes of boatmen we have named there are others in East Bengal who are also distinguished by some peculiarities —the boatmen of Sylhet, Backergunge and Furreedpore for example. Again, the boatmen of West Bengal who navigate the Ganges and its tributaries are quite a distinct class of boatmen from any of the Eastern districts. They sing much better than our critic's friends of East Bengal. They usually come in contact with a larger number of educated and polished gentlemen than any boatmen of East Bengal can ever hope to do, and it may be said the former move in better society. They are therefore expected to be better educated and more civilized than their fellow-laborers in the eastern districts and yet their songs indicate no tunes of musical merit. If there is any thing for which their songs attract notice it is their point and peculiar epigrammatic beauty. But perhaps Mr. Clarke bad the rare good fortune to fall in with a class of musically educated boatmen. What however surprises us most is that his proteges sang songs in Sanscrit. He says :—

"When I had travelling in my boat Koylash Chunder Sen (Additional Deputy Inspector of Schools in Dacca) I got the boatmen to repeat the words to him. Koylash Chunder told me that the words were Sanscrit that the boatmen very imperfectly understood them themselves, and gave me some account of the legend of which I took no note."

It is very difficult to maintain one's gravity in arguing with a person who can be so credulous. Cannot our critic favor us with one or two of the songs which so charmed him? But a few words will suffice. He cannot deny that the popular songs of a nation must be composed in the language spoken by the people. Can he refer to a period when Sanscrit was the spoken language of the masses of Bengal, and of East Bengal in particular? Where did the boatmen learn Sanscrit songs? We know of very few *Pandits* who can recite extempore Sanscrit songs. But the writer betrays himself when he says that "the boatmen often sing very nicely in tune though their voices may be rough and their style uncultured, &c." Ignorant and uneducated people may mispronounce Sanscrit, but if they sing in Sanscrit it cannot be in uncultured style unless the songs be of their own composing. We fear Mr. Clarke's short stay in East Bengal has made a *Bangal* of him, and we fear that his Deputy treated him with a canard.

We now come to the discussion of our critic's remarks on our musical notation, which he condemns by saying "that the nationalist Bengali musical notation is valueless and ought to be superseded at once by the stave." To say the truth we do not very clearly understand the gist of his objection. We may, however, tell him that the Indian notation as far as it goes is all that we require. It is simple, convenient, and sufficient for all practical purposes. What the Europeans express in eleven lines by the great stave of eleven we do the same in three lines only,—the great stave of eleven is arbitrarily divided into two halves as the Europeans use both the hands. We beg Mr. Clarke to bear in mind that the notation he condemns is based on the original Sanscrit notation, of which he will find a full exposition by Sir William Jones in the Asiatic Researches; many of the signs and symbols of that notation have now become obsolete or have been entirely lost. What we have done is simply this, we have endeavoured to introduce such improvements in the system as are necessary to adapt it to modern requirements. In the original Sanscrit notation Hindu Music was represented by means of one line with certain signs and symbols and the initials of the seven notes; we now use three lines for three octaves. The reason of this innovation is, that the three octaves being the three natural ones are best represented by three lines, though one line would do and might still be used in the same way as the Tonic-sol-fa method of the Europeans. It will be remembered that the Greeks represented three octaves by three different letters. Now it will be seen that in representing the three octaves the Europeans not only require the stave of five lines but also use many ledger-lines for the notes, or they use the great stave of eleven lines. Now we put it to Mr. Clarke to say which is simpler—the stave of three or the stave of eleven, and which would occupy lesser space?

There is a great diversity of opinion among English musicians regarding the stave in use. Nathan in his History of Music says :—

"In the eighteenth century a staff of four lines was in general use, which may be met with at this period in some of the old church music."

Again Curwen says :—

"The old way of "noting" or writing music called the old "notation," uses a ladder of five lines and four spaces, which is called the "staff." On this certain marks are placed which represent the tones. These marks are placed higher or lower on the lines and spaces as the tones are higher or lower in pitch. The difficulty of the old notation, to the singer, arises from its not shewing *plainly* and *promptly*, which is the key-tone Doh, which the third of the scale, Me, which is the fourth, Fah, &c. For, on the preception of key-relationship, the power of the singer depends. When once the Tonic Solfa-ist has heard the key-tone and knows that a certain note before him is Ray or Soh, &c., he can sing it. * * * But until he sees the key-relationship of a tone he is at a loss. No information as to its absolute pitch, or its distance in pitch from the last tone sing, apart from key-relationship, can supply to him that clear and accurate preconception of the tone to be struck, to which he has been accustomed." To remove this difficulty the author offers some hints, the repetition of which in this place is deemed unnecessary. When the staff of five is still imperfect even in English music how can it be sufficient for Hindu Music which is rich in Rágas and which abounds in *Murchhanás, Tálas*, &c. ? And yet Mr. Clarke says that the Bengali notation ought at once to be superseded by the English stave.

Every nation that has a music of its own has also its own system of notation for writing it. Whether that system be an advanced one or not, it cannot be correctly expressed in the notation of another nation, however improved and scientific it may be. And even in such a case the notation will have to be studied separately. Under such circumstances we do not understand how the introduction of a foreign notation can save us the trouble of learning it. Anglicized as we have become in many respects, we confess we prefer our national system of notation for our national music. The English system of notation, it needs be observed, is imperfect and insufficient for the purposes of Hindu Music for the simple reason that the genius of Hindu Music is distinct from that of European music. We cannot, therefore, subscribe to Mr. Clarke's opinion that "if it was essential to represent quarter-tones, some modification of the stave would be far more preferable to the nationalist notation, and that the common European stave can represent fully the Bengali melodies and ought to be generally adopted." When it is admitted that some modification is necessary for the quarter-tones alone and some more for the *Murchhanâs* and the varieties of *Tâla* &c., we cannot understand with what consistency we are asked to have recourse to a foreign and hybrid notation, in preference to our national system. Indeed, we fail to perceive the force of the *ipsi dixit* that a Bengali who knew no English might play a melody from an English or French piece of music, when it is not denied that he must submit to the difficult task of studying the English stave without knowing the language, and learn the modifying signs not only for the quarter-tones but also for other innumerable varieties of *Tálas*, &c., referred to above. It may from this be imagined what a deal of trouble he must undergo in order to understand a single Rága. But why impose upon him this heavy work when in the three-lined Hindu notation—in spite of the signs for Srooties, &c., which, however, are very distinctly marked upon the *Swaragráma*—he has only to mark the different *swaras* in their initial order in the three *Saptakas* placed separately each in its proper place, and the whole thing is at the perfect command of the learner ? Only three lines mark the three sorts of natural sounds, namely, the chest, the throat, and the head sounds. Is not this simple and clear ? To give a clearer idea of this we give below a diagram of our *Swaragráma* of the *Saptakas* which is so natural and at the same time sufficient for all practical purposes.

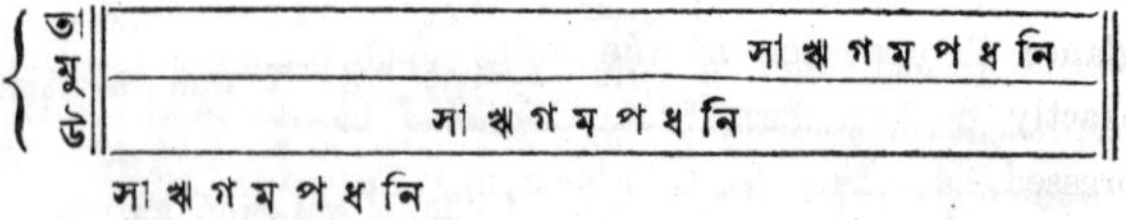

Now mark the contrast in the English notation. Here is a diagram of eleven lines.

Let us examine, as far as practicable, both the English and the Indian systems of notation from the diagrams given below in order to judge of their comparative merits and of the facilities for comprehension which they respectively afford. We will take the English notation first, and, foreigners as we are, we cannot help remarking that to our understanding it is complicated. In order to express an octave it is required in the European notation to have seven or eight lines or steps indicative of the position of notes that constitute an octave.

Thus upon the lowest of these lines or steps, the lowest note *c* must have been placed ; upon the line above it, the next note *d* ; upon the third line, the note *e*, and so on. In this case, which however is the most natural, so many lines are necessary that it is next to impossible to perceive at a glance the position of the notes upon them, and such will exactly be the case if our *Saptakas* be required to be expressed according to this system. To remove this inconvenience, the number of lines is limited to five, and why? Firstly, because an odd number of lines, as Dr. Marx says, has the advantage of an equi-distant middle line, which divides the staff into two equal parts and thereby facilitates its reading. Secondly, because a less number than five, say three lines together, with their spaces do not afford even a sufficient number of spaces for a single octave, while a greater number than five, say seven, will be unnecessary. In order to obtain a sufficient number of degrees, the spaces between the lines above and below them are also employed as places for notes. These five lines together are called a staff, which is now in use among the Europeans. These five lines together with the spaces between, below and above them, separate places for eleven different notes as will be seen in the next diagram drawn below :

1. 2. 3. 4. 5. 6. 7. 8. 9. 10. 11.

Here the note representing the lowest sound has the lowest place below the first line, while that representing the highest sound is placed above the last or fifth line. But the insufficiency of this system for the purposes of Hindu Music is at once apparent. As the ledger-lines usually drawn are no more than the long ones, then five-lines staff is altogether insufficient even for English music. The ledger-lines, however, are thus used for the purpose of representing the notes above the 11th as shewn here :

11. 12. 13. 14. 15.

c d a g f a c

Recourse is had to the same expedient when the lower sounds are required to be noted. Thus there will be no end of such lines, and how complicated and cumbrous it would look when our *Saptakas* are noted with the *Srooties* and the different varieties of *Tálas*. For, besides the *Swaras*, for which an almost infinite number of ledger-lines will have to be drawn, there must also be used numberless different signs to represent the *Srooties*, &c., along with the signs for the different clefs. Yet we have not done, we must know what sound is really represented by a note standing upon a certain line or space. For these various purposes they remove the notes as it is impossible for them from the nature of the staff to have a fixed position. For instance, if it had been determined that the first line of the staff in the last example quoted above should be the place for one lined c, then we should at once know that the note on the first space must be *d*, on the second line *e*, and that below the first line be small b; for the notes follow each other in the same order as the sounds themselves. But it is obvious that if one more note than one lined *c* were to be placed on the first line, all the other notes would change their places. If, for instance, *e* instead of *c* were to occupy the first line, then the notes *d* and *f* would stand below and above it, and *g* would have its place on the second line. This is indeed a complicated and confounding method. The situation of a note must be definitely fixed, if the object be to determine the respective places of the rest. The English musicians use for this purpose certain signs called clefs, which have been introduced to point out a certain line as the fixed place of a certain note. Of such clefs there are at present in use three, and there may be more in future. These three are first G or treble clef, sometimes called the violin clef, the C clef, and the F or bass clef. The form of G or treble clef is as shewn below :—

If we required to note in this clef the small *f*, we should have to place it upon a third ledger-line below the staff; the three-lined *a* would have its situation over the fourth ledger-line above the staff, and so on. Here the English musicians use *g* as the first note, which would be impossible in our *Swaragráma*. For *G* corresponds to our प, and प cannot form the base or the first note of the षड्जादि स्वरा, षड्ज according to the Sanskrit authorities is always to be taken as the first. Further, we do not understand why they have used here *G* instead of *C*, which is the recognized fundamental note, and this *c* they use on the ledger-line. Again, the first note must, as a matter of course, occupy the first line, but the *g*, although taken here as the first note, must stand on the second line. Altogether this is a complex method for us to understand, however plain it may appear to Europeans. Moreover, in the first diagrām drawn above, it is shewn that *e*

takes the first line, and therefore *e* naturally forms the clef. But in reality it does not do so. Formerly in France they used *G* as the first note and upon the first line; but we do not know why they have changed its position. The *C* clef shows, that the line which it occupies is the fixed place of one lined *c*. It occurs in this form :

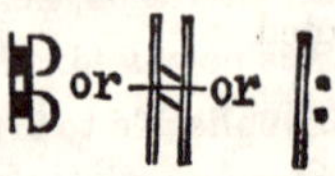

And this again is employed in three different ways, as canto, alto, and tenor clefs. The canto clef places one-lined *c* upon the first line. Here is a table of its notation.

c g a b c d e f g a b c d e f g a b c

This table may be extended by means of ledger-lines below or above the staff, according to the preceding directions. The alto clef places the one-lined *c* upon the third line and the tenor clef places the one-lined *c* upon the fourth line. But in the former case the *F* will be on the first line, which corresponds to our मध्यम, and in the latter case *e* will be on the first line, which corresponds to गान्धार, therefore the two are inapplicable to our षड्ज. Of the annexed two diagrams, the first represents the sounds of the notes of alto clef and the second presents the notes of the tenor clef.

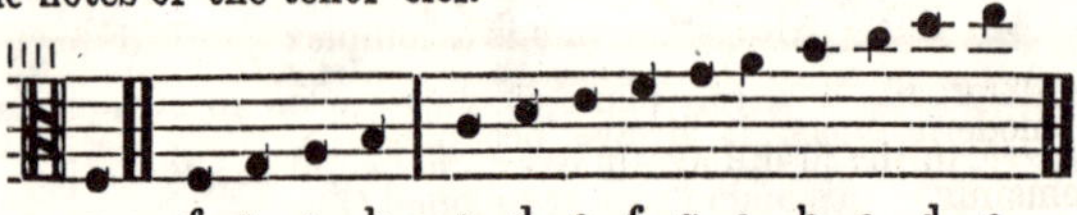

c f g a b c d e f g a b c d e

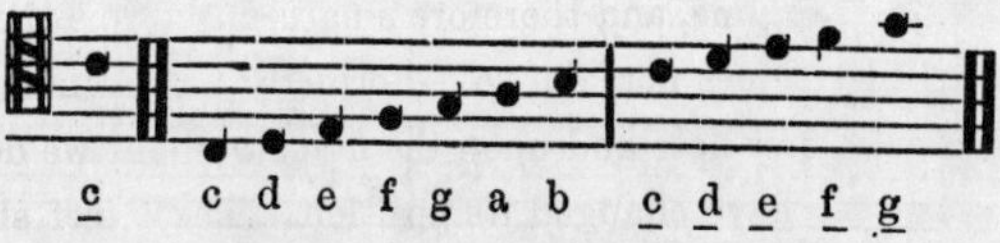

These are the three ways in which the *C* clef is now employed. The ancients used it in the second also, and we cannot account for the modern alteration, neither do we understand which of the three clefs is now used. It may be asked why the first canto clef is inapplicable to Hindu Music, since the one-lined c may stand for षड्ज; the answer is that the one-lined c corresponds to षड्ज, not in the उदारा or the lowest *Saptaka*, but in the स्वरित् or मुदारा *Saptaka*. In Hindu music, whether vocal or instrumental, we commence our *gráma* from the lowest or the उदारा सप्तक. But the discant or canto is the highest of the four principal voices. Here we may observe in passing that in noting our three octaves, which are natural, when divided and sub-divided as in the European music, an endless number of ledger-lines must be used. And will the innovation be an improvement upon our system? Supposing it were, it would change the character of Hindu music, which does not admit of any minute divisions and sub-divisions.

We now come to the third clef, *F* or Bass clef, which is represented in the form here shown, and indicates that the line which it encircles is a seat of small *f*.

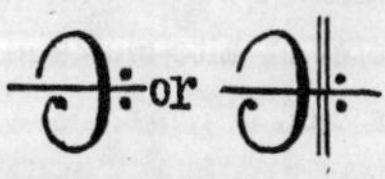

In modern music it always occupies the fourth line and the remaining lines and spaces are named thus :—

Contra Great.

f . A B C D E F · G A B c d e f g a b c d e

When it is required to extend its range, it is found insufficient, and innumerable additional ledger-lines have to be drawn. Thus contra *G* being situated below the third ledger-line, they require an additional ledger-line for the notation of contra *F;* above the staff, a third ledger-line must be drawn for one-lined *g,* a fourth for *b,* and so on. In old English music, however, we occasionally meet with Bass clef upon the third line, and also upon the fifth. Thus there has been a change already, and we know not how many more might take place in future. These are the clefs—but what is the use of so many clefs? Will not the numerous gradations of clefs in use prove perplexing and misleading? Will not one be sufficient, as Weber says, "indeed we might employ only a single line." To this perhaps it might be urged that the use of one clef would necessitate the multiplication of ledger-lines both below and above the staff, as in the Bass clef; for example, two ledger-lines are required for one-lined *e;* five ledger-lines for two-lined *c,* and perhaps not less than nine ledger-lines for three-lined *c,* all which is avoided by the use of the clefs. Admitting the explanation to be reasonable, why have the Europeans then in modern music discarded not only the *G* clef upon the first line, but also the *C* clef upon the second line, and *F* clef upon the third and fifth lines—and according to many the reduction is just. Really, all this is a puzzle to us—is this the system which is to solve our difficulties ?

All these divisions and sub-divisions together with so many clefs and varieties of lined notes have been derived from the great stave of eleven, and, notwithstanding all these innovations and modifications, they cannot, as Dr. Weber remarks, represent more than three octaves, originally noted down in the simplest forms of the stave of eleven lines. Again, the English musicians divide this stave into two equal parts, the reason of which is inexplicable to us. Perhaps it is done in order that the performer on a pianoforte might use both the hands, or it may be for male and female voices being used in harmony. But all that we say is mere guess—the correct explanation may be best furnished by Europeans. But whatever the reason, no such division is admissible in Hindu Music in which the melody requires that the series of tones should come in succession ; nor have we any instrument like the pianoforte which to be tuned requires two hands for two kinds of tones at one and the same time. From the above explanations it will be evident how complicated Hindu Music will become, if noted after the European fashion, while the contrast will be remarkably favorable to our national system of notation.

We will now enter upon the examination of the Hindu system of notation. In the English notation, of which we have furnished but a rough sketch, the lines used are in proportion to the number of tones in an octave, which are eight; sometimes so many as eleven or twelve lines are used, perhaps with the view of making them correspond to the number of strings in a harp, or for other reasons which are unknown to us. In the Hindu system of notation we generally use three lines for the three *saptakas* in common use amongst us. सा ऋ ग म प ध नि corresponding to C D E F G A B, are the seven notes which together constitute a *saptaka.* There may be more than three *saptakas* in Hindu Music; but they are not in general use. The three lines on which the *saptakas* are placed indicate by their position three kinds of sounds, *viz.,* उदारा, मुदारा and तारा. We do not require different clefs, nor changes in the situation of our notes for different purposes, as we always make षड्ज the base or the first note of the *saptakas*: षड्ज or c in European music has its position fixed and permanently settled.

This peculiarity enables us to avoid the introduction of different clefs, the use of numberless ledger-lines, and the change of situation of the notes. We have three *saptakas* in common use, for which only three lines and nothing more are required.

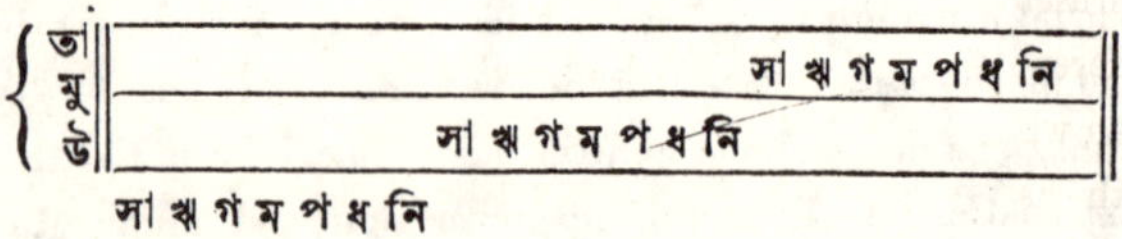

In the foregoing diagram, shewing the notation of Hindu Music, the lowest or the first line has the lowest *saptaka,* and the third or the uppermost line has the highest *saptaka.* If it were necessary to use more *saptakas,* we could use dots under each note to mark their position, either below the first or above the uppermost line. Thus, if we place one dot under सा on the uppermost line, it will show that it has a place in one *saptaka* above that line; and if we put a dot under सा on the lowest line, it will shew that it has a place in a *saptaka* next below that line. Similarly two or more dots will represent as many *saptakas* besides the natural ones, either above the uppermost or below the lowest or first line.

This is all that we require for the purpose of forming the basis of our notation, and from all that has been said, the reader will form an idea of the simplicity of our notation as contrasted with that of the Europeans. To guard against misapprehension, we must say that our object is not to establish the superiority of the Hindu system over the European, but merely to show that our system, as it is, is quite sufficient for all practical purposes, and that the introduction of the European system will not be an improvement. We will here add that if we have recourse to the division of scale by means of clefs, one line for each *saptaka* will be sufficient. From what has been said of the notations of different nations, it will be remarked that each nation, for the complete representation of the differences of their music, must use different signs. If the Europeans use lesser number of signs than what we require, it is simply because they have to do with harmony, while we, for the sake of melody, must use a variety of signs to represent *Srooties*, *Murchchhanâs*, *Tâlas* &c. So our notation, as we have shewn, is adapted to our requirements, and is both simpler and easier of comprehension than the English; while it dispenses with the necessity of adopting the stave. We cannot, however, give our assent to the view of Mr. Clarke's so-called progressive party, that "by adopting, if possible, the European stave for the representation of Bengali melodies, the Bengali musicians of course would save themselves the labor of learning one notation more," that "a Bengali who knew no English might play a melody from an English or French piece of music." For this dissent we have the best of reasons. In the European notation we cannot use all the signs necessary for the full representation of our music without making it indistinct and cumbrous. Some of the signs we refer to are *Bikshepa* and *Prakshepa*, which are in frequent use in vocal music ; the varieties of *Krintanas*, such as *Murchchhanā-krintana, Spars'a-krintana, Gamaka-krintana, A's'a-krintana*, &c., the varieties of *Chheras* or अष्टालङ्कार which are of very frequent use in our *Vina-Setára*, and the sign known by the name of झारा which in the Mahomedan instruments, the *Rabáb*, the *Sarode*, &c., in several strings used in various ways, greatly contribute to the grace and ornamentation of our music ; the *Spars'a*, the varieties of *A's'a*, such as *Gamaka-A's'a, Murchchhanā A's'a, &c.* These and several others are not represented in the notation of the so-called progressive party, and their not representing them does not make the representation the less necessary, if for nothing else, at least for the preservation of the integrity of our system of music. They may ignore them, but we are prepared practically to prove their existence whenever we may be called upon to do so. Again, that which we hold to be the very foundation-stone of Hindu Music, we mean the *Srooties*, or the quarter-tones of the Europeans, in which Mr. Clarke has pledged his disbelief, and in expressing which we take a special pride, finds no place in the system of the misnamed progressive party, who are victims of self-practised delusions. All these signs when mentioned in the Sanskrit works on music must be expressed either vocally or by means of instruments, and if we fail, it is plain we are ignorant of the method. The adopted notation of the progressive party, even in its improved state, is still as incomplete as it can possibly be. The numerical signs introduced in it require to be explained for the comprehension of different nations, and so will the several new signs created expressive of the peculiarities of our music, which is distinct from the music of other nations, and that in the languages of those nations. Will it be possible for an Englishman or Frenchman, who knows no Bengali, to play a melody from a piece of Bengali music as represented by these notations ? The signs, moreover, have been differently used for the purpose of representing our music, and how will the Englishman or the Frenchman make them out without special instruction ? For instance, they use the sign of *Soma* for the English pause, while this *Soma* is the very starting point in Hindu Music, and is as difficult of comprehension to the European as the *Rāga.* We could point out other anomalies, but what we have already done will suffice.

Above all, the notation in question has been formed on the treble clef, but not only one such clef but all the clefs divided as they are, are quite insufficient for the representation of the *A'lápa* of a *Rāga.* The *A'lápa* consists of four divisions,— आस्थायी, अन्तरा, सञ्चारी and आभोग, and these four divisions together constitute what is called a *Tána* (तान), without which the *Rāga* is incomplete.* It is thus evident that Mr. Clarke's assertion "that if it was essential to represent quarter-tones, some modification of the staff would be far more preferable to the nationalist's notation &c.," is barely an assertion, and does not admit of proof.

We think we have adduced sufficient evidence in this part of our discussion to justify us in pronouncing Mr. Clarke's

---

* An account of these divisions will be found in Sir William Jones' Works on Hindu Music ; also in *Sangita Ratnávali* in Sanscrit.

theory about the adaptation of the English system of notation to the music of all nations as wholly arbitrary. Every civilized nation, that has a music of its own, has also a system of notation adapted to the peculiarities of that music. If we attempt to replace it by the European system of notation, we will be under the necessity of expressing those peculiarities by means of new signs. Take the Chinese music as an illustration. The Chinese have a notation of their own with distinguishing peculiarities. They have adopted nine different characters, which are enumerated in French by DeGuignes as *ho, se, y, chang, tche, kung, fan, licon,* and *an.** There they write in a line downwards. They note down each with a character of their own, and DeGuignes says it is impossible to set them down correctly in the European system of notation. Take again Japan. As far back as the year 1611, the musical lines of the Japanese were pricked.† Captain Turner was informed that the Buddhist priests in Thibet had their music written in characters which they studied. Nor are the Egyptians and Hebrews without a contrivance of their own.‡ Java and other islands of the Indian sea possess some kinds of notation quite sufficient for the musical requirements of the different nationalities.§ The Burmese and the Siamese appear to have made as great a proficiency in music as any other Asiatic nation. They are naturally very fond of it, and the style of their music is, for the most part, extremely lively, and may not sound unpleasant to the European ear. Their pieces of music are

---

* They have also been translated into English by the Rev. E. W. Style.

† Howard Malcolm's Travels in South Eastern Asia.

‡ Historical, Technical and Literary Description of Oriental Music and Musical Instruments by Villoteau.

§ Opus cit.

very numerous. They exhibit as many as hundred and fifty tunes written in their own character.* In Ceylon too, music appears to be cultivated with great ardour. There are pieces of music to be seen in regular notes written in the Pali language. The Turks are not without a system or rule. Their music has not only all the tunes and sounds corresponding to ours, but, possessing quarter-tones, it is very rich in materials, and consequently highly melodious and difficult of reduction to a regular scale even in their national system of notation. The Turkish people play in unison or in octaves, which practice though hostile to harmony in the musical sense of the word, is productive of a grand musical effect, and is very imposing.† The Arabs divide their music into two parts—the *telif* (composition) or music considered in its relation to melody, and the *ikaa* (cadence of sounds) or the measured cessation of melody regarding instrumental music only. They have four principal modes from which are derived eight others, and they have also six composite modes formed by union of these. Their manner of noting music is by forming an oblong rectangle, divided by seven lines perpendicular to its sides, representing together with the two extreme lines eight intervals. Each of these lines is of a different color, which must be remembered as well the name as the interval. They use in their music smaller intervals than our semitones. The notes of their scale (which are designated by the numbers from one to seven—*yek, du, si, tschar, peni, sehesch, heft*, or, as in European music, by the first seven letters of the Alphabet, which are in the Arabic, *alif, be, gim, dal, ha, wain, zain*,) are subdivided into seventeen one-third tones, and in

* Howard Malcolm.

† See The Harmonicon, Vol. II.

rendering this scale in the European system of notation, new signs will have to be invented for the quarter-tones. But from the sixth to the minor seventh a—b flat will be semi-tones, while in their scale only one-third tone, &c. Thus, it is impossible to represent Arabic music in the European system of notation, notwithstanding the invention of new signs for quarter-tones.*

The Persian music very much resembles ours. It has also its own notation, the reduction of which to the European scale is as difficult and impracticable as that of ours. Now we leave it to Mr. Clarke to determine the result of representing the music of different nations on the face of the earth by one common notation, *i. e.*, the European with newly invented signs according to the requirements of each. We fear we must defer the prospect of an universal language of music till the milleneum arrives. If an attempt be made to adapt the English notation to the music of the different nations, it will be necessary, we believe, according to Mr. Clarke's plan, to make sub-divisions in order to cover the wants and peculiarities of each nation, but then the result will not be that "a Bengali who knew no English might play a melody from an English or French piece of music." But the difficulty we have just represented is not all. As the different systems of music of different nations are not equally progressive, (and some are not at all progressive) the new signs we have referred to will have to be modified, altered or extended according to the stages of progress and development of the original music. We will ask Mr. Clarke to bear in mind how much alteration has European music

* A Treatise on Arabic Music, translated from the Arabic by Eli Smith.

undergone in the course of the last 500 years, and how much more it is destined to undergo. Had the European system been an immutable or a system, what necessitated John Curwen's modifications (which by the bye closely resembles the ancient Sanscrit notation) and what guarantee have we that they will stop here? From what we have already adduced it may now be safely assumed as an established fact that, except by the systems of notation invented by them, the music of the oriental nations cannot be represented by the European notation. In this opinion we are well supported by Ambros, who says that "respecting the national songs which have hitherto been published, it must be observed that in all of them the original character of the music has been greatly altered, if not obliterated, by the arrangement of melodies for the pianoforte, or by the unwarranted addition of accompaniments of some kind. In many instances where the songs are usually performed in unison, they retain, when harmonized, but faint traces of their former characteristics. Even in instances where an accompaniment originally exists, its peculiarities are often so entirely disregarded in the arrangement that it becomes almost another composition." And as to the inapplicability of the European notation, what has been said of the music of other oriental nations is equally true of Hindu Music. The difficulty of adopting the foreign notation arises as much from the modifications necessary for the quarter-tones, as for various other causes too intricate for enumeration. We will cite a few more authorities in support of the views advocated by us. "A great difference," says Willard, "prevails between the music of Europe and that of the oriental nations in respect to time, in which it resembles more the system of the Greeks and other ancient nations than the measures peculiar to the music of modern Europe." Again, another writer says, "nor are the ancient Hindu airs known to the Europeans from the impossibility of setting them according to our system of notation. The Hindus have quarter-tones, a fact which renders it still more difficult to express their music by our own system."* Mr. Whitten, in his lecture on the music of the ancients, delivered at the Calcutta Normal School, took the same view of the question. His words were as follows: "Few of the Hindu airs are known to Europeans, and it has been found impossible to set them to music according to the modern system of notation, as we have neither staves nor musical characters whereby the sounds may be accurately expressed."† Another writer, an equally independent authority, goes on to say, that "considerable difficulty is found in setting to music the *Rágas* and *Ráginís,* as our system does not supply notes or signs sufficiently expressive of the almost imperceptible elevations and depressions of the voice in these melodies; of which the time is broken and irregular, the modulations frequent and very wild."‡

It is thus generally admitted that Hindu Music, from its nature, does not admit of being represented by the European system of notation. Mr. Clarke may, therefore, well regale in the enjoyment of his pleasing visions supported by the distinguished authority of his progressive friends, and will

* Oriental Collections by W. Ouseley Esq.

† Orchestra, March 14th 1868.

‡ Oriental Collections by Sir W. Ouseley. Mr. Clarke himself has given an indirect demonstration of the difficulty of representing Hindu Music by the European notation in the three lines appended to his article, and we are glad to find that Mr. Aldis takes our view of the case.

we hope have the goodness to practically illustrate his theory with their invaluable aid as to how the Hindu system of notation may be superseded by the European.

We will conclude with a few words, pointing out certain errors into which Mr. Clarke has, perhaps unwittingly, fallen in respect to certain musical facts and personal questions. In discussing the question of notation he incidentally mentions that the notation in use is not the Bengali notation but an invention of four years ago, taken up by "a small but rich party in Calcutta." We are sorry to say, that in making this statement our critic is entirely mistaken, or has allowed himself to be misled by the party to which he has apparently surrendered his critical judgment. If he had referred to the published works of his countrymen, he would have discovered its mistake. Amongst others we would take the liberty to recommend for his perusal Sir W. Jones' works on Hindu Music. The notation in use is not one of four years' invention, but of an age anterior to the commencement of the authentic history. In proof of its antiquity we annex a facsimile of a printed form of notation, written in the oldest Sanskrit character of वसन्त राग।

ANCIENT SANSCRIT NOTATION

VASANTA.

वसंतः

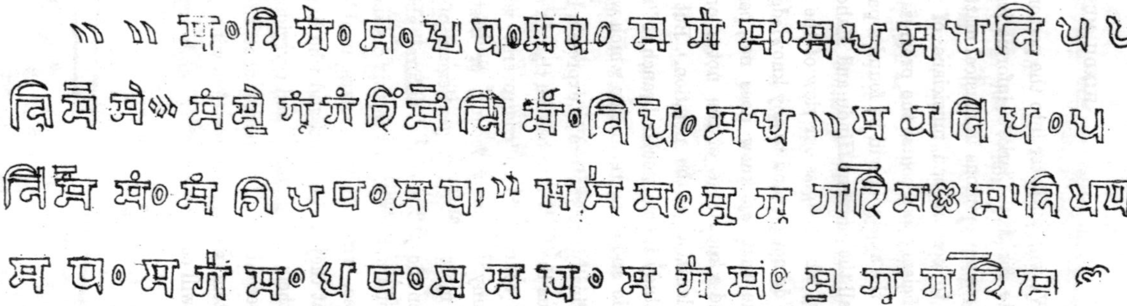

We will not enter into the personal question, but we may state for Mr. Clarke's information that the party which shares our opinions in musical matters is nearly as numerous as to comprehend musicians of all degrees of taste and proficiency—of course the progressive party only excepted. In the appendix will be found a paper containing autographs of all the eminent Hindu and Mahomedan musicians of the day, who endorse our view of the question under discussion. We do not pretend to any knowledge of English music—the little that we know does not, perhaps, extend to much beyond a knowledge of the notes on a harmonium and the explanation of the notation. But we have taken the pains to study the particular branch of music in which we take pride and pleasure, and on which we have presumed to write.

Finally, we venture to express a hope that Mr. Clarke will do us the justice to believe that in all that we have said in the course of this controversy we have not been actuated by any unfriendly feeling, or hostile spirit. What grieves us most is that a gentleman of Mr. Clarke's erudition, scientific attainments, natural abilities, and high character, should have imported in this discussion the party spirit of those, who are themselves unable to understand or explain what they write about, and who have made him an exponent of their crude views and egregious misconceptions. If this paper satisfies Mr. Clarke that in advocating the national system we are simply following reason, truth, and history, we will consider ourselves amply repaid.

श्रीगणेशाय नमः।

कदीमजमानेसें यो आजतक हिन्दुस्तानमे इल्म सङ्गीतके यो हमारे नजदीक तमाम दुनियाके सङ्गीतसे अच्छा अवर वड़ाहै, उस्के आलिम अवर पण्डितने इष् इल्मकी वुनियाद्को के जो अवाजहै, तिनचिज पर कायम कीया है। एक सुर, जिस्की सात किस्म। दोसरे तालकी, जिस्की बऊत किस्म है। तसरी लय, जिसे जमाना कहते है। इसुरको तरकीव दीया है श्रुति, मूर्छना अवर सम्पूर्ण अवर असम्पूर्णसें अवर तालको तरकीव दीया है। सम, अतीत, अवर विषम अवर अनागतसें मात्राके हिसावपर अवर लयको तकसीम किया है। दुरुत, मध, विलम्बित पर पस हम लोग आजतक उनयी कायदापर इस इल्मकी वरतावमे लाये है। अवर जोके श्रुति अवाजसे पयदा ऊइहै अव उसे सुर वनायाहै। इस्वास्ते इस्कोहम सुरकी वुनीयाद ओ मूल कहते है। अवर इन सुरोंके चढ़ाने, उँतारने अवर वदल्नेंसे हरेक रकमकी रागरागिणी पयदा होती है; पस अव जानना चाहिये इस् इल्मका प्रकाश होना दोचिजसे होता है। एक गलेसें, जीसे जीस्के गाना कहते है।

दोसरा यन्त्रसें, जेसे जीस्को वजाना कहते है। लेकीन गाना पहिले, अवर जड़ है अवर कण्ठ उस्के पयदा हूश्की जगा है की जीस्को गानेवाले ओस्ताद सातों सुरोंकी तरकीव कोमल, मध्यकोमल, अतिकोमल, तिवर,मध्यतिवर, अतितिवर अवर हरेकीस्की राग-रागिणी की अलाप उस्के फयलायके वहूत अछीतरह कायदोंसे हरेक तरकीवत देखलायकर अदां करतेहे वगयर दोसेरेको मदतके अवर एकाम कुदरती है वरखीलाफ यन्त्रके केओ गलेका नकल है अवर हाथका मोहताज है जैसे वीणा रवाव सीतार सरोद ओगयरह की वे दोसरेकी मदतके कोइ तरकीव सुरोंकी उस्मे जाहिर नही होती पस यो सकस हूस्मे कहे केसुरोंकी तक्सीम गलेसे यैसी नही होसकती येसें यन्त्रसें सो उस्का दावा गलत है चाहे इयोरोपका पण्डित इस इल्मका हो चाहे हूशीयाकाहो ओसे चाहीये हमारे पास आवे हम उस्को वहूततरेसे सुरोंका हीसाव गलेसे कर देखा-वेगें वेतरदूत् अवर फीकरके अवर एवात मसुर नही है असल के असलीहि है, नकल नकलहि है, याने जो चीजके असलसे अछी जाहिर होगी, नकलसें नही होणी, पस गला आसल है यन्त्र उस्की नकलहै पस इस इल्मकी वारिकी अवर

सुरोंका हीसाव अवर लय घटाव वढ़ाब कीतावमे पढ़नेसे कवही मालुम नही होताहै खाली नाम जानना जवतक् गलेसे वहुत रोज वरसों रीयाज न कीया हो जयसे वड़े वड़े ओस्ताद गानेवाले भारतवर्षके क्या हिन्दु क्या मुसलमान जव इनोने वरसों इस् इल्ममे रात दिन मेहनतका है तव उस्को मिलाना अवर उक्सी तक्सीम अवर जाननेसो मोस्कील काम मोनासीव इस्के है। की अपने अपने इल्म अवर अक्कीलकी योर्सें अपने अपने कानोमे मालुम करलेते है। अगर कोइ वड़े लायक सक्स इल्मके नामके जानेवाले डांड़ी माजी लोगेंाके गानेको जो विलकुल सव इल्मसें जाहिल होते है; सुन्कर ए समझोंगे हिन्दु-स्तानका सवसे अच्छा एही गानाहै तो हम अवर उनकी समझकी वहुत् तारीफ करते है, क्यो नही जीस्की जयसी अक्कील उस्की ओसीही समझ उनको सवाय अवर क्या कहै। तमाम भारतवर्षमे उत्तम अवर वेहतर सङ्गीतका एकीतरह चलन है; जैसे सव लोग वरते आवे है, वर्त्तोंओ करते है, सीरीफ फरक जवान और तरकीवका है। पस् हम ए कहते है, की यो श्रीयुत वाबु क्षेत्रमोहन गोस्वा-मीने भारतवर्षके इस्पुराने इल्म सङ्गीतके सुरोके

घटाने अवर वढ़ाने लीखने अवर वरतामे लानेका हीसाव इस इल्मकी संस्कृत अवर फारसीकि कीताबोंके कायदोसे आजसरेनौ दुरस्तकायमकीया है, ओहि सुरोंका हीसाव ओगयरह हम सव लोगोंकी रायके मोताविक है, कायदेसें वाहर नही है, इस्मे क्या हिन्दु, क्या मुसलमान गायक गुणीहिकी एहि मतहै, पस जो लोगके इस् इल्मको खुव जान्ते है अवर ओस्ताद है,उमेद इस्तहरीरकी लेनेकी तस्दीक पर अपनी दस्तखत फर मावेतो निहाएत मेहरवानी और इनायत होगी ॥ १ ॥

PROFESSOR MOWLA BUX,
Of Bombay.

श्रीकालीप्रसन्न वन्द्योपाध्याय,
सेक्रेटारी वङ्गसङ्गीतविद्यालय।

श्रीजोयत्लाप्रसाद दीच्छत, ध्रुपदिया। सुकलकान्ताप्रसाद ध्रुपदिया। दसखतहरिनाथ मीसर, ध्रुपदिया। दसखतगङ्गाप्रसाद मिश्र, ध्रुपदिया। दसखतवद्रीमिसीर, ध्रुपदिया। वाल्गोवीन्द मिश्र, ध्रुपदिया। श्रीशिवरामकुमार खेयालिया।

قدیم زمانه سے جو آج تک ہندوستان مین علم
سنگیت مروج ہي اور جو ہمارے نزدیک تمام عالم
کي سنگیت سے اچھا اور بڑا ہي اوسکے عالم اور نیدٓیون
نے اس علم کي بنیاد کو که جو آواز ہي تین چیز
پر قائم کیا ہي ایک سر که اوسکے سات قسم ہي
دوسرے تال که اُسکي بہت قسم ہي تیسرے لے
که جسے زمانه کہتي ہین پس سر کو ترکیب دیا ہي
سروتي اور سور جہنا اور سنپورن اور اسنپورن سے اور
تال کو ترکیب دیا ہي سم اور استیت اور بے سم
اور اناگت سے ما ترونکي حساب پر اور لے کو تقسیم
کیا ہي درت مده بلنپت پر پس ہم لوگ آج تک
اونہین قاعدون پر اس علم کو بر تاوین لاتي ہین اور
چونکه سرتي آواز سے پیدا ہوتي ہي اور اُس سے سر
بنا ہی اسواسطے اسکو ہم سب لوگ سُوکي بنیاد اور
اصل کہتي ہین اور انہین سرونکي چڑہائي اور اوتارني
اور بدلني سے ہرایک قسم کي راگ وراگني پیدا ہوتي
ہین پس اب خاندنا چاہیئے که اس علم کا ظہور دو چیز
سے ہو تا ہي ایک گلو سے که اُسے گانا کہتي ہي دوسرا

جنتر اور ساز سے که اوسے بجانا کہتے ہین لیکن گانا
اول اور اصل ہي اور گلا اوسکي پیدایش کے جگہه ہي
که جس سے گانے والے اوستاد سات سرونکي ترکیب
کومل مدہ آتے کومل تیورمدہ تیورآتي تیور اور ہریک
قسم کے راگ راگني کے الاپ اور اُسکي سرونکے پہلاو
کو بہت اچھي طرح قاعدون سے ہرایک کا فرق دکھلا
کر ادا کرتي ہی بغیر دوسریکي مدد کي اور یہه امر
قدرتي ہي برخلاف جنتر کي که وہ گلے کي نقل ہي
اور ہاتھه کا محتاج ہي جیسي بین رباب ستار سرود
وغیرہ که بغیر دوسریکي مدد کے کوئي ترکیب سرون
کي اُس سے ظاہر نہین ہوتي بس جو شخص یہه
کہي که سرونکي تقسیم گلے سے ایسي نہین ہو سکتي
جیسي ساز سے سو اُسکا دعوي غلط ہی خواہ یورپ
کا پندت اس علم کا ہو خواہ ایشیا کا مناسب اُسکو که
ہمارے پاس آوے ہم اُسکو بہت اچھي طرح سے سرون
کا حساب گلے سے کر دکھائینگي بلا تردد اور کیا یہه
بات مشہور نہین ہي که اصل اصل ہي ہي نقل نقل
ہي ہي یعنے جو چیز که اصل سے اچھي ظاہر ہو گي وہ
نقل سے نہ ہوگي یعنے گلا اصل ہي ساز اُسکي نقل ہي
پس اس علم کي باریکیان اور سرونکا حساب اور لي کا
گھتا ویرہا و فقط کتاب مین پڑہي سنے کبھی نہین
معلوم ہوتا ہي خالي نام جانتا ہي جب تک که گلے

سے بہت برسون ریاض نہ کیا ہو چنانچہ بڑي بڑي
اوستان گانیے والے ہندوستانکے کیا ہندو کیا مسلمان جب
اونہونے برسون اس علم مین رات دن محنت کی ہي
تب اونہونے سرونکا ملانا اور اوسکي تقسیم اور جتني
مشکل کام متعلق اسکي ہین اپني اپني علم اور عقل
کے زور سے اپني اپني کامونمین معلوم کیا ہي اگر کوئي
بڑي لائق شخص اس علم کی نام کے جاني والي
ڈانڑي مانجھي لوگونکا گانا کہ جو باالکل سب علم سے
جاہل ہوتي ہین سنکر یہہ کہین اور سمجھین کہ
ہندوستان کا عمدہ اور سب سے بہتر گانا ہي تو ہم
اونکي سمجھہ کے بہت تعریف کرتي ہین کیون نہو
جسکي جیسي عقل اوسکي ویسي ہي سمجھہ اونکو
سوائے اسکي اور کیا کہین تمام ہندوستان مین اُتم اور
اعلي سنگیت کا ایک ہي چلن ہي کہ جسے سب لوگ
بڑتي آئے ہین اور برتاو کرتي ہین صرف فرق زبان
اور ترکیب کا ہي پس اب ہم یہہ کہتي ہین کہ جو
سري حکیت بابو کہترموہن گسائین نے بہارت برش
کے اس پراني علم سنگیت کي سرونکا گہتاو اور بڑہاو
اور لکہني کا حساب سنکرت اور فارسی کے کتابونکي
قاعدون سے ازسرنو درست کیا اور قایم کیا ہي وہی
سرونکا حساب و غیرہ ہم سب لوگونکي راي کے مطابق
ہي اور قاعدہ سے باہر نہین اسمین کیا ہندو کیا مسلمان

کالگ گنتي نسب کے ایک ہي مت ہي پس جو حضرات که اس علم کو خوب جانتي ہین اور اوستاد ہین اونکي خدمت مین عرض ہي که اس تحریر تصدیق پر اپني دستخط فرماوین نہایت احسان ہوگافقط

---

* العبد کالي پرشن بنداپادھاے سکرتري اسکول سنگیت بنگاله بدیالي *

* العبــد *

* احمد خان خیالي *

* العبــد *

* علیجان خیالي *

* العبــد *

* محمد خان بین کار*

* العبــد *

* تاج خان دھرپدي *

* البعــد *

* احمد خان دھرپدي دترانه سراي *

* العبــد *

* حیدر خان دھرپدي دترانه سراي *

* العبــد *

* حکیم غلام محمد قانون نواز *

* العبــد *

* نعمت الله خان عفي عنه سرود نواز *

* العبــــد *

* غلام حسين خان دهوپدي *

* العبــــد *

* جنون خان سوز خوان *

* العبــــد *

* عيوض علي خان سوز خوان *

* العبــــد *

* عنايت حسين خان دهرپدي *

* العبــــد *

* احسان علی خان خيالي *

ON THE

MUSICAL SCALES OF DIFFERENT NATIONS

FROM

"*An Introduction*

TO THE STUDY OF

NATIONAL MUSIC;"

BY

CARL ENGEL.

ON THE

MUSICAL SCALES OF DIFFERENT NATIONS.

THE seven intervals of the Hindu scale—*sa, ri, ga, ma, pa, dha, ni,*—which nearly correspond with our diatonic major scale, are subdivided into twenty-two *Srooti,* corresponding to quarter-tones, but not quite exactly, since there are only 22 instead of 24 in the compass of an octave.

Whole tone.	Whole tone.	Semi-tone.	Whole tone.	Whole tone.	Whole tone.	Semi-tone.
4 *Srooti.*	3 *Srooti.*	2 *Srooti.*	4 *Srooti.*	4 *Srooti.*	3 *Srooti.*	2 *Srooti.*

sa *ri* *ga* *ma* *pa* *dha* *ni* *sa*

(*c*) (*d*) (*e*) (*f*) (*g*) (*a*) (*b*) (*c*)

Sir William Jones considers *sa* identical with our *a*, so that the syllables *sa, ri, ga, ma, pa, dha, ni,* would represent our scale of a major, a, b, c ♯, d, e, f ♯, g ♯. Other writers on Hindu music take *sa* to be synonymous with *c*, as has been done in the above illustrations of the scale. Captain Willard observes that Sir W. Jones, in making the *Khuruj** to correspond to *a*, "appears to be guided more by alphabetical arrangement of letters than by any connexion it may have with musical arrangement. If the *Khuruj* is tuned *ut* or *c*, it seems to me to be more systematic, it being

* *Khuruj* is the name given to *sa*, the fundamental note of the scale.

the key-note of the natural key. The musicians of Hindustan never appear to have had any determined pitch by which their instruments were regulated, each person tuning his own to a certain height, adapted by guess to the power of the instrument and quality of the strings, the capacity of the voice intended to be accompanied, and other adventitious circumstances."* This question, however, is not of much importance in our inquiry. More remarkable is the fact that two of the *whole tones* in the Hindu scale, *viz.*, those from the second to the third, *ri—ga,* and from the sixth to the seventh, *dha—ni,* comprise only three *Srooti,* while the other whole tones comprise four. In certain cases the performer to some extent obviates inequality, by enlarging a small whole tone with a *Srooti* borrowed from the next tone of the scale.

The general name for the Hindu scale is *Thăt. Rắgas* and *Rắginees* are melodies founded upon certain scales, or rather *modes,* which are formed either by substituting for the *prime* another interval of the scale as fundamental note, or *tonic,* as in our ancient Church modes; or by considering certain intervals of the scale as inessential; or by omitting one or two intervals entirely. In illustration I subjoin a few specimens of scales selected from a number given in Sir W. Jones's essay 'On the Musical Modes of the Hindus.'† Two of them, called *Todi* and *Saindhavi,* resemble, it will be seen, the former the Dorian, and the latter the Phrygian mode. Those intervals which in the scales called *Bhairava, Tacca,* and *Maravi* are written as crotchets, are

---

* A treatise on the Music of Hindustan by Captain N. Augustus Willard. Calcutta, page 27.

† Asiatic Researches, Vol. III, p. 55.

inessential, and may be skipped by the performer. Intervals entirely omitted (as in *Maravi* and *Hindola*) are indicated thus—

In the music of the Arabs we also meet with smaller intervals than our semi-tones. The notes of the Arabic scale, which are designated by the numbers from 1 to 7, *yek, du, sí, tschar, peni, schesch, heft,* (or also, as in our own music, by the first seven letters of the alphabet, which are in the Arabic *alif, be, gim, dal, he, wan, zain,*) are subdivided into seventeen *one-third-tones.*

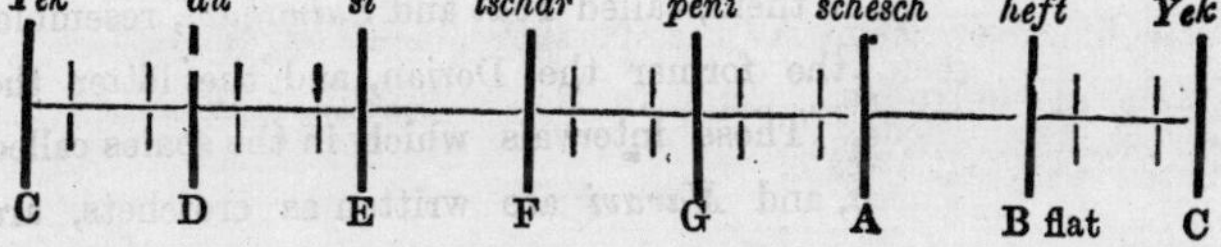

In rendering this scale in our notation, I shall employ signs similar to those previously adopted in the examples with quarter tones. Thus, $\frac{1}{3}\sharp$ before a note raises it a one-third-tone, and $\frac{2}{3}\sharp$ two one-third-tones; $\frac{1}{3}\natural$ before B indicates that the interval is a one-third-tone higher than B flat, and $\frac{2}{3}\natural$ that it is two one-third-tones higher than B flat. The minims indicate the diatonic intervals, which, it will be seen, differ from ours in so far as the *seventh* is *minor*, and the two steps from the third to the fourth *e—f*, and from the sixth to the minor seventh, *a—b* flat, which in our notation would be semi-tones, are in the Arabic scale only *one-third*-tones. The intervals written as crotchets denote the intermediate one-third tones between the respective diatonic intervals.

ARABIC INTERVALS.

The Persians appear to have employed at an early period smaller intervals than semi-tones. After the conquest of Persia by the Arabs, about the middle of the seventh century of our Christian era, the music of the Persians and Arabs, became, so to say, amalgamated, and there are still treatises extant of early Arabian and Persian theorists, in which the system of one-third-tones is exhibited. Afterwards, however, some of the Persian Musicians adopted a system of twelve semi-tones in the compass of an octave, like our chromatic scale.

THE SAMAN CHANTS

FROM

The Arsheyabrahmana,

BY

A. C. BURNELL, PH. D

THE SAMAN CHANTS.

THE music of the *Sâman Chants* has been so often mentioned by me, that I shall try to give an idea of it, as it is now sung by the *Sâma Veda* priests. Here, as in other respects, there are numerous *Câkhá* differences and I shall, therefore, follow the practice of the *Kauthumí Câkhá*, the only one of which I have been able to obtain sufficient information. The art is very nearly extinct, and this is a good reason for describing it, especially as the only European who studied it in India—Dr. Haug—is now no more.

The foundation of these Chants being unquestionably very old, they are, as might be expected, on an imperfect scale of notes, but modes do not appear to be used, except one. The *Sáman Chants* resemble in some respects the Gregorian or Plain Chant, and the two kinds of music approach one another in many points; the *Sáman*, however, being the older and less cultivated, one occasionally meets with passages which are forbidden by the rules of the Plain Chant, and are, to a foreigner's ear, by no means pleasing.[1]

The notation, as has been already remarked[2] varies exceedingly, accordingly as the MSS. come from different parts of India, and it is not too much to say that it would be almost impossible to find two MSS. which precisely agree. MSS. of the ganas are only copied by professional *Sâma-*

---

1 cfr. P. 370 of Helmholtz, "Die Lehre von den Tonemp-findungen," (3rd ed.) as to the development of taste as regards Music.

2 Above PP. XXVI and XXVII.

Veda priests for their own use, and present no kind of interest to the public; every copyist, therefore, follows a different plan in details, for almost every one adds marks and signs of his own to assist him in chanting the notes.

It would be useless to give the complicated notation as used in the S. Indian MSS. and which I have already mentioned, for these letters amount to several hundreds. The principle of the modern notation by numbers is far more simple. The seven notes are marked by the numerals 1, 2, 3, 4, 5, 6 and the last (really never used) by 7 or ⌢. Of these the first = F and the rest E, D, C, B, A, G.[1]

It is necessary to point out (as there has been much confusion on this point) that the gánas are not *accented* in the ordinary sense of the word, or like the other *Vedas*; but that the marks which form such a prominent feature in the text are actually *musical notes.*[2]

The difficulty in understanding their true nature has arisen out of the attempts to classify the notes, and also to connect them, phonetically, with the accents. It is not difficult to understand this by comparison with similar attempts of the mediæval students of music. Thus Hugbaud

---

1 I have ascertained this by means of a standard pitch-pipe. It is also the doctrine of the *Nàradacixà* (adhy. ii.) according to oral information:

> Yah Sámagánám Prathamah Sa Venor madhyamasvarah
> Yo dvitiyah Sa Gándháras, tritiyas tv rishabha smrita.

The common Hindu scale corresponds with the European key of C, but Sir W. Jones has (as evidently might be done) put it in the key of A, for which I can find no sufficient reason; and, in fact, he is thus led into inconsistency (As. Res. iii.)

2 These notes should be as just mentioned; but I have seen MSS. in which the accent marks were used, and this misled me (Cat. P. 45), and the practice is, admittedly, wrong.

(840-930 A.D.) classified the notes of the Plain Chant in the following way :—

So, La, Si, Ut grades	*Ri, Mi, Fa, Sol* finales	*La, Si, Ut, Re,* superiores	*Mi,Fa,Sol,La* excellentes

In the Indian books on music there is a somewhat similar classification of the notes :

Udátta	*Anudátta*	*Svarita*
Nisháda, gándhára.	*Rishabha, Dhaivata.*	*Shadja, Madhyama, Pancama.*

The three sthánas represent three octaves.

The names of the seven notes differ, and some have several names. The oldest list that I know of is probably that in the *Sámavidhána Bráhmana*[2]—*krushta, Prathama, dvitiya, tritiya, caturtha, pancama* and *shashtha* or *antya*. In the later works (*e.g.*, *Sáyanas* C. on the *Arsheyabráhmana*) the numbers *prathama, etc.*, are used[3]; these again partly correspond to the *shadja, rishabha, gándhára, madhyama, pancama dhaivata* and *nisháda* of usual music, but in reverse order, *i. e.*, the first note of the Hindu ordinary music is the fourth of the *Sáma* priests, and the scale *ascends*, the reverse of the scale of the last. In S. India the names are usually given as *prathama, etc.*, *mandra* (5th) *anusvarya* (6th) and *atisvarya* (7th).

---

1 Dela Fage, "Cours complet di Plain Chant," P. 691.

2 See i., 1, 8 of my edition (P. 5).

3 So in the *Svaraparibháshá*. *Mandra* is, nowever, the most usual name for the fifth *svara*. In the *Sámatantra* (by i, ii, 3—" ucco gan") gi, ji, *di*, di, stand for the first five svaras. The *antya* is not mentioned (S. T. I., i, 1.)

4 That the *krushta* is the first note, and that it is generally called *prathama* there can be no doubt. Sáyana (in his C. on the Arsheya br.) mentions *krushta* repeatedly (*e. g.*, in I, 16 and 17) where the *Saman* has the first note marked.

Besides the seven simple notes (*prakriti*), there are seven others (*vikriti*)[1] which express constantly recurring groups of notes or modifications, and the necessity for which has evidently arisen from the system of notation by numbers. There are : '*prenkha*' which adds two mátrá to the preceding syllable and ends with the second *svara*, it is marked प्र, or in S. Indian MSS. 'pre' sometime occurs. '*Namana*' which consists of the first three notes (one, two and three) ; '*karshana*' is either up the scale (marked Λ) or down (marked V) and includes all the notes between these marked. 'Vinata' is marked by 'vi' or *S* and consists of 1 and 2 ; where '*Vinata*' occurs in the *Grāmageyagāna*, *Prenkha* is put in the *Uha*. The two remaining *vikritis* are embellishments : *Atyutkrama* =4565, *Samprasárana*=2345. There are many other terms of the art, but only '*abhigāta*' requires to be noticed. This consists in a repetition of the note with a short a ; it appears to be marked in the *Bibliotheca Indica* edition of the *Sáma-Veda* by 7. As is everywhere the case in Sanskrit literature, the *Sáma Veda* priests have a long vocabulary of technical terms, but I shall not attempt to explain them, as most have arisen out of the peculiar notation, and it would not be possible to make them intelligible in a short space.

With these explanations it is now possible to give a specimen of the *Sāma Veda* chants noted according to the Plain Chant system which will best suit the purpose. It must be remarked, however, that the Chant is continuous, and not staccato, and that, in one respect, there is a total want of resemblance to the Plain Chant—the value of the notes or time depends chiefly on the words ; in the adaptations of a

1 These are purely modern.

Gautamasya parkah (1., 1.1)

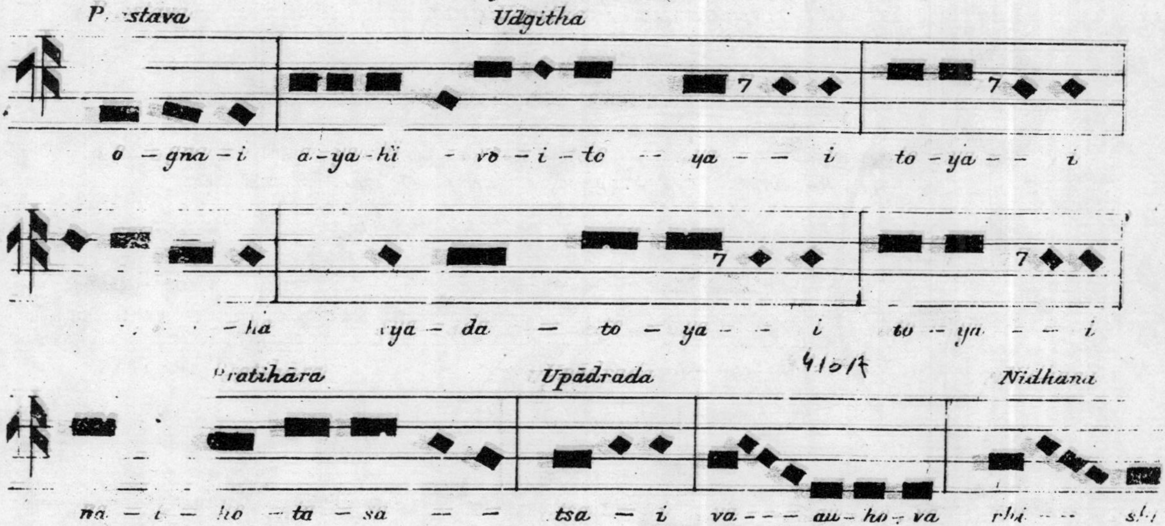

Expl. 7 indicates that the note before is prolonged one mātrā.

Kacyapasya barhishyam (1., 1. 2).

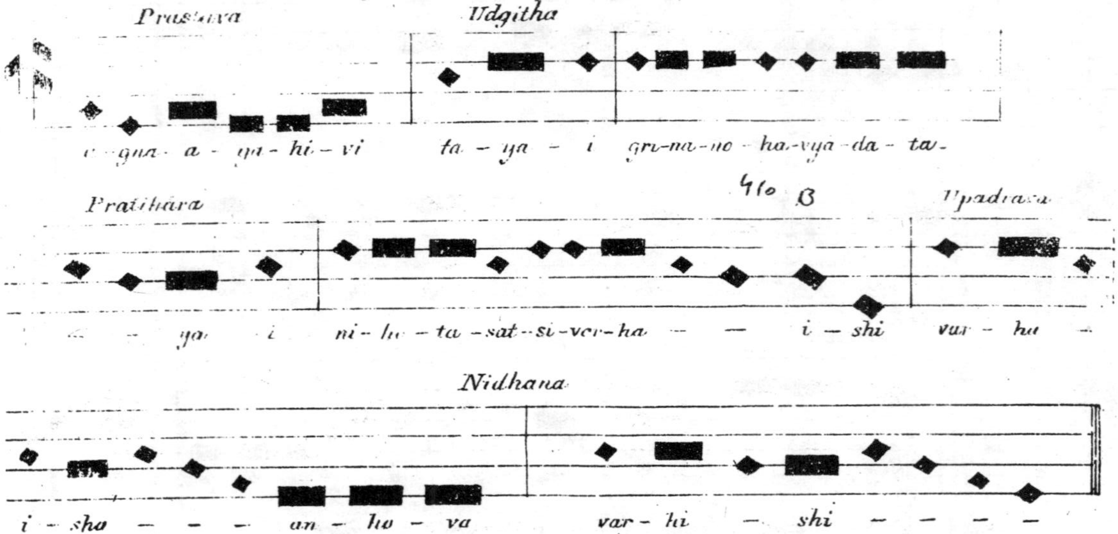

Sáman to different words, the length of the notes is made up by the modifications of the words and insertion or omission of letters. Notes are, sometimes, *Dirgha* or *Vriddha,* and the former are alone marked—in N. Indian MSS. usually by the letter r, in S. Indian MSS. by O. *Vriddha* notes are emphasized; *Dirgha* notes are prolonged beyond the usual length. Where there is a group of notes and a number over each one, these upper numbers give the length in (*Mátrá*).[1] The bar or division (*Parvan*) marks the notes to be sung with one breath. The length of the note depends on the vowel, and not on the length of the syllable according to prosody; thus in 'citra' the first note is short, the last note in each *parvan* is always *Vriddha.*

If I be right in assuming that the S. Indian letter notation is the oldest—and there are many reasons in favour of this, and none (so far as I can see) against it—it is obvious that such chants can never have been thus preserved exactly without alteration, for the letters do not show the place of the notes on the text, and there are other indications of this. For instance, the syllable 'hum' which so often occurs in the *Sāman* was called originally (as the Brahmanas prove) *hinkara,* and 'him' must, therefore, have been the original sound. Again the *Phullasútrā* shows that some *Cákhás* sang certain *Sáman* to more notes than others. Again, it is difficult to trace much in common between what are nominally the same chants as sung by members of different *Cákhās.* This consideration affords a probable explanation of the

1 The above explanation will enable any one to note the *Sáma Veda* chants (as *e. g.* printed in the B. I. edition) in the European way. In some cases notes seem to be made sharp or flat, but I have not been able to learn any rule as regards these.

assertion (in the *Puránas*) that there were formerly countless ('a thousand') *Cákhâs* of the *Sáma Veda*; it was inevitable that endless differences should arise in course of time, as the *Sámavedins* gradually arrived at a better appreciation of melody. I am not sure that the chants are not modified even at the present day; some priests, at all events, use embellishments which others reject.

Thus the *Sâma Veda* contains the 'incantamenta' of Ancient India as Profr. V. Roth appropriately has termed them[1]; and it is, therefore, of great interest as the best preserved record of a phase of belief of which we find traces in the histories of the civilization of all nations. The ascription of a magical effect to music is remarkable, and our word 'incantation' is still a witness to it among the Latins; the German held the same belief.[2]

Brief and imperfect as this outline necessarily is, I think it will be found sufficient to show what the oldest Indian music was. The ancient music of nations even nearer than India has not as yet attracted any interest,[3] and the best historians of this art have not always had access to unquestionable information. When more important work that I have in hand is done, if ever it be done, I hope to return to this subject, and to elucidate it so far as my imperfect acquaintance with the theory of music will permit.

---

1 "Der Atharbaveda in kaschmir," P. 9.

2 J. Grimm, "*Deutsche Mythologie*" pp. 987 ffg. The myths which have obvious reference to music are numerous and interesting, but little has, as yet, been done to illustrate them.

3 *e. g.* Greek music has been but little studied.

THE HINDU THEORY OF MUSIC

FROM

"*What is Music*

BY

ISAAC L. RICE,

Pianist and Professor, New York.

THE HINDU THEORY OF MUSIC

THE musical system which next claims our attention is that of the ancient Hindoos. Though unlike that of the Chinese, it is no less curious and interesting. The latter attempted to account for the power of music over the emotions by a mystic symbolical system. But it was not the characteristic of the Hindoos to enter into such geognostic mysteries. They, too, were susceptible to the influence of the music, and to a very great degree ; but they were too indolent to seek for the natural cause of the phenomenon—they had a simpler way of doing things. Why spend your existence in the futile effort to untie a knot, when you can cut it, and sever its most intricate ramifications at a single blow ?

2. Music is the invention of the great God Mahada-krishna, who caused five *Rágas* to spring from his five heads. The sixth owed its existence to Parbuti. Afterwards Brahma himself created thirty *Rágìnis.* Each *Rága* was then personified in a god who protected and governed it, each *Rágini* in a nymph. The *Rágas* were the primary modes, the *Rágini*s the secondary ones. Later, *Sarasvati,* the spouse of Brahma, presented mankind with the most beautiful of instruments—the *Víná.* The demi-god Nárada was elected to teach its use. Then Mahada-krishna endowed the *Rágas* with the power of magic. The *Rágas,* in turn, endowed the *Ráginis.* Men, animals and inanimate nature were henceforth compelled to obey them. One *Rága* was possessed of the power of raising clouds and producing rain. A songstress versed in that mode at one time saved Bengal from an

imminent famine by intoning. Another *Rága* could cause the sun to vanish. One charmed serpents, another lions and tigers. All heaven is filled with music. The great God Indra is surrounded by Gandharvas ; they accompany him in war and sing his praise in peace. Yea, the terrible Shiva himself was charmed by the magic of Ravana's *Vínâ*. Music is the pier of prayer and sacrifice—it is god-compelling.

3. The original system was much elaborated in the course of time, so that it grew to contain no less than sixteen thousand modes, each of which was governed by one of the sixteen thousand nymphs, who attempted to gain the love of Mahada-krishna during his incarnation. The nymphs are governed by the thirty *Ráginis*, the *Ráginis* by the six *Rágas*, the *Rágas* by Krishna himself. Now, as certain *Ráginis* had affinities for certain *Rágas*, it was conceived that a general marriage had taken place—that each *Rága* had been wedded to five *Ráginis*, and that eight sons had been born in each family ; that each of the forty-eight sons, called *Putras*, had taken a nymph for a spouse, whereupon the immediate family of the *Rágas* comprised one hundred and thirty-two heads, all chief modes.

4. Later, the *Rágas* were construed as being also gods of the seasons. This was done, because there appeared to be a great analogy between the frame of mind produced by each of the *Rágas*, and the one natural to one of the six seasons into which the Hindu year was divided. The joyful strains of one *Rága* were symbolical of the season of blooming ; the gay characteristics of another, of the ripening of the fruits; while the sad and melancholy melodies of another, of the fading and falling leaves. In time it came to be considered a grave offence to the presiding *Rága* of the

season, if melodies in any but one of the modes subject to his control were intoned.

How differently the Chinese and the Hindus accounted for the emotive power of music! On the one hand, the gloomy mysteries of the numbers and the elements; on the other, the bright, fantastic, gorgeous heaven of sunshine, marriages, and pleasures! And yet, who knows but that the Hindu philosophers, who established such a flowery system, were thinkers fully as deep as the Chinese sages —that their original conception and hidden meaning were not as spiritual as those of modern days? It was the spirit of the age to call a force a God—that is to say, to personify the ideal, the spiritual. The first theoreticians, probably, used the word *Rága* as a sober name, signifying mode. As the tones increased in variety, and by the aid of modulation, changes of rhythm, &c., appeared to become almost unmanageable, or rather irreducible to any system; they were compelled to limit them to a certain number of modes fit for practical use, and this number became in course of time extended to sixteen thousand by some calculation, of which we are ignorant. Then came mythological philosphy. The tones, with their wonderful effect on the soul, must have originated in heaven. The next step was to specify how and where they originated, by whom they were propagated, and then the wildest speculations on the subject were the order of the day. The peculiar poetical character of the ancient Hindu showed itself in the question "What is music?" as part of the question "What is Nature?"

THE INDIAN ART OF MUSIC

FROM

The Imperial Gazetteer of India.

BY

THE HON'BLE W. W. HUNTER, C. I. E., L. L. D.;

Director-General of Statistics for the Government of India,

President, Education Committee of India.

THE INDIAN ART OF MUSIC.

Indian music.

THE Indian art of Music (*Gandharva-veda*) was destined to exercise a wider influence. A regular system of notation had been worked out before the age of Pánini (350 B.C.?) and the seven notes were designated by their initial letters. This notation passed from the Bráhmans through the Persians to Arabia, and was thence introduced into European music by Guido d' Arezzo at the beginning of the 11th century.* Some, indeed, suppose that our modern word *gamut* comes not from the Greek letter, gamma, but from the Indian *gámu* (in Prákrit; in Sanskrit, *gráma*), literally 'a musical scale.' Hindu music, after a period of excessive elaboration, sank under the Muhammadan dynasties into a state of arrested dèvelopment. Of the 36 chief musicians in the time of Akbar, only five were Hindus. Not content with tones and semi-tones, the Indian musicians employ a more minute sub-division, together with a number of sonal modifications, which the Western ear neither recognises nor enjoys. Thus they divide the octave into 22 sub-tones, instead of the 12 semi-tones of the European scale. This is one of several fundamental differences, but it alone suffices to render Indian music barbaric to us; giving it the effect of a ballad in a minor key sung intentionally out of tune.

---

* Von Bholen, *Das alte Indien*, ii, 195 (1830); Benfy's *Indien* (Ersch & Gruber's *Encyclopædie*, xvii, 1840); quoted by Weber, *Hist. Ind. Lit.*, p. 272, foot-note 315, (1878).

Its peculiarities.

Melodies which the Indian composer pronounces to be the perfection of harmony, and which have for ages touched the hearts and fired the imagination of Indian audiences, are condemned as discord by the European critic. The Hindu ear has been trained to recognise modifications of sound which the European ear refuses to take pleasure in ; our ears, on the other hand, have been taught to expect harmonic combinations for which Indian music substitutes different combinations of its own. The Indian musician declines altogether to be judged by the few simple Hindu airs which the English ear can appreciate. It is, indeed, impossible to adequately represent the Indian system by the European notation, and the full range of its effects can only be produced on Indian instruments—a vast collection of sound-producers, slowly elaborated during 2,000 years to suit the special requirements of Hindu music. The complicated structure of its musical modes (*rágs*) rests upon three separate systems, one of which consists of five, the other of six, and the other of seven notes. It preserves in a living state some of the earlier forms which puzzle the student of Greek music, side by side with the most complicated developments. Patriotic Hindus have of late endeavoured to create a musical revival upon the old Sanskrit basis. Within the past ten years, Rajah Sourindra Mohun Tagore of Calcutta has published a series of interesting works on Indian Music in the English tongue, adopting as far as possible the European notation. He has organized an orchestra to illustrate the art ; and presented complete collections of Hindu instruments to the Conservatoire at Paris,

Revival of Hindu Music.

and to other institutions in Europe. One of the earliest subjects which the new movement took as its theme, was the celebration of the Queen of England and her ancestors, in a Sanskrit volume entitled the Victoria-Gítika (Calcutta, 1875). No Englishman has yet brought an adequate acquaintance with the *technique* of Indian instrumentation to the study of Hindu music. The art still awaits investigation by some eminent Western professor; and the contempt with which Europeans in India regard it merely proves their ignorance of the system on which Hindu music is built up.

END OF PART II.